FROM
VIETNAM NASHO
TO
CATCHING
SCHOOL CROOKS

From Vietnam Nasho to Catching School Crooks
© 2024 Colin O'Neill

All Rights Reserved. No part of this book may be reproduced in any form or by any electronic or mechanical means including information storage and retrieval systems, without permission in writing from the author. The only exception is by a reviewer, who may quote short excerpts in a review.

This book is a work of non-fiction. This publication is designed to provide accurate and authoritative information in regards to the subject matter covered. It is sold with the understanding that neither the author nor the publisher is engaged in rendering legal, investment, accounting, or other professional services. For privacy reasons, some names, locations, and dates may have been changed.

These are the memories of the author, from their perspective, and they have tried to represent events as faithfully as possible.

Printed in Australia

Cover and internal design by Book Burrow

www.bookburrow.com.au

Images in this book are copyright approved for use by author

First printing: November 2024

Paperback ISBN 978-1-7637606-2-2

eBook ISBN 978-1-7637606-3-9

Publisher: Lightning Source

Distributed by Lightning Source Global

A catalogue record for this work is available from the National Library of Australia

FROM VIETNAM NASHO TO CATCHING SCHOOL CROOKS

A MEMOIR BY
COLIN O'NEILL

Contents

Early Days	1
Family Issues	9
Exemplary Student	12
Police Department 1965 -1967	24
National Service Luck of the Draw	34
Army Training	50
Vietnam is Waiting	62
Good Morning Vung Tau	71
Life in a War Zone	82
Reality of War	92
Fun and Frivolity	114
The Dat	130
Winning Hearts and Minds	145
Attack on the Village of Ngai Giao	153
Leaving Vietnam in One Wakey	161
Allied Withdrawal from Vietnam	188
End of the Vietnam War Postscript	194
Police Department 1969 -1974	207
Crime in Schools An Overview	222
School Security	229
Every Contact Leaves a Trace	256
Silent School Intruder Detection	263
Catching School Crooks	272
Comedy 'Arrest' Capers	298

A New Direction	311
An Eventful Year	323
Two Defining Arrests	335
Crime has no Boundaries	344
Not a Good Year	358
School Arson Out of Control	367
Laurie Ratz	376
Operation Firebug Frankston High School Fires	380
Rogues Gallery	389
The Final Chapter	415
Acknowledgements	425
Bibliography	429
Reports & Articles	432
Website Publications	437
Reference Websites	439
Transcript of Interviews	440
Newspaper References	441
About the Author	449

1

Early Days

Little did I know when I came into this world on Friday, 21 March, 1947, that Hopalong Cassidy, along with his horse Topper, would be my first boyhood heroes. My favourite pastime was attending the Saturday afternoon flicks in Buckley Street, Essendon, where I would boo at the baddies and then laugh along with the antics of my other childhood heroes, The Three Stooges featuring Larry, Curly and Shemp and sometimes, Moe.

I believed Hopalong was a real-life hero, not a fictional character played by actor, William Boyd. One good thing I liked about him was he didn't drink alcohol and his favourite drink was sarsaparilla. Curly, also known as the "dog loving stooge", was my favourite because he was known to all as a protector of dogs. There was even a clause in his Columbia Pictures contract stating he could have two dogs on set at one time. I remember, in one short film you could see one of his dogs invade the set, much to our amusement.

My other boyhood hero was Captain Biggles. I loved nothing better than listening to the "Adventures of Biggles", on the radio. His tales, entertaining to young boys like me, told of his amazing feats flying planes in the early days of combat.

Aircraft included Sopwith Camels during World War One, Hawker Hurricanes and Spitfires in World War Two.

Living in Deakin Street, Essendon had its advantages. It was easy to catch the bus in Buckley Street, then travel to the pictures with a shilling in my pocket. I think the bus fare was threepence with the rest being spent on lollies and ice cream only because we always managed to sneak into the picture theatre without paying.

My early days, before attending Aberfeldie Primary School, was spent tormenting my good mate and neighbour, Johnnie "Johnno" Foster. We went to the local Essendon kindergarten and I had much pleasure telling Johnno there was no such person as Father Christmas/Santa Claus. This was then followed by tying his wrists to the Hills Hoist in our back yard and spinning him around, so his feet didn't touch the ground with him screaming to get down, as I laughed uncontrollably. My mother was certainly not impressed and yelled at me to cut him down, or else.

I think Johnno may have had his revenge when I fell off Mum's Singer sewing machine while watching a truck unload sand in the vacant allotment at the back of our house. This resulted in me nursing a broken arm, a trip to the Royal Children's Hospital in Dad's FJ Holden with my new sister screaming in the back. The FJ was based on the earlier model known as the FX and was manufactured in Australia by Holden from 1953.

I also suffered from blocked sinuses and the medical treatment in those days was to stick a large needle up your nose to try and puncture or clear the blockage. Talk about painful! The fairy godmother would always visit and Dad's favourite trick to extract any loose baby tooth, was to tie a piece of string around it, with the other end tied to a door which was then slammed shut to complete the extraction.

I was a mad Essendon supporter and went to the football on a regular basis. We lived quite a distance from the ground, so I had to catch the bus. These were the days when the Bombers played at Windy Hill. One of my favourite players at the time was Jack Clarke who played over 260 games for Essendon. These were the days when the Bombers played at Windy Hill in the Victorian Football League. In those days, you could go into the rooms after the game without any problems and, as a little six-year-old kid, I was allowed to speak with Jack and tell him how good he was.

I was shattered when my other idol, John Coleman, injured his knee at the early age of 25 in 1953 and never played again. He played a total of 98 games for the Bombers and kicked an amazing total of 537 goals. John could have kicked more but Essendon initially rejected him for two seasons in 1947 and 1948 as they thought he wasn't good enough. He returned to Hastings in the Mornington Football League and kicked 296 goals in 37 games, including a bag of 23 goals in one game against Sorrento in August, 1948. John went on to coach the Bombers to premierships in 1962 and 1965.

Aberfeldie Primary School was a 10-minute walk from home and, even after I dislocated my thumb in the playground, I walked home after recess, consuming the free bottle of milk, which we normally drank in our playtime. Free milk was introduced in schools by the Australian Government in 1951 to allegedly improve the nutrition of children. The only problem was, by recess, it had been left in the hot sun and attacked by the local bird population, in particular, crows.

Mum took me to the doctors to put my thumb back

in place but only after a general anaesthetic because I was a wimp! Of course, I told Jack Clarke I injured my thumb playing football for the school side, but somehow, I don't think he believed me, as I was only seven years old at the time. Mum and Dad would give me two bob pocket money on the basis that I stopped tormenting Johnno, but if it wasn't spent on going to the pictures, it was saved for cracker night. This night, known as Guy Fawkes night, was and still is, celebrated on 5 November.

Everyone loved cracker night and I was no exception. Setting up a bonfire, with Guy Fawkes sitting in an old chair at the top, was held in high esteem, much like Christmas and birthdays. I would go to the local milk bar or newsagent near school to buy skyrockets, Tom Thumb bungers and penny bungers but my favourites were the three penny bungers.

The local neighbourhood would attend the bonfire and watch as the kids let off all the firecrackers, while "oohing" and "ahhing" as the rockets would take off into the night sky. What they didn't know, of course, was Johnno and I and, I suspect, numerous other kids, would love nothing more than placing a penny or three penny bunger in a letter box and watch it blow to smithereens. Of course, the purchase and use of private fireworks is now banned so no longer do we have the issues of blistered or burnt fingers we all suffered, not to mention the destruction of neighbourhood property.

In those days, we also used to have cracker gun fights. You would have a stainless-steel pipe with a handle underneath, a hole in the top to put your marble down the end, then you would place the penny bunger in with the wick up. We used to build forts and mock bunkers in the adjacent creek and all hell would break loose. How we never killed one another defies logic! I vividly remember, when the local constabulary called in home one day to tell my parents, 'Enough is enough,' bringing an end to our cracker gun fights.

Johnno and I had to turn to other devious past-times to amuse ourselves and, unfortunately, the local bread delivery was at the top of our list. The horse-drawn baker's cart was painted in bright colours with the name of the bakery on the side. The delivery man would stop at each house, hop down, load the bread into a wicker basket and then deliver the loaf or loaves of bread. Sometimes, if you were lucky, you might score a fresh bun or the baker would place you into the seat of the cart and you held the reins as the horse went from house to house.

Unfortunately, this all came to an abrupt end when Johnno and I thought firing our marble-filled cracker guns into the back of the bread cart would be great fun. We were at the top of the hill in Deakin Street when we saw the baker's cart delivering the bread towards the bottom of the hill. We aimed our cracker guns at the back of it and fired. I hit the rear of the cart with the marble, causing the horse to take off at an extremely fast pace with the very annoyed baker running down Deakin Street trying to catch him. Johnno missed as he was never a good shot and we laughed all the way home.

A disgusting pastime, but Johnno (only him!) would catch frogs and then tie them to the penny bungers. When I think about this now, I cringe. Of course, it resulted in the frogs being blown up but we were just bored kids, filling in time by getting into mischief in the fifties. One of my other favourite pastimes was attending the Royal Melbourne Show at the Flemington showgrounds. My attraction to this annual event dissipated the year my uncle Jack and his good mate, Eric, took me with them but left me sitting alone eating many bags of liquorice. Mum had to subsequently take me to the doctor, who diagnosed an overloaded stomach.

A very young and newly crowned Queen Elizabeth visited Melbourne in February 1954 and I recall Mum taking me to the Essendon train station where we all waved as her Majesty and Prince Philip, seated on the back of a rail carriage, waved back as they passed through, much to everyone's delight. Her Majesty also attended a lively pageant at the Melbourne Cricket Ground where 17,000 children participated in dancing around maypoles in their warm welcome to our Queen.

Australian television was then launched from TCN 9 in Sydney on 16 September, 1956 by Bruce Gyngell, when he uttered those telling and famous words, 'Good evening and welcome to television.'

I still enjoyed listening to Captain Biggles but another favourite radio program was an evening variety segment with Jack Davey as compere. His signature greeting was, 'Hi ho, everybody.' One of his contestants in 1955 was a sprightly lad named John Howard, who would later become Prime Minister of Australia.

This was quickly followed by GTV9, conducting its first broadcast on 27 September, 1956 with 80 minutes of cartoons followed by a John Wayne film. The program was hosted by Geoff Corke then followed by daily test pattern transmissions. Mum would take us down to Puckle Street, Moonee Ponds where we would join a group of people watching a flickering black and white television in the front of a shop window.

Around this time, only about five per cent of the population owned a black and white television, which would cost hundreds of pounds. I can remember watching the Mickey Mouse Club with Annette Funicello as the most popular musketeer.

Unfortunately, poor old Hopalong Cassidy had been replaced in my book of heroes by the Lone Ranger, his horse Silver and, of course, his side-kick, Tonto the Indian.

I also remember a program called Pick a Box, hosted by Bob Dyer and his wife, Dolly. It was initially a multi-question trivia quiz radio program, with two contestants, in the late 1940s. The same format was adopted for television in 1957, with the catch phrase at the end, 'The money or the box?'

If you selected the wrong box, you would win a booby prize. Two well-known contestants were Frank Partridge, who was the last Australian to win a Victoria Cross in World War Two, followed some years later by Barry Jones, who would go on to a successful career in Australian politics. Barry was so knowledgeable, he would often take issue with Bob Dyer on the correct answer. Barry was proven right every time.

Melbourne was the host city for the 1956 Summer Olympics with 72 nations competing mainly at the Melbourne Cricket Ground. Around this time, a youth subculture, known as the bodgies and widgies, came to light in Australia. They were influenced by the English Teddy Boys who were bodgies with long hair and rode motor bikes or drove cars with mag wheels and hot mufflers. The widgie was a teenage female, commonly with short hair and wearing jeans, the counterpart to the bodgie.

They were certainly known for recalcitrant behaviour, which resulted in Victoria Police forming the Bodgies and Widgies Squad, consisting of plain clothes police. Their task was to cause as much disruption to the subculture as possible. They were very similar to today's police taskforces dealing with outlaw motorcycle gangs, the latter, of course, being on a much higher criminal level.

This happy period in my life, however, was about to dramatically change.

2

Family Issues

Issues concerning family can be, to say the least, a very stressful and an emotional time for all involved. Unfortunately, family law has not always been the way it is today under the *Family Law Act*.

In the 1950s, before *the Matrimonial Causes Act 1959* (Cth) and the *Commonwealth Marriages Act 1961* (Cth) came into force, marriage and divorce were managed by the states and you had to prove marital fault. The 1959 Act provided 14 grounds for divorce, which included: adultery, desertion and even habitual drunkenness. In other words, you still needed evidence to support the claim of marital fault or wait five years of separation before applying for divorce, which would then give you a no-fault ground.

My parents had been married for nearly 10 years after Dad returned from service with the Australian Army, following the end of World War Two. He was a foreman printer and very mechanically minded but unfortunately, he didn't pass this down to his son. I still can't put two pieces of wood together with a hammer and nail, but Dad was very astute and certainly mechanically adapt.

I remember his FJ Holden with some fondness. He would

always be working on his cars and probably a few other things at the same time. Being an extremely cluey man, Dad would buy motor vehicles to rebuild or fix them up, lovingly tinkering over them in the back yard of Deakin Street. I recall he wasn't home a lot, leaving Mum to look after my three-year-old sister and me practically singlehanded.

About 1956, Mum became disenchanted with their marriage and began to suspect Dad was being a bit of a lad. To prove marital fault in those years, a spouse would often have to engage a solicitor or private investigator to find some evidence. This process was expensive, making it very difficult to obtain the relevant grounds for a divorce. Unbeknownst to me during this time and, given that Mum had no source of income, she had one of her brothers follow my father to gather any evidence to support the claim of marital fault.

Just before Mum and Dad separated, a couple living in Deakin Street, Essendon had moved up to Gerang Gerung to buy and run a hotel. Mum had become friends with them and, upon hearing of her marriage problems, they asked Mum to work in their hotel. Mum agreed because things obviously weren't easy for her trying to raise a family of two young children on her own. It was a pretty gutsy and scary effort by my mother to separate from her husband and take off with her children.

Gerang Gerung, with a population around 190, was a rural location situated on the Western Highway and the Horsham to Adelaide railway line. Its name is believed to come from the Aboriginal word meaning, leaf or branch. The hotel was situated near the railway line and there was not much else in the town, apart from the primary school, public hall, post office and milk bar.

Mum enrolled me in the local primary school and I have fond memories of the year we spent living at the hotel, apart from being bullied on a regular basis by the local lads. I found myself involved in many fights, lost most of them but overall, I behaved myself. Missing Essendon and Windy Hill, I soon stumbled across the local country football club where I would always attend the Saturday home game. I think Gerang Gerung played in the Richmond colours and I used to run out with the team as a mascot. My favourite recollections of living in Gerang Gerung were definitely the footy matches.

I loved the half-time break as the locals would all turn up with a plate of sandwiches, scones and cakes. Gerang Gerung's main social function was the local football match. I can still taste those cakes the women used to bake and the sarsaparilla, as I always loved sarsaparilla, just like Hopalong Cassidy.

I fell in love for the very first time! She was the publican's daughter and a few years older than me. I also had a motherless pet lamb that I looked after until it was big enough to return to the rest of the sheep. It was absolutely heartbreaking when I said goodbye and I cried for days.

We subsequently moved back to Reservoir to live with my nanna in late 1957 and the hotel closed the following year.

3

Exemplary Student

Reservoir is approximately 12 kilometres north of Melbourne's central business district and its local government area is the City of Darebin. As an established suburb, it contained a number of weatherboard and standard brick homes. My nanna's home was in a block of very small flats in Lane Crescent. It became rather crowded with Mum, Susan and me, Nanna and Mum's younger brother, Jack, all living together. My grandfather had passed away from a heart attack in 1953 and Nanna had not remarried at this stage.

I was then enrolled to complete Grade Six at Reservoir Primary School in Duffy Street. Prior to starting at my new school, my mother reminded me of the bullying I was subjected to at Gerang Gerung Primary School and told me I had to stick up for myself or cop more physical abuse from other students. I took this to heart and, after being punched regularly at playtime by a certain large local lad, who went on to play for Collingwood when he was older, I planned my revenge.

This involved waiting in bushes in a laneway near Lane Crescent where he walked home from school. After he went past me, I came up behind him and belted him unmercifully, which, of course, is now known as a coward's punch. However, it had the desired effect and he never bullied me again. When starting Form One the following year, I was soon to learn the bullying and fights would continue.

One of my other favourite games, apart from belting the local lad, was playing cherry bobs at school during recess. This involved throwing a cherry bob, or pip, into an area set up by other kids and, if successful hitting out the cherry stones on the other side of the line, you would take all the cherry bobs. If you weren't successful, the student who set up the game would take your cherry bobs. The winner would be the kid with the most cherry bobs.

Apart from this mind-boggling past time, I did attend class but was more interested in football, cricket and motor car racing. My dad, on one of his then rare visitations, took me to Albert Park Circuit in Melbourne to watch Englishman, Stirling Moss, win the Grand Prix, with Jack Brabham, a well-known Australian racing car driver, finishing second.

My first job earning "proper" pocket money was delivering newspapers on my bike for the local newsagent. That job didn't last long as I decided my last delivery was too far to cycle as I was tired, so I never made it. I forgot the householder could see me up the road and with him yelling, 'I want my paper,' I furiously pedalled home.

I had a slight health issue when our local medical practitioner, Dr Alex Mitchell, detected a heart murmur but after further specialist advice, it was determined not to be a major concern. I did use it as an excuse to extract some sympathy from Mum when she wanted some odd jobs done, pleading that I had a "stressful heart". Needless to say, it only worked a few times. I somehow passed Grade Six with flying colours then started Form One at Keon Park Technical School, which at that stage, had not been completely built.

We were being schooled in temporary accommodation when my first year commenced at Northcote Primary School in Helen Street. To attend class, I had to walk to the railway station then board the train to Northcote. The school relocated to its new home and buildings in Hughes Parade, Keon Park, for the start of Form Two in 1960.

Keon Park was a residential estate between Reservoir and Thomastown and was situated close to the Keon Park railway station and near the J. C. Donath Reserve. The school buildings were of light timber construction in a H pattern with a separate trade block and the canteen at one end. Little did I know during my four years at this school, I would revisit it many years later and certainly in a different capacity from when I was a student.

We then moved from Reservoir to East Preston as Mum was working in a cake shop next door to the East Preston tram terminus. It was very convenient as we were living in a nearby milk bar. I kept up the newspaper tradition by selling them at the tram terminus before I began working after hours for the local butcher, Harry Broom. I unfortunately lost that job when I decided to dispose of the butcher's pamphlets I was supposed to deliver to each household. Despite my excuse that they somehow fell down a drain, Harry, understandably, was not impressed and I lost the job. I then tried working at the local Preston Drive-In, which also didn't last long.

My parents reconciled and remarried, resulting in me being very confused about life and wondering what the hell was going on. My father had actually married someone else after leaving Mum and the first question I raised was, 'Have I got any half brothers or sisters?'

To this day I am not aware of any, but you never know.

We moved from our Preston residence above the shop to Malpas Street, East Preston, which was just down the road from the tram terminus.

The bullying continued at school and I found myself having to contend with the Younger brothers. Donny Younger was a piece of work and he loved nothing better than grabbing someone in a headlock and spitting in their ear. One fight I found myself in came to an abrupt stop, with me falling off the end of the trade block onto the ground below as we wrestled and fought.

When fights started, everyone would yell out, 'fight, fight, fight,' and kids would gather to see who got belted. I had learnt a few tricks from my uncle Jack who had taken me to my first boxing match at Festival Hall in 1959, when over 7,000 spectators witnessed George Bracken, the Australian Lightweight Champion, beat David Oved on points.

The other "highlight" I found in my four years of technical education was the introduction of corporal punishment by the teaching fraternity. Students would get the strap on regular occasions where they would have to stand and hold out both hands. If they had been very disruptive in class, which was often the case with me, they would get "six of the best".

If I knew then, what I know now, it's a wonder I didn't turn around and head butt one of the teachers. In those days, the strap was on the go all the time and you would cop six of the best and sometimes more. Talking in class, back chatting the teacher or simply not paying attention were the norm for the strap and when you were hit, you were really hit, leaving you with numb hands for hours.

I don't recall getting the strap in primary school but I know in tech school it was on a regular basis. If they did that now, they would be sued. It was not until 1983 when it was finally abolished; one of the first major policy decisions of the newly elected Victorian John Cain Labor Government.

The school allowed me to further my education by undertaking excursions to Queensland and Tasmania. On the trip to Queensland, we had a short stopover at the Sydney railway station and I was proud as punch when a well-known rock and roll singer by the name of Johnny O'Keefe arrived at the station. When he saw my school cap, he tried it on his head, much to my amazement!

He was a delight and was known as J.O.K or The Wild One. He had a total of 29 top 40 hits in Australia from 1953 until his untimely death in 1978. His hits included the signature tune Wild One and he entertained Australian soldiers at Nui Dat in South Vietnam in August 1969. JOK was also called up in 1952 and served with the RAAF at Richmond Air Base in New South Wales.

On my return from Queensland, I somehow won a prize to appear on the Channel Nine Tarax Show, hosted by Geoff Corke also known as King Corky and King of the Kids and, of course, the show promoted Tarax soft drinks. I won a five-pound voucher to spend at Clive Fairbairn sports store and proudly took my new cricket batting gloves to school the next day. The Tarax Show was previously hosted by Happy Hammond and I loved Professor Ratbaggy, who was played by Ernie Carroll. He went on to star as Ossie Ostrich in Hey Hey, It's Saturday.

I then came down with an attack of the mumps, which is a contagious viral infection with painful swelling of the salivary glands. Mum took me to our local doctor who recommended a stay in bed for a few days and to ensure I was kept very warm.

I took that literally and when Mum came home from work that afternoon, she found me in a very smelly room in a lather of sweat with soaked sheets. I had closed up my bedroom with a kerosene heater going full blast. These types of heaters were very popular in those days but we were not warned they should not be used indoors due to the toxic fumes and the potential fire hazard.

To say I was a poor student, based on my results, is an understatement but I admit I was hopeless. I managed a score of four out of 100 in one solid geometry exam and when I asked the teacher where I went wrong, he laughed and said, 'O'Neill, the only thing you got right was spelling your name.'

A bit rough but I had the last laugh. At the end of Form Four when I received my report card, I changed the four to 44 in the same pen colour because, although it was still a fail, it didn't look as bad as my original mark of four, for just getting my name right.

One student at Keon Park Tech was Len Thompson who won a Brownlow Medal for best and fairest in Australian Rules football and played a remarkable 301 games. I remember Len in Form Four. We would line up at morning assembly where we would ask 6ft 6in Len how the weather was up there as he was literally head and shoulders above all the other students.

One of my other mates was Ian Thomson, who happened to be the brother of Alan "Froggy" Thomson who went on to play test cricket for Australia in 1970 -71. He was also a VFL umpire in the days of only one field umpire. I used to face Froggy in his parents' garage, with him bowling off his front leg like a frog with a windmill action from the middle of the road. I had much pleasure in belting him all over the park (the street), albeit with a tennis ball.

I had also tried to convince my peers around me at the time that my uncle was in fact, Norman O'Neill, who played test cricket for Australia and had scored a memorable 181 in the tied test against West Indies in the 1960-61 tour to Australia. I suspect my batting in the garage wasn't up to the standard of my favourite "uncle" though. My batting, however, was up to scratch playing cricket in Malpas Street or our back yard with my mate, Ross Clark, who lived just up the road. I remember belting a huge six which unfortunately went through the window of a neighbour's house. It had to be paid for by my parents because our neighbour was definitely not impressed.

As Ross also went to Keon Park Tech, we would often ride our bikes together to school. This came to an abrupt halt one morning when I was trying to catch up to Ross. I put my head down and pedalled furiously, only to crash into the back of a stationery bus. That bus then became our mode of transport from the East Preston tram terminus to Hughes Parade, Keon Park.

Riding the bus did have its attraction, despite the hefty return fare, as a very attractive young lass would sit at the back of the bus in her very short mini skirt. Thankfully, we had our school bags to cover up our "embarrassment" when we got off the bus. Ross and I would often watch Preston Football Club play at Cramer Street Oval, where his brother Greg played in the firsts. Preston's nickname was The Bull Ants and they competed in the Victorian Football Association (VFA), winning the 1963 premiership when they defeated Waverley. At the time, little did we know that some years later, Ross and I would both be conscripted to serve in Vietnam, but sadly only one of us would survive the rigours of war.

Mum had now decided that perhaps a technical school was

not right for me and I should try a high school. It was obvious high school was going to be a better choice as I wasn't really made for a career in woodwork and sheet metal. I continued life's journey in 1963 by commencing Form Five at Reservoir High School in Plenty Road, Reservoir. I had grand plans of becoming a fighter pilot, which was every boy's dream.

Every young boy with visions of grandiose adventures wants to fly aeroplanes and I desperately wanted to be a jet fighter pilot but it wasn't to be. I actually sat the test to become an air force pilot but I didn't do well. The best position they could offer me was as a clerk, but when I failed that test, it finally hit me that my dream career of becoming a pilot would never eventuate. I've been up in many planes and helicopters ever since, of course, but not flying them. My fascination with flying was most likely due to watching the Russian cosmonaut, Yuri Gagarin, being the first human to be blasted into space on 12 April, 1961, followed by the first woman, Valentina Tereshkova, on 16 June, 1963.

I spent two years completing fifth form as I failed my first year quite dismally, passing only three subjects. I therefore couldn't receive a Leaving Certificate to qualify for Form Six Matriculation, which was the entry required for university. Apart from my poor academic record, I remember 1963 very well because United States President John F. Kennedy (JFK) was assassinated by Lee Harvey Oswald on 22 November, 1963, a critical time in respect to America's participation in the Vietnam War. Apparently, Kennedy was considering a total withdrawal of American forces at the time.

His alleged murderer didn't last long because two days later, when being escorted by police to the local jail, Oswald died two hours after being shot. His convicted killer, Jack "Sparky"

Ruby, subsequently died in prison four years later, while waiting for a new trial on appeal. Being a cricket tragic, another vivid memory, two weeks after the assassination of JFK, was the no-balling of Ian Meckiff for "chucking" the ball at the Brisbane test match, effectively ending his cricket career.

Little did we know at the time though, the JFK assassination would be followed by a further three in the 1960s, including President Kennedy's brother, Senator Robert F. Kennedy, who was assassinated on 5 June, 1968. His death would occur only two months after the fatal shooting of Martin Luther King Jr and during a volatile period in America in opposition to the Vietnam War. Malcolm X, a well-known human rights activist was assassinated some three years earlier in 1965.

In 1964, I repeated my schooling year in order to obtain my leaving certificate. As far as I was concerned, life was more about playing school football and cricket. On Saturdays, I played with Regent Football Club and church cricket with Regent Presbyterian in the junior competition and for one season only, I tried to play baseball with the Preston Baseball Club. I did have the dubious honour of being the highest scorer in one cricket game on a matting wicket when I made three magnificent runs, after we were bowled out for a total score of 10 runs with sundries making up the total. One of my so-called mates from high school, Graeme Cuthbert, took 9/1 but he didn't get me out.

My favourite pastimes were girls, in particular, Janise, who was my first "proper" love, and socialising at local dances. During one of my so-called liaisons with a local girl called Rhonda, my 10-year-old sister, Susan, interrupted us when she stormed into my room at the rear of our Malpas Street home, screaming out to keep the noise down.

One school football match playing against Heidelberg High School resulted in me being knocked out, waking up in hospital and missing out on seeing a group called the Beatles, much to my immense disappointment. I returned to school on the Monday only to be lambasted by our acting school principal, Wes Muir, who at an assembly, without naming me, said words to the effect, 'It would appear we have a student who would rather start a fight in a school football match, bringing our school into disrepute.' On he went with all the other students pointing at me and laughing, even though I had no recollection of what had happened.

Our sports master, Kevin Hardiman, was also not impressed and deliberately omitted me from the next school match as a harsh punishment. Mr Hardiman previously played a number of games with Essendon in the VFL and went on to be local mayor of Preston and later became president of the Victorian ALP.

I did, however, get a mention in the 1964 school magazine edition of Amphora, when the captain of our sport schoolhouse, called Yan Yean, mentioned me, not only for my sporting achievements with the school, but my so-called help as senior house vice-captain. Thankfully, he did not mention my attempt at cross county running for the school when somehow, I got lost in my first run, went the wrong way and arrived back at the finish line an hour and half later.

I was very embarrassed as I had trained very hard for my sojourn into running. With a couple of mates, including Ross Pitman, we would train by running 24 miles from the East Preston Tram Terminus into the city and back again. The glamour of being mentioned as having a consistent season at both football and cricket still didn't help my academic achievements as I only just scraped through with two extra subjects to finally receive my Leaving Certificate.

The bodgies had now graduated to be known as rockers or greasers. In those days, you were either a rocker or their nemesis, a mod jazzer, who preferred traditional jazz and rhythm and blues. Later in the 1960s, they were described as hippies. There was also a group known as the sharpies who roamed in gangs. They were somewhat desperate to maintain the subculture that flourished with all the long hairs doing the stomp. So, they would line up and do what became known as the sharpie shuffle, often resulting in violent confrontations.

In one weekend alone, Victoria Police conducted a special operation to try and stamp out the violence, particularly around dance halls. I decided to be more moderate and became a jazzer, so I grew my hair long, covering my high forehead with a fringe, much like the Beatle type of haircut. I also wore a skivvy.

My favourite pastime outside school was to attend dances on a Friday night at a place called Opus, or the Gasworks, in Kew. I always wore my skivvy, a duffle coat and Fletcher Jones pants. Those were the days of Judy Jacques, who I adored. She was a much-recognised popular jazz singer with a powerful voice. She first appeared at the Pakenham Hotel at the mere age of eleven when she sang, Smoke Gets in Your Eyes. By 1963 – 64, her long shiny blonde hair with a fringe was the go-to look for most girls. Judy appeared on Bandstand, including a live performance at the Myer Music Bowl in 1965 and with Johnny O'Keefe at Pentridge Prison.

After I finished school, sporting my long hair and skivvy, I applied to join the police force. I failed the height requirement by about a quarter of an inch as you had to be at least five foot, nine inches. This was abolished four years later in 1969. The sergeant at the St Kilda Road police depot said at least one inch of that height was made up with my hair in any event, which I had deliberately grown even longer to cover up my high forehead and receding hair line.

Taking the alternative option at nearly 18 years of age, I joined the public service in February 1965 and had the choice of either the Motor Registration Branch (MRB, now known as VicRoads), or the Police Department as an unsworn public servant. Of course, I took the latter as it was the best and only option available due to my height, or lack thereof, to join the police as a sworn member.

4

Police Department 1965-1967

With some trepidation on 1 February, 1965, I boarded tram number 88 from the East Preston tram terminus to commence the one-hour journey to Police Headquarters in Russell Street. Constructed in the 1940s, this building was styled like a New York skyscraper. It was adjacent to what was known as the Old Melbourne Goal, which housed the watch house, police garage and the city courts. The building also included the police theatrette / ballroom on the ground floor and was used by police when conducting line ups, which I would later experience firsthand.

The Chief Commissioner of Police was Rupert Arnold who had been appointed in November, 1963, leading to further appointments of three assistant commissioners for Crime, General (uniform branch) and Traffic and Technical Departments. Following his appointment, the Police Motor Boating Squad was established and a refurbished building at Spring Street, Melbourne housed the Forensic Science Laboratory (FSL), Detective Training School (DTS) and the Licensing, Gaming and Vice Squad.

The FSL was staffed by serving police members and public servants. Their role was providing forensic examination support in prosecuting offenders involved in various crime scenes, including homicides and arson. The new method of detecting speeding motorists was the amphometer, which was a device laid over a stretch of road for a fixed distance to measure the speed of a vehicle. I can say with hand on my heart, I drove over the set cables on the road on a number of occasions but was always within the speed limit.

On arrival at Russell Street, I was told I would be working in Despatch situated next to the Central Correspondence Bureau (CCB) on the first floor. I spent the first day sorting and delivering mail to a number of different sections of the police force but the fourth floor was to become my favourite as the police gym was located there. This was to be regularly visited by me for sparring sessions over many years.

Indeed, it was used by Ken "Crusher" Webb who was well known for his other endeavours and, apart from working in the police drawing office, was also an actor and professional wrestler. He appeared in the television show Homicide and the main Russell Street building was used in the opening to this fictional police drama. Crusher was certainly an interesting character and was the double used or should I say, hanged, in the movie starring Mick Jagger as Ned Kelly. Both Crusher and his offsider, Kelvin Peart, who finished second in the 1971 Stawell Gift, had great fun throwing me around the police gym, not only when we were wresting but also with gloves on.

In those days, I fancied myself as a boxer and, without my knowledge, they wrote in large dark letters on my carry bag, "Colin O'Neill–The Boxer". Going home that night on the tram, I wondered why other passengers were looking at my bag and then at me, before breaking into smirks and fits of laughter.

Crusher soon found his match in police officer, Alan "Yabby" Jeans, who regularly attended the gym. I did wrestle Yabby on one occasion but being small and very skinny, I was no match. Yabby was a lovely man and after playing 77 games for St Kilda in the Victorian Football League, he took over as senior coach, leading them to successive grand finals in 1965 and, of course, the winning premiership in 1966 against Collingwood.

My failure at school where it took two years to obtain my leaving certificate, did not deter me from wanting a higher education. In March 1965, I enrolled with Taylors College for its classes in Form Six Matriculation. Taylors was a night school in Flinders Street, Melbourne, which also provided specialised university courses and my plan was to go on to bigger and better things.

That didn't quite work out as well as I planned, however, as I selected a higher maths subject, together with physics and chemistry, which clearly I had no idea about. After three weeks of classes on a Tuesday night, I found I was being better educated by having a few drinks at the City Court Hotel before closing at 6pm. We would down a few beers in the last hour, saving our empty glasses before the last call for final drinks came, then we would gulp them down by 6pm.

I recall one occasion when I had a few too many after knocking off work at our finishing time of 4.36pm. I went to the City Court for the usual "six o'clock swill", caught the tram home and sat in the laneway near home at the rear of Malpas Street to sober up. I then walked into our lounge room two hours later, told my parents night school was great then fell into bed. Taylors didn't last long after that and I finished my short foray in higher education.

I subsequently obtained my driver's licence, mainly thanks to, not only my father for his driving lessons, but the police officer at Heidelberg Police station. One of the advantages of working in police despatch was to meet various public servants and police officers: two being First Constables Les Reading and his driver, Wally Saville. They would call in each day to pick up the mail I had sorted for delivery to various police stations. Wally, on learning I was about to attend the police station for a licence test, contacted the testing officer and asked him to look after me.

My licence test involved one trip around the block and, despite making an error, well, a few errors, I somehow obtained my licence. Les and Wally both had a larrikin streak and they "arrested" me one day walking down Collins Street in the city. They both thought it was hilarious, placing me in the back of their police divvy van, telling all those walking past that I had been a very bad boy, then proceeded to drive me back to Russell Street, laughing all the way.

I purchased my first car, a Volkswagen Beetle, on hire purchase and it would stay with me for the next 10 years, despite several accidents which, of course, were not caused by my erratic driving. By this time, the six o'clock swill was no more as it was abolished in Victoria on 1 February, 1966, with hotel trading hours being extended to 10pm. Restricted trading hours had already been abolished in other states many years earlier, apart from South Australia, who followed suit in 1967.

These restricted hours had been in place since World War One and stemmed from legislation to look after the interests of our soldiers. They were then maintained by our government, again supposedly acting in the better interests of our people.

Decimal currency was also changed 14 days after Victoria abolished early closing. On 14 February, 1966, the Australian dollar replaced our pound, with a conversion rate of two dollars to the pound and coins in denominations of 1, 2, 5, 10, 20 and 50 cents. I don't think these two milestones were in any way related, though!

In late 1966, I was transferred for a very short period to Dawson Street, Brunswick, which housed the Police Traffic Branch where I worked in Penalties Payment. I returned to Russell Street in late February 1967, not long after the last person to be hanged in Victoria, Ronald Ryan, met his fate on 3 February, 1967.

On 19 December, 1965, Ryan had escaped from Pentridge Prison in Coburg, Victoria with his good mate and fellow prisoner, Peter Walker. He was later convicted of the murder of warder, George Hodson. Ryan's hanging was met with much public contempt, particularly from those who vehemently opposed capital punishment. It was subsequently abolished in all Australian states by 1985.

When our Premier, Henry Bolte, copped a particular flogging at the time from both constituents and the press, he simply responded by saying, 'If I thought the law was wrong, I would change it.'

He would face further controversy later in life when, following a serious traffic accident, his hospital blood samples were substituted and he was never prosecuted for drink driving.

Talking of drink driving, I unfortunately had a too few many one night at the Summerhill Hotel in Reservoir and, after leaving, I flipped my VW beetle onto its side. I still drove it back home only after a local resident came out on hearing the noise and helped me right the vehicle. Dad, quite rightly, was not impressed as he knew I had been drinking.

This was followed by another prang when I drove into the rear of a vehicle in Cramer Street, Preston, but this time it was thanks to my sister who distracted my concentration. My parents were not suitably impressed, so I moved out into rented accommodation in Malvern with Fred Jobson, who I worked with at Police Headquarters. The change of address only lasted three weeks as I missed the comforts of home. The only shining light during this period was playing in a winning cricket premiership with East Preston Cricket Club and making 70 in the final, only to be run out in the second dig for a duck. Celebrations, of course, continued long into the night at the Gowerville Hotel in Preston.

On my return to Russell Street, I thought I would be promoted out of Despatch, due to being the "favourite son" of the officer in charge of the Central Correspondence Bureau, Len Richter. Sadly, it was not the case and I languished there until I was called up for National Service in July 1967. During this time, a young police officer by the name of Rex Hunt was just commencing his first year in the police force and would call in to pick up the mail for delivery to Prahran police station.

Rex, who always had a smile on his face, would later go on to play over 200 games of football with various clubs, including Richmond, in the VFL. He also became a football commentator and had his own fishing and wildlife programs. Later in the early 1970s, Rex and I would play cricket together for Prahran Police in the mid-week competition and I always thought he was a better cricketer than footballer.

It was also during this period I came to know quite a few

other police officers, including members of the consorting and homicide squads. In those days, they had, shall we say, quite a different method of police interrogation, including the way they conducted line ups for a witness to a crime to identify the offender. Jack Ford was a well-known Victorian homicide police inspector at the time and he and his colleagues had arrested a criminal identity and deadly gunman by the name of James (Jim) "Machine Gun" Bazley or "Iceman".

Bazley, well known for committing armed robberies and extreme acts of violence, was shot during the frenzied war between the painters and dockers but, somehow, he survived relatively unscathed. This unionised group from the Federated Painters and Dockers Union ruled their patch during the 1960s, generally with members standing over other members and also the public, with sawn off shotguns.

It was common practice in those days for certain police members to call on public servants, usually unsworn members, to participate in a line up. On this particular day, I was in the police auditorium for a line up conducted by Inspector Ford. The alleged guilty culprit was none other than Bazley, who, at the end of the line-up, was handcuffed and looking very unkempt alongside a dozen or so well-dressed public servants.

A number of witnesses were brought in, one at a time, to look along the group of men, including me, and asked to point the alleged perpetrator out if they could identify who shot or assaulted them. However, Bazley's reputation proceeded him and, lo and behold, not one witness was able to identify Bazley, much to the annoyance of Ford. Bazley, despite his fearsome reputation, did have a soft side. He and his wife bred poodles. She was also the sister of another well-known gunman by the name of Horatio Morris.

Justice, however, finally caught up with Bazley and also Ford, with Bazley being sentenced to nine years in prison for conspiracy to murder a then potential liberal politician, Donald Mackay, who was killed in a Griffith pub carpark. This was followed by a sentence of life imprisonment for his participation in the murders of two drug couriers, Douglas and Isabel Wilson, at Rye in 1979, so his poodle breeding days came to an abrupt end. Bazley died at the ripe old age of 92 in 2018, still professing his innocence in respect to the murder of Donald Mackay, whose remains were never found.

Ford, on the other hand, together with the Head of the Police Traffic Branch, Superintendent Jack Mathews, were both convicted and sentenced to lengthy jail terms, following the 1970 Abortion Inquiry, conducted by William Kaye, QC. They were named by Peggy Berman, a receptionist at an East Melbourne abortion clinic, after their level of corruption had extended over nine years of bribes.

Such was their greed that both Mathews and Ford arrived at her hospital bed where she was being treated for cancer, wanting their weekly bribe and stuck empty envelopes under her pillow. They were both jailed for five years, together with Detective Martin Jacobsen who was sentenced to three years. Another police officer, Detective Sgt Frank "Bluey" Adams, was acquitted. His alleged role was to tip off the 30 or so abortion doctors of any pending police raid.

Little did we know any of this at the time of the police line-up, in which I participated, let alone what lay ahead for me.

Left: A quiet and well dressed toddler with Mum.
Right: I loved spending time with my paternal Grandpa.

With Susan, Nanna and Mum.

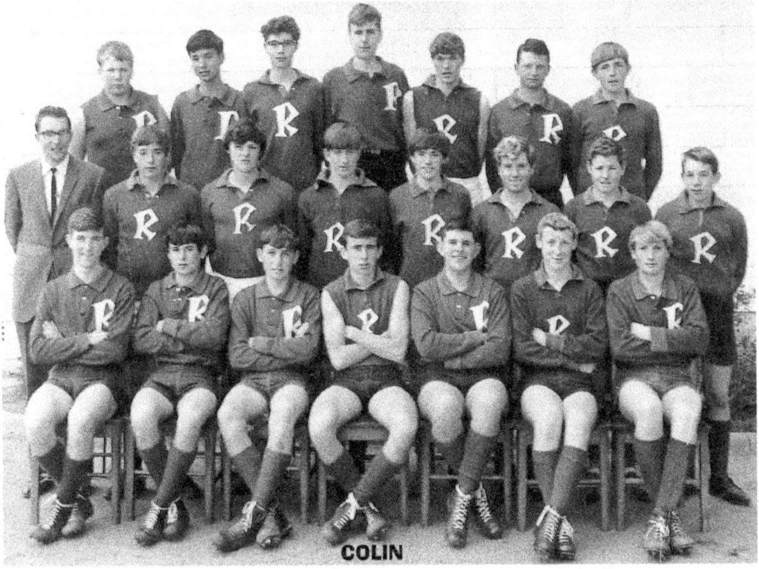

Captain of Reservoir High School Football Team.

With Mum, Dad and Susan outside our family home in Preston.

5

National Service Luck of the Draw

National Service was an Australian tradition from Federation in 1911 but in the days of World Wars One and Two, it was more aptly described as conscription, or volunteer forces to serve overseas. Following the commencement of the Korean War in 1950, together with a conflict in Malaysia, and the strength of the Viet Minh insurgents against the French in Vietnam, Australia was in a difficult position. It did not have sufficient numbers to serve in the regular services to address any possible threat to its borders.

As a consequence, the Menzies Government recommenced conscription, supported by all political parties. The first ballot was for the period 1951-1959 where all young men, on turning 18, were called up under legislation at the time, courtesy of the *National Service Act 1951* (Cth), where they could elect to nominate a service preference. Overall, most served in units close to their place of residence for the standard 176 days of recruit training, followed by roles as reservists for a further five years. The requirement was slowly reduced around 1957 and call up was now by birthday ballot. In November 1959,

National Service was discontinued and by June 1960, any further obligation ceased.

In July 1956, a deadline was put in place by the Geneva Accords requiring South and North Vietnam to be under one government. It was met with a number of obstacles, including election fraud. Over the next few years, North Vietnam leaders carried out a campaign of subversion and sabotage. By 1962, life in South Vietnam and its security were at peril. It was well known that support by Australia for South Vietnam in 1962 was at the beckoning of a number of nations, including the United States of America, to try to curb the increasing problem of communism throughout Asia.

Being an ally to the United States, Australia's support for the South Vietnamese government was implemented by our government, so the specialist unit, known as the Australian Army Training Team Vietnam (AATTV) with 30 military advisers, was dispatched to South Vietnam on 31 July, 1962. In reality, this was the commencement of Australia's participation in the Vietnam War, the conflict between North and South Vietnam. Their role was mainly in a training and advisory capacity as part of the U.S. Military Command, including its special forces, but they also worked in the field with various other local units, including the South Vietnamese Army (ARVN). By September, 1964 they had 73 personnel in South Vietnam.

Unfortunately, the first Australian to lose his life was adviser, Sergeant William Hacking, who died on 1 June 1963, following an accidental weapon discharge when it became entangled in vegetation near Hue. This was followed by the first Australian battle casualty, when on 6 July, 1964, Warrant Officer Kevin Conway, also with the AATTV, was killed in action at Nam Dong, 30 miles from Da Nang.

By August 1964, the South Vietnamese Port of Vung Tau saw the arrival of Caribou aircraft flown by the Royal Australian Air Force, followed by a major escalation by the United States of America to address the ever-increasing insurgency into South Vietnam by the North Vietnamese. As part of the American build up, the US Government expected, or should we say, requested friendly nations such as Australia, to provide logistical support to curb what the Australian people were led to believe was the rise of communism and the threat to its sovereignty.

Once again, recruiting was an issue so in November, 1964, the Menzies Government reintroduced a National Service scheme via the *National Service Act 1964* (Cth) (the Act). This time, the criteria was for all males aged 20 to be registered with the Department of Labour and National Service (DLNS) then drafted, following the luck of the draw by way of a birthday ballot. If your date marble came out, you were called up to serve two years full time in the Australian Army, including as required, special overseas service or, to put it more bluntly, combat duties in Vietnam.

The Act, however, exempted by definition Aboriginal and Torres Strait Islanders peoples, members of the permanent armed forces, including the regular army and former members who had served at least two years, together with various other exemptions, including United Nations employees and personnel from foreign governments permanently residing in Australia.

In respect to Indigenous Australians, they could still join the armed services and, thankfully, they were then treated as equals, being paid the same salary and not suffering any further discrimination. This, however, wasn't the case in 1914, when many were rejected on the grounds of race as they weren't considered "white enough". However, World War One recruiting officers soon decided that, with the increasing casualties and lack of numbers, Indigenous recruits were acceptable to fight for their country.

Many of our Indigenous Australians enlisted with the profound hope that fighting for their country would bring about a change in equality for all. Sadly, when they returned home from overseas duty, Aboriginal servicemen received little recognition from the Australian public.

These injustices were only righted, to a degree, on 27 May, 1967 when our country voted to amend our constitution so all Australians, including Aboriginal and Torres Strait Islander people, were counted as part of our population, so the Commonwealth could enact laws for our Indigenous population with an amendment to section 51 of our constitution. A staggering 90.6 per cent were in favour, with all states and territories voting in a majority and it was deemed to be one of the most successful national referendums in our history. Regardless, enrolment and voting in our elections was not made compulsory for Indigenous Australians until 1984.

Following an amendment, by way of the *Defence Act 1965* (Cth) in March, 1966, Prime Minister Harold Holt announced that conscripts would be sent to Vietnam as required, to serve with units of the Australian Regular Army. Upon discharge after two years, service was to continue for a further three years as part-time army reservists. The National Service scheme did not include a ballot for the navy and air force.

On 10 March, 1965, the first ballot draw took place. As expected, 2,100 20-year-old men were selected from an estimated 100,000 eligible for the ballot. Members of the Citizens Military forces (CMF) were exempt as were theology students. Apprentices and students drawn from the ballot could have their two-year service deferred until they finished their studies by way of temporary deferments, including those alleging executional hardship.

Under the Act, failure to register was deemed an offence and the offender could be fined up to 50 pounds. If you were absent from Australia and not an ordinary resident, you were required to register within 14 days on returning home.

There were a number of loopholes and inconsistencies. You could obtain an indefinite deferment if you married before being called up, if you had a serious criminal record and posed a potential security risk, or if you joined the CMF on a part-time basis for six years or its equivalent in the navy or airforce. It wasn't long before the loopholes were addressed by the government. As an example, young men would often join the CMF, or its equivalent, before their age group ballot and, as deemed to be balloted out, would then immediately resign afterwards. Ballots were then held every four to six weeks following the closure of each registration period and generally held under government supervision, with each marble drawn by a well-known or distinguished citizen.

After the ceremony of the first marble being drawn, the remainder of the ballot was closed to representatives of the media. Once the ballot had been drawn and a person's marble came out, they could claim an exemption based on physical or mental disability but only those disabilities as prescribed by legislation. Section 29A of the Act allowed persons with conscientious beliefs on non-religious grounds, which prevented them from serving, to apply for an exemption which then had to ultimately go before the courts for adjudication.

The ballot inconsistencies included the method of carrying

out the draft, where some potential conscripts born on certain days were more likely to be drafted than those born on other dates. For example, if you were born on 30 June, you were more likely to be conscripted than if you were born on 1 January. One glaring issue the government also failed to account for and adjust, were the numbers during leap years between 1965 and 1972.

Some potential conscripts ultimately became known as "conscientious objectors", which added to the political and social dissent at the time. A number of objectors were either fined or sent to jail to serve their period of national service behind bars. One conscript, in particular, after being found not to have any such conscience, was ordered to Vietnam, subsequently went absent without leave and then served a prison sentence.

A number of others declared they would defend Australia to the hilt if it was attacked, but would, in no way, serve in Vietnam. They failed to comply with their call up notice, with one being convicted and sentenced to two years imprisonment after the Act was amended to impose a two-year jail term for draft resisters.

A protest movement known as Save our Sons (SOS) was also established, mainly comprising of mothers whose sons were old enough to be conscripted. They protested, sometimes by way of silent vigils in public places such as the Shrine of Remembrance, or they would hand out leaflets at army barracks or railway stations, supported by the Draft Resisters Union when National Servicemen would leave to begin their two years of conscription.

Some SOS members were arrested and five were ultimately sentenced to 14 days incarceration at Fairlea women's prison for the "terrible crime" of handing out leaflets to men about to register for national service. Other protesters would walk down main city streets carrying placards that read "No call up", "Conscription is immoral", "We oppose the callup" and, of course, "Make love not war".

The Draft Resisters Unions and the Youth Campaign Against Conscription's main aim was to repeal the Act and bring an immediate end to Australia's support for the Vietnam War. This was open to members who blatantly refused to comply with the Act and demonstrated using the tactic of holding draft card burning rallies. The Monash University Labour Club, under the control of Maoists in fierce opposition to the war in Vietnam, set up a committee to raise funds to be sent to The National Liberation Front of South Vietnam, more famously known as the Viet Cong.

One well known journalist and television presenter, Simon Townsend, was subsequently tried in court for his conscientious stance to the Vietnam War. He served a period of imprisonment in Long Bay Goal, was court-martialled and served a further one month in an army prison. Albert Langer, also a well-known political activist in the 1960s, led a group in stern opposition to the Vietnam War, resulting in many who failed to accept call up. Despite still being prosecuted, he had the option to undertake civilian work, which ultimately, was found by the government to be totally unworkable.

Resistance to the draft was also occurring in the United States. In 1966, well known American professional boxer, Muhammad Ali (Ali), born Cassius Marcellus Clay Jnr, refused to be drafted into the armed forces, due to, not only his religious beliefs, but in stark opposition to the Vietnam War. He did not box for another four years after being found guilty of draft evasion, but did avoid jail. Ali was held in high esteem as a consequence of his conscientious objections and not just because of his boxing prowess.

Despite intervention in Australia by the Returned Services League of Australia (RSL) and other pressure groups, draft resisters were still subject to convictions and civil imprisonment continued. The Australian government, despite all this unrest, had already sent a task force, the first battalion known as the Royal Australian Regiment (1RAR), to support the US 173rd Airborne Brigade in Bien Hoa province, arriving at Vung Tau on 8 June, 1965 on the HMAS Sydney.

1RAR was involved in numerous engagements with the Viet Cong, including the Battle of Gang Toi where two Australian soldiers were deemed killed but missing in action following the fighting. This was followed by a further two battalions despatched in 1966. These included conscripts, together with RAAF squadrons of Canberra jet bombers and helicopters, further supported by the Royal Australian Navy patrolling off the coast of North Vietnam.

Between 1963 and May 1965, Australia lost 36 regular soldiers as a consequence of the Vietnam War. On 24 May, 1965 the Australian public was further saddened by the death of Errol Noack, the first National Service conscript to be killed in action.

Private Noack, who had only been in the country for a mere 10 days, had experienced 10 hours of combat when he lost his life, shot during Operation Hardihood. At the time, the Australian public was told he was killed by enemy fire, but it emerged at the end of the war that he was a victim of friendly fire. The sadness for his family extended to the manner in which they were advised of his death. The Minister for the Army, Malcolm Fraser, accompanied by an army officer and chaplain, hand delivered a cable to Noack's father.

Some months later, on 13 November, 1965, Warrant Officer Kevin Wheatley of the AATTV was killed in action and was posthumously awarded the Victoria Cross (VC) for his bravery in defending a wounded soldier. This courageous soldier would be one of four Australian soldiers to be awarded the VC during the Vietnam War.

A budding young test cricketer, Doug Walters, who made 100 in his first test and followed two weeks later with another 100, was called up on 20 April, 1966 and served the compulsory two years. He missed out on serving in Vietnam, despite declaring he was more than prepared to go if required and despite the public opposition to the war.

Other notable sportsmen to be subsequently drafted but who did not serve in Vietnam, included the Richmond football champion, Royce Hart and Constable Rex Hunt, who was also making a name for himself at the time with Richmond, Bernie Quinlan, a Footscray footballer and Brownlow medallist, and Kevin Sheedy, later to become a much heralded senior AFL coach. Essendon Football Club had a total of six players conscripted to Vietnam, including Keith Gent who was posted to 7RAR but wounded in action near Long Binh. On his return to Australia, his playing days were effectively over.

Test cricketer, Tony Dell, who played two tests for Australia in 1971 and 1973, was conscripted and served with the 2nd Battalion, Royal Australian Regiment (2RAR) in Vietnam in 1968. He was involved in a number of enemy contacts around the Australian base at Nui Dat and, as a consequence of his military service, founded the Post Traumatic Stress Disorder Group (PTSD) known as Stand Tall for PTS in 2010.

Australian motor racing driver identity, Peter Brock, was also drafted into the Australian army and served two years in the medical corps but made his views, in opposition to sending conscripts to the Vietnam War, well known. Following his discharge in 1967, he would eventually have a distinguished racing career, winning the Bathurst 1000 nine times amongst other honours, including being inducted into the V8 Supercars Hall of Fame. The local sporting fraternity also conscripted included boxing champions, Henry and Leon Nissen. However, their father was certainly antiwar as he was involved in a demonstration outside Pentridge prison in support of John Zarb, who was imprisoned as a conscientious objector.

Interestingly, Ross Case, another famous sportsman who won two grand slam tennis titles, failed the medical examination when called up for National Service. The DLNS, in a typical bureaucratic explanation, put out a press release stating, those who were rejected as unfit were not unnecessarily unfit for normal activity, including sport, but obviously did not meet the army's high benchmark.

Former Australian Deputy Prime Minister, Tim Fischer, was conscripted in 1966, served with 1RAR as a second lieutenant and was wounded in the Battle of Coral-Balmoral during May and June 1968. He, in fact, extended his national service by nine months so he could serve with the battalion in Vietnam. Mr Fischer was the first post-Vietnam conscript to be elected to parliament, however, he used the 50th anniversary of the first intake, that took place on 30 June, 1965, to make a number of statements on the irregularities of the conscript ballot methodology.

Shortly after Harold Holt became Australian Prime Minister on 22 January, 1966, he announced the 1st Battalion, Royal Australian Regiment was to be replaced by the 1st Australian Task Force (1ATF) and to be based at Nui Dat in

Phouc Tuy Province. This had the effect of tripling the number of Australians serving in Vietnam to approximately 4,500, of which 1,500 were conscripts mainly with 5RAR and 6RAR.

Mr Holt had visited the United States to discuss the war with President Lyndon Baines Johnson (LBJ), whose famous speech on 30 June, 1966 resulted in the slogan, "All the way with LBJ". This visit confirmed the Australian government's unwavering support for the US Vietnam War policy. Just prior to Holt's suspected drowning off Portsea, Victoria on 17 December, 1967, Australia had over 8,000 personnel in South Vietnam and it was always his belief that, by increasing the number of foreign troops in South Vietnam, this would ultimately lead to victory and resolve the threat of communism.

The enemy, at this time mainly consisted of the 274 Main Force Regiment, also known as the Dong Nai Regiment of the North Vietnamese Army (NVA). It consisted of two very experienced battalions of approximately 2,000 soldiers, supported by mortar and machine gun units, together with engineers and equipped well enough to carry out hit and run assaults at will on our military and the South Vietnamese Army (SVA).

This was very evident when, in November, 1965, its 275 Regiment successfully annihilated a SVA Ranger battalion only five kilometres from Nui Dat. The NVA was also supported by a Viet Cong (VC) mobile battalion, known as D445, with an estimated 500 VC and further reinforced with approximately 400 numerous guerrillas who also had the support of various infrastructures in villages and hamlets which assisted the VC.

At home, opposition to the Vietnam War escalated further, particularly after the Battle of Long Tan on 18 August, 1966. Eighteen Australians were killed, 11 of who were National

Servicemen. One third of Australians from D Company 6RAR were either killed or wounded and were evacuated to 2 Field Ambulance in Vung Tau. On the previous night, the Australian Army base of Nui Dat (also referred to as "the Dat") was subjected to the VC's relentless mortar and rifle attack, lasting over 22 minutes and wounding 24 Australians.

Nui Dat, southeast of Saigon, was selected as the site for the Australian Task Force operations with Vung Tau serving as its logistical base some 26 kilometres away by road. The base was set up mainly by national service conscripts, together with army regulars, including infantry and engineers. It was also supported by a battery from the Royal New Zealand Artillery and a small number of US troops.

Like Australia, the involvement of New Zealand in the Vietnam War from 1964 was fiercely opposed at home with widespread anti- Vietnam War rallies, but their government decided to become involved over what were cold war concerns, support under the ANZUS Alliance and, of course, opposition to the Southeast Asia communists. From a basic military point of view, Nui Dat was suitable for the Australian military and its counterparts to base its task force operations in opposition to the VC, which now had 5,000 fighters located in the surrounding hills, making the province, in particular the roads, subject to repeated ambushes.

It is fair to say, by the time the base was established in 1966, after erecting barbed wire, digging pits, laying claymore mines around the circumference of the 12-kilometre base and prior to the Battle of Long Tan, the province was very much controlled by the VC. The barrage rained into Nui Dat by the VC, resulted in a planned outdoor concert for the soldiers, featuring Col Joye, a well-known rock and roll artist, supported by a young singer called Little Pattie, to be abandoned as the diggers had more pressing problems to address. The next morning, D Company of 6RAR left Nui Dat to join B Company and intense fighting took place in the Long Tan rubber plantation. One hundred and eight diggers from D Company fought and held off an estimated 2000 soldiers from North Vietnamese combat units.

At the time, there was some thought that the real mission of the opposing forces was to attack the Australian army base at Nui Dat, which had been hit with mortars and recoilless rifles a few nights earlier. Long Tan was approximately 2,500 metres outside the range of artillery from Nui Dat. The battle was to make headlines, not only in Australia, but also the United States.

Both sides claimed victory and Harold Holt, congratulated the Australian troops on a well won victory, as did General William Westmoreland, a well-known and decorated United States soldier. The casualties of the Viet Cong and People's Army of Vietnam were in the order of 245 dead with three captured but many of the dead and injured were removed as they withdrew from the battle.

The battle further fuelled criticism and unrest in Australia to a point where the government later reduced the number of conscripts to 50 per cent of any unit, much to the chagrin of 1ATF at the time, who were left to make some immediate structure reorganisation. The anti-war protestors' movement continued to grow, not only in Australia but in the United States.

In Australia, it was not helped by a visit from the President, Johnson. I recall the motorcade traveling down Bourke Street, Melbourne, and onlookers waved along with 'All the way with LBJ', or perhaps we all simply booed him like thousands did, as part of the demonstration in opposition to the Vietnam War.

It didn't help LBJ's case, seeking support for the war, when the Premier of NSW, Robert Askin, told his driver to 'run the bastards over' as protestors lay down in front of his vehicle during the motorcade.

It was against this backdrop and after being promoted, or perhaps just "transferred" from Despatch to the Supply Branch of Victoria Police, that my day of reckoning was about to take place. My recollection of the National Service draw, or lottery, which took place in early April, 1967, I was sitting at home watching the ballot on television when it was announced which birth dates had been plucked from the barrel. My luck had run out as 21 March was drawn from the barrel by some unknown dignitary.

I was destined to keep the O'Neill military tradition alive and follow in the footsteps of my father, Thomas Edward O'Neill, who served as transport driver VX 84067 in the Australian army during World War Two, and his father, Thomas O'Neill Snr, who served with the British Army as Lance Sergeant 3701425 during World War One with the 2nd battalion of the Kings Own Royal Regiment. Grandpa was so proud I was to continue the O'Neill history of serving in the military, not that I was all that convinced at the time.

Although I was reasonably healthy and quite fit, having played both cricket and football, the required standard of fitness for National Service was deemed to be the same for any potential voluntary applicant for acceptance in the Regular Army. I did, however, have bad acne and wondered whether this would preclude me for being unfit as approximately 35 per cent of young men examined generally failed the medical. If, of course, you failed to report for the medical, or in any way lied about your current health, you could be fined heavily.

The medical was conducted after work about three weeks later by a civilian doctor in Bell Street, Preston. I was questioned about my general health, had a urine test conducted and a chest x-ray taken. The only concern was my acne and I was referred for a further medical examination some weeks later. It was not uncommon though for a number of pending draftees, who were opposed to the Vietnam War, to take various concoctions prior to the examination in order to be rejected. On this particular night, a number of those waiting for their examination, openly boasted about consuming large amounts of sugar, apparently in an attempt to fail the urine test.

Although I may have been a borderline case and not because of any sugar intake, I was somehow passed as suitable following the second examination and aptitude test. Interestingly, a Morgan Gallup Poll in May, 1967 determined that 62 per cent of those polled were, in fact, in favour of continuing Australia's involvement in the Vietnam War.

I had no grounds to apply for a deferment and, in many ways, I was looking forward to a new chapter in my very short life, albeit with some trepidation. Weeks later, I received a letter by way of a formal call up notice from the DNLS advising I had been called up for 'National Service with the Military Forces of the Commonwealth'. I was to report for service at the army barracks in Swan Street, Richmond on 7 July, 1967 and present a copy of my call up notice and certificate of registration.

That morning, before my parents drove me to the depot, I decided to cut my hair, especially the fringe, although I was to discover it was unnecessary as the army barbers were about to have a good crack at me in any event. We arrived at Swan Street to be met by a Save our Sons protest. After a cursory medical examination, we were all immediately loaded onto military buses for the two-hour drive to Puckapunyal to commence an initial three months of recruit training at 2 Recruit Training Battalion (2RTB). Conscripts from other Australian states would be sent to either 1 Recruit Training Battalion (1RTB) at Kapooka or 3 Recruit Training Battalion (3RTB) Singleton in New South Wales. Little did we all know what was ahead for us.

6

Army Training

The Puckapunyal Army Base, commonly referred to as "Pucka", is situated approximately 115 kilometres from Melbourne along the Hume Highway and 10 kilometres west of Seymour in Central Victoria. It was the recruit training base for all conscripts, other than those from Queensland and New South Wales, and was also the base for the 1st Armoured Regiment. The actual base itself was generally flat, apart from a large hill overlooking it, commonly referred to as "One Tit Hill". The base housed married officers in brand new three-bedroom brick homes at Milton Bay Close on the outskirts of the facility.

It is believed the word "Puckapunyal" was the name taken from the Aboriginal people known as the Taungurung and translated as "The Middle Hill", "Place of Exile" and "Valley of the Winds". It has often been described as one of the most desolate and barren military grounds in the southern hemisphere. I was to subsequently find out, it was prone to extreme bouts of weather.

We were to be trained by experienced soldiers at 2RTB and for the next twelve weeks, we would be accommodated in army huts, each one divided into four cubicles, generally housing around 12 to 15 trainees. At any one time, the army base would home up to 4,000 soldiers. We were to be paid the same wages as regular servicemen, approximately $35 per week and if you were married, it increased to $45 per week.

The other bonus provided to you was free board, including meals and uniforms, together with medical, dental and hospital treatment, as required. You were eligible for three weeks annual leave and following two years' service, an additional seven days leave or pay. If you served overseas, you would also be eligible for a war service home loan pursuant to the War Service Homes Act 1918 (Cth). The majority of trainees were usually well educated with many graduating from Form Six.

I arrived at Pucka around 2pm with my solitary suitcase in hand, to be "warmly" greeted by a sergeant. He took one look at us, all meekly lined up after alighting from the bus and yelled, 'I've never seen such a scruffy looking bunch of mongrels. I'll soon knock you guys into shape.'

He then walked along the line of very nervous looking conscripts and asked each to provide a short life history, including employment.

When I said I worked for Victoria Police, everyone laughed as they thought I meant as a serving police officer. He said, 'You a copper? You're too little.'

I replied, 'No, I was a public servant.' The laughs intensified more when the chap alongside me told the sergeant his employment was as a "mattress tester".

We were then marched down to the Q store, after a medical and dental examination, to obtain our mandatory uniforms consisting of a slouch hat, fatigues, which were dark green trousers, shirt and a jumper, together with GP boots and PT gear. I had a big head, so the slouch hat I was originally issued was too small for me. Others had jumpers that were too large but it was bad luck. You also received a towel, a bar of soap, a razor blade, eating utensils and a pay book before being presented for a haircut. The barber took one look at me and muttered, 'Where do I start with this head?'

I finished up with very short back and sides. I must admit though, when he finished shearing me, I looked a lot better than when I first walked in and at the end of my first day in the army, I became a third intake recruit with C Company, 13th training platoon, 2RTB with army number 3791976. The battalion was made up of four companies called Alpha, Bravo, Charlie and Delta, based on the NATO phonetic alphabet.

Our instructors, very experienced regular non-commissioned veterans (NCO), had previously served in the Malayan conflict and some already in Vietnam. They generally had no patience, were largely intolerant of all and sundry but at the same time showed glimmers of fairness on the odd occasion. On the other hand, the second lieutenant in charge of the platoon as our commander, was very young and a conscript with no military experience, apart from three months officer training. He received his commission for no other reason than his education qualifications and was a good fit for all conscripts, although it was always his way or the highway.

My life was now very regimented. I was not only just a number but always yelled at by either the platoon commander or his lackey sergeant.

'Recruit O'Neill, straighten up. I tell you what to do and how to do it, your life is now under my control.'

I always responded with, 'Yes, Sir,' or 'No, Sir.'

Our days usually commenced at the sound of the first post revelry around 5.30am. It was followed by a line up, usually using our bedding to keep warm, before quickly making the perfect bed known as the "fart sack". Then came showering, dressing immaculately, relentlessly polishing our boots, cleaning our rifles and after breakfast, we were usually running or being taught to march properly around the parade ground, or charging up and down One Tit Hill.

Our 16-hour days would generally finish around late evening. Some nights we would have to attend lectures, map reading classes and towards the end of recruits, an introduction to war and its origins, including, of course, Vietnam. We had to spit polish our boots nightly and were also required to sit a test to see if any of us were officer material in order to be transferred to the Officer Training Unit at Scheyville. It's fair to say I failed that test miserably.

To maintain our sense of humour and as a bit of light relief, we would play sport on a Thursday, usually football and boxing. Sunday was our day of rest provided, without fail, you maintained to meticulous army standard, your spit polished toe on each boot, freshly ironed uniform with name badge pinned straight over and above the left pocket, shiny brass buckle, clean rifle, webbings and kit.

Training included an introduction to various weapons of war, in particular the self-loading rifle (SLR), M60 machine gun (M60) and the MK2 grenade (MK2). The SLR loaded with 7.62 cartridges was the weapon of choice in the Vietnam War and generally preferred by infantry soldiers over the 5.56 calibre American M16 Armalite.

The SLR had an overall range of about 750 metres and weighed approximately four kilos. I had fired a number of weapons, mainly shotguns and .22 rifles, before joining the army, as I often went rabbit hunting with my father.

I believed I was experienced with guns but after firing the

SLR for the first time, it literally knocked me backwards, much to my and the instructing NCO's amazement. He even asked me if I had ever fired a gun before! There was a real kick behind the weapon and we all had earplugs, as the noise was deafening. I finished with bruises on my right shoulder but once I got used to firing the SLR and spending a lot of time on the range, it eventually became quite easy.

However, before we actually got to the range, we were taught about our weapon and instructed about safety: how to dismantle it, how to clean it, how to put it back together. It got to the stage where the instructor would blow a whistle and we had a minute to dismantle the SLR and put it back together.

It was repetitive training all the time, until eventually, we became competent using the weapon. We used to have competitions to see who was the quickest in dismantling their SLR and putting it back together.

Another practical examination of our skills was when the instructor would place the dismantled SLR on the ground, mix up all the parts of the rifle and then ask us to identify each part, before having to reassemble it. We were told by the duty sergeant that our rifle was our best friend and we had to treat it better than we would treat our girlfriend.

When being instructed on how to use the MK 2 grenade at the rifle range, my initial embarrassment with the SLR was to pale into insignificance. Another trainee, lying on his back between two sandbags, pulled the pin, promptly froze and wouldn't let the grenade go. In a panic, the sergeant barked out for all of us to run while he, quietly and with some patience, took the grenade without the pin from the offending culprit and lobbed it away in the air – exactly what the recruit was expected to do but failed miserably.

The M60 was an interesting weapon and even though it could be fired at a short range from the shoulder, it was generally used from the ground and worked by a gunner, assistant gunner and the bearer of ammunition. What they didn't tell the recruits was, occasionally it would go into what can only be described as a "runaway weapon". It would go into automatic mode and continue firing without any pressure on the trigger. This happened on the firing range as well, causing everyone to scurry for cover. Once again, our training instructor came to the rescue.

After four weeks of constant marching parades, bayonet practice and relentless physical training (PT), including the mandatory push ups if we started to slack off, we were allowed to have visitors on a Sunday. After eight weeks, a four day leave pass was granted, with our sergeant handing out condoms which I placed in my wallet. I had been out one particular night, returned home and somehow the condom was sitting alongside my bed, still in its packet. My mother came in, saw it and was absolutely horrified and disgusted. There I was, at 20 years of age, old enough to be in the army yet my mother was shocked at seeing a condom on my bedside table. Things were very different back then.

It was a bonus, however, to leave camp, see your family, girlfriend and enjoy decent food. The army food was supposedly nutritious but, shall we say, not very appealing. At one stage, I did have to work in the mess peeling potatoes for some infraction that supposedly I was responsible for.

On return, we now had to elect our two preferences for what corps we preferred to serve in. I always had some fascination with medical procedures and hospitals, so I decided to be a medic.

Dad's words before I left were, 'Whatever you do, don't go into infantry.'

It was probably the best advice he's ever given me, so I elected the Medical Corps (RAAMC) with my second preference being the Dental Corps (RAADC).

Why I put that as my second preference, I don't know. I wanted to be a medic preferably with a battalion because, at this point, Vietnam was a constant reality of knowing that approximately 50 per cent of conscripts would see active duty in Vietnam. I got Dental Corps and suffice to say, I was shattered.

Absolutely bloody shattered. *The Dental Corps? What?*

I phoned my father and said, 'You're not going to believe this, I'm in the Dental Corps.'

He replied, 'So?'

I shouted, 'Oh, give me a break!'

He then stated, 'Now listen, you stay where you are. Stay where you are, you'll get a couple of stripes, you will go to Vietnam and have an experience that will always stay with you.'

I wasn't convinced so I went to see the platoon sergeant and I politely said, 'I'm not happy about this and want to change to infantry.'

The overall largest proportion of conscripts would be assigned, as I was later to find out, as a "crunchy", with the Royal Australian Regiment. It was the nickname given, based on the infantryman "crunching" through the jungle terrain.

He said, 'Well, recruit, you're in the Dental Corps and that's it. Nothing is going to change.' I was stuck in the Dental Corps, and now known as a "Fang Warrior".

He was the same sergeant who had called me into his office earlier to enquire if I was trying to grow a goatee.

He said, 'Recruit, your appearance lately is leaving me with some concern.'

I had a small scar under my chin, due to falling out of a tree after having quite a few drinks, so I had difficulty shaving. I tried to explain this to him, but to no avail. He was also previously concerned about my marching or drill practice on the parade ground, which we did relentlessly. Because I had broken my arm as a young child, I had trouble straightening it, which obviously was not to his liking as a strict drill sergeant.

This sergeant also had a habit of visiting our hut after we had made our beds, tidied up our lockers and left for morning parade. If he found one bed not made properly with regulation or "hospital" creases at the end of the mattress on each side, or any locker left untidy and not in pristine condition, he and other non-commissioned officers would leave the hut as though a hurricane had hit it! We all learnt very quickly to make sure our hut was spotless and to this day, I still know how to make a bed with the 45-degree angle hospital corner.

With only a few weeks left in basic training, we also had to elect our preference for service. We were given two choices, Vietnam or regular army and possible service in Malaysia, which meant we would have to sign on for another year, so I ticked Vietnam. There was a rumour going around Pucka that some platoons had been given a choice, where those who elected Vietnam would take one pace forward in a platoon line up. That didn't work very well as many of the larrikins in the platoon would take one step back, leaving those in front supposedly volunteering.

In the interim, we continued to climb ropes and all sorts of obstacles, further rifle practice, dismantling our weapons, relentlessly cleaning them and putting them back together and, of course, throwing grenades without any further mishaps. As part of our graduation day, we had to practice marching onto the parade ground with our rifle, then practice with the lowering of the flag.

One day, when the sergeant was coming along the line to inspect everything, I realised I hadn't put the safety catch on my SLR. Panicking inside, I slowly pulled it down and clicked it on. Of course, he heard it and just screamed at the top of his lungs, 'How dare you not have the safety catch on!'

My poor memory resulted in me spending the whole night on guard duty, and, of course, to carefully watch over the parade ground that I had 'insulted with an unsafe weapon'.

After three long, hard and tiring months, I finally got through the graduation parade. I left Pucka with a piece of paper titled, "2RTB March Out Pro Forma" stating my new rank of Private, or colloquially known as a "baggy arse", my army number 3791976, address of my new unit and that I was leaving Pucka by driving my Volkswagen beetle, Reg No JGA 989. With a white strip around and along the left side of my wind burnt face from the slouch hat strapping, I departed begrudgingly and drove to the School of Army Health in Healesville.

My fellow conscripts, also now with the rank of private and not recruit, were sent for three months training at various locations throughout Australia. Those in the Engineering Corps were sent to the School of Military Engineering in Casula, N.S.W, guys in the Artillery Corps joined regiments at either Holsworthy, N.S.W. and Wacol, Queensland and, if you were lucky enough to be posted to infantry, you would start your training at the Infantry Training Centre, Singleton, N.S.W.

The Armoured Corps training was at Puckapunyal and others were posted to specialist corps such as Psychology and Education, or the Catering Corps. As the majority of national servicemen were posted to infantry, this allowed the government to increase the Royal Australian Regiment to nine battalions.

The School of Army Health for Medical and Dental Corpsmen was first established at Puckapunyal in 1949, then moved to Portsea before settling at what was known as the Summerleigh Lodge. Healesville is located 65 kilometres from Melbourne in the foothills south of the Great Dividing Range. It was chosen for, not only its location, but access to suitable training areas in the adjacent mountains. It was to be the home for the Royal Australian Army Medical Corps (RAAMC) and of course the Dental Corps (RAADC), of which I was now a somewhat reluctant member.

Our training was to take place over three months and included all areas of dental work. Our role would mainly be assisting the supervising dentist who had the rank of captain. The majority of us were national servicemen. We were taught basic medical first aid and procedures and trained alongside the soon-to-be medics. I enjoyed this part of the training as my ambition had not wavered from becoming a medic.

Our accommodation was in tents and after about two weeks of constant rain and cold, a number of us moved into more suitable housing in the Healesville township. If we didn't, we all thought we'd start to rust from the constant rain. I am not sure if this was approved by the major in charge of the school but we seemed to exist without any issues and would travel each day to and from the base to our accommodation.

Part of our training included a mock vehicle accident, not that we knew it at the time. One day during class, one of the instructors ran in to tell us there had been an accident out the front on the main road opposite the school. We were ordered to race out and assist the "dying and injured". We saw two cars which appeared to have crashed into one another and bodies were lying by the side of the road. A number of the trainee medics actually collapsed and fainted upon seeing all the "blood" and "injuries".

This resulted in the instructors determining it wasn't such a good idea, so the supposed training drill was called off, obviously to treat the soldiers who had collapsed. The event was to be discussed at great length with some laughter in the boozer that night. Training was eventually completed after three months before we were sent back to Puckapunyal to await our fate.

The dental unit at Puckapunyal consisted of both army dentists with the rank of captain. Because of a shortage of army dentists and given that the army demanded all soldiers had to be dental fit, civilian dentists from Seymour would come to the unit to assist. My days were not filled with much excitement, other than playing football, boxing in the army gym, gazing "lovingly" at One Tit Hill and assisting with teeth extractions, fillings and overall normal dental procedures.

Three months as a private ended when I received notification in the mail that I was to be sent to Vietnam but only after I attended a jungle training course (JTC). After I was handed the envelope by the major in charge of the dental unit, I finally knew my fate.

As part of preparing for duty in Vietnam, I was required to have two injections: one for cholera and one for yellow fever. To say I had a reaction is an understatement as I spent a few days in bed in the army hut next door to the dental unit, suffering from acute flu-like symptoms and struggling to raise my arm.

When I telephoned my parents to tell them the news of my Vietnam duty, my mother was not impressed because she always believed I had volunteered. Dad proved to be correct though, when he originally advised me not to transfer to the infantry and that I would go to Vietnam and have an experience I would never forget.

7

Vietnam is Waiting

Prior to three weeks of JTC, the Vietnam War witnessed a major escalation and was subject to one of its most intense and largest military campaigns, known as Operation Coburg, which saw heavy fighting between 1 ATF, the communist forces of the Viet Cong, together with the North Vietnamese People's Army of Vietnam. Operation Coburg was commenced on 24 January, 1968 by the Australian forces and supported by New Zealand soldiers with fighting around Long Binh and Bien Hoa. This planned military operation was, however, unable to prevent what occurred in the late-night hours on 30 January, 1968 which was to be known as the "Tet Offensive".

The South Vietnamese Army of the Republic of Vietnam and the United States Armed Forces, together with their allies, were the focus of surprise military attacks, not only against these armed forces, but also the civilian population. The VC were going from house to house in the battle at Hue and arresting civil servants, teachers, religious leaders and any South Vietnamese civilian allegedly connected with the allied forces.

Although the Vietnam War was overall portrayed as a conflict between the United States and North Vietnam, the ARVN from the outset, were carrying the brunt of the conflict long before the Allied nations got involved. They even established and modified the use of M113 Armoured Personnel Carriers (APCs) where they were awarded the United States Presidential Unit Citation for exceptional heroism.

The ARVN, however, would suffer the highest number killed in action, totalling 254,000 recorded deaths from 1960 to 1974, compared to 58,000 U.S Troops killed during the war. The ARVN were not without complaints about its overall performance as many of its units were considered to be lacking motivation and direction. Overall, it meant the Allied forces did the bulk of the fighting.

The Battle of Hue, also known as the "Siege of Hue", launched by North Vietnam and the Viet Cong, was a major miliary engagement, but the combined forces of both the ARVN and Americans resulted in the city of Hue being recaptured after one month of heavy fighting with literally thousands of civilians killed and wounded, including 668 allied troops killed in action.

The name Tet was derived from the Lunar New Year Festival called *Te'T Nguyen D'an* and was commenced by the North Vietnamese, due to the majority of ARVN forces on leave during the festive and holiday period.

The Tet Offensive was all over South Vietnam where 80,000 PAVN and VC attacked more than 100 towns and cities and provincial capitals. This included Saigon, which was the main intent of the offensive, where 35 VC battalions attacked the Tan Son Nhut International Airport and Air Base, the Presidential Palace, the U.S Embassy and the National Radio Station.

The fighting in Saigon produced one of the most famous and chilling images of the Vietnam War. A photograph was taken of the execution of a VC prisoner by a senior ranking officer of ARVN, when he placed his pistol against the head of the prisoner and shot him dead in full view of the local population. Other images included the attack on the U.S Embassy where VC soldiers had occupation for nearly six hours until US paratroopers landed on its roof by helicopter and took control.

Overall, allied forces lost over 3,000 during the offensive. Australian troops were also subject to attacks at its base at Nui Dat in Phouc Tuy province, on targets around Baria, in particular its hospital which was almost destroyed. Fortunately, these attacks were driven back following heavy street fighting never seen before by Australian troops. The fighting at Baria saw Australian troops engaged in many heavy street battles, inflicting heavy causalities and the VC attack was defeated.

As a consequence of Operation Coburg and the Tet Offensive, 17 Australians and two New Zealanders were killed in action, and 61 Australians and 15 New Zealanders were wounded, with many being medevacked to 8 Field Ambulance at Vung Tau.

Following the Tet Offensive, support for the US effort had already been declining. There was a further downturn in public opinion to a point where US President Johnson determined he would not run for re-election. In any event, by early February, 1968, the communist party came to the conclusion that their miliary objectives had failed and they stopped any more attacks on their selected targets.

On January, 1968, prior to the TET Offensive and following the disappearance of Harold Holt, who was believed to have drowned off Portsea, John Gorton was elected as the new Australian Prime Minister. He announced that Australia would not increase the number of troops being sent to Vietnam.

Gorton had a reputation as a strict anti-communist and he continued the Australian involvement in the Vietnam War, albeit slowly reducing the number of troops due to the ongoing dissent and opposition to the war by the citizens of Australia.

It was against this backdrop that my three weeks of the jungle training course began in late February, 1968 at the Holsworthy Army Barracks, located in the outer south side of Sydney. Part of the Holsworthy Military reserve had been a training area and artillery range for the Australian Army since World War One and following World War Two, formed the major base for the Australian army in New South Wales.

The camp was well known for its gullies, creeks and thick woodlands, which I was about to experience. I travelled to Holsworthy by train from Spencer Street, Melbourne in full military uniform and carrying my trusty SLR rifle by my side, but without ammunition.

Training consisted of surviving in jungle warfare as all soldiers, regardless of their corps posting, had no choice when called on, to use a weapon when the need arose. We had weapon training and slept in little tents at night without cover. It was here that I was introduced to a F1 submachine gun, which I would carry for the first few months in Vietnam.

The F1 replaced the Owen machine carbine and had a very distinct top mounted 34 round magazine with a 9mm calibre cartridge. We would be trained to walk through a mock village where targets would suddenly pop up and if it was the enemy, you had to let go a burst of rounds. If they were villagers with little children, the idea was not to unleash a spray of bullets.

I was one of many who shot a number of "innocent villagers". When a target quickly popped up, your first instinct was to let go a few rounds. It was interesting watching our instructors demonstrate the relative power of each weapon, notably the SLR compared to the F1. They placed a 44-gallon drum full of water 100 metres away and fired a few 7.62 mm rounds to see it explode, leaving basically nothing. They then set up an army great coat over a drum and from about 35 metres, fired a few 9mm rounds from the F1. On examination, these rounds had not penetrated the coat and either bounced off or were embedded in its fabric. Mind you, I suspect the Viet Cong would not be wearing great coats but it certainly demonstrated the relative strength of each weapon, or lack thereof.

We would camp out for days, generally near a river and part of the training was to load your gear on a raft and push it across. I remember one occasion where a water snake showed a lot of interest in me and, when I was alerted to this, I paddled very quickly to reach the other side. Training also consisted of climbing up and down ropes, crawling under barb wire, attending classes, usually at night and being introduced to what to expect in Vietnam. Topics were booby traps, mines, snakes, other aggressive inhabitants, like ants, our personal hygiene, taking malaria tablets and in particular, the dangers we faced with exposure to venereal disease from the local bar girls.

Map reading exercises were also part of our education and it was not one of my better endeavours. We were taken out by helicopter on one occasion to the middle of nowhere and I was tasked to get us back safely to the army base. Of course, that didn't happen and after what seemed like an eternity, we were rescued and taken back to camp.

Overall, I enjoyed the three weeks of intense training and returned home by train to Spencer Street station, again with my SLR by my side, but this time I had with me, a few left over live rounds of 7.62mm ammunition. It was probably not a good idea, but what the heck, I was in uniform. I excitedly took Dad up to the hills past Epping where he was most impressed when he let off a few rounds into a 44-gallon drum, which we took with us to raise the excitement level. I showed him how powerful the SLR was, with a small entry hole at the front and the back of the drum blown to smithereens.

It still amazes me to this day that in the 1960s, you could travel on public transport with a rifle by your side and no one would look sideways at you. It was accepted without question.

My love of boxing had not abated and on 26 February, 1968, I watched with delight and pride as Lionel Rose, Australian Bantamweight champion, beat Fighting Harada in Tokyo on points to win the World Bantamweight title. Lionel became the first Aboriginal Australian to win a world championship and was so highly regarded, he was welcomed home at Melbourne Town Hall by a crowd of over 10,000.

Lionel went on to defend his title on three separate occasions. In March, 1969, he beat Alan Rudkin, but then lost to Ruben Olivares five months later. I must admit, I looked up to Lionel, as we all did. Sadly, I would cross paths with him many years later in very unfortunate circumstances, but he was certainly a lovable rogue. One of my other idols was Johnny "Fammo" Famechon, who went on to win the WBC featherweight title when he defeated Cuban Jose Legra. Fammo also successfully defended his title against Fighting Harada in July, 1969 in a split points decision, then knocked him out in the 14th round six months later in a rematch.

I quickly became engaged to my girlfriend, Marjorie, did a last Will and Testament, and Dad put my VW up on blocks, before I commenced a week's pre-embarkation leave. This was prior to departing for Vietnam on a date to be determined in April, 1968, at the ripe age of 21.

In the meantime, sporadic fighting continued in Saigon until March, 1968 with some areas of the capital, in particular, Cholon, left badly damaged due to heavy U.S. artillery and bombing strikes, which resulted in the deaths of hundreds of civilians. The dissent for the Vietnam War again escalated, following what was deemed the My Lai massacre in Son Tinh District, taking place on 16 March, 1968, and resulting in the mass murder of an estimated 347 to 504 unarmed South Vietnamese civilians by US army soldiers, including families of adults, their children and livestock.

It was also alleged some women suffered the indignity of being gang-raped before being killed and their bodies then mutilated. A total of 26 soldiers were charged but only one, platoon leader, Lieutenant William Calley Jr, was convicted and sentenced to life imprisonment. Calley only served three and a half years under house arrest until President Nixon commuted his life sentence.

Whilst fighting continued to escalate in South Vietnam, a leading newspaper's front page screamed out that Normie Rowe, a young pop sensation, had been conscripted into the army and was about to commence his national service at Puckapunyal. Normie arrived at the Swan Street barracks in a Rolls Royce with his screaming fans weeping as he boarded the army bus. Little did Normie know at the time but he too would serve with some distinction in Vietnam as a trooper with the 3rd Calvary Regiment in 1969. However, his army service effectively ended his career as a much-loved pop singer, thanks to raging anti-war sentiments.

I reported to Watsons Bay, New South Wales, in early April

1968 after travelling again from Spencer Street, Melbourne, but still with no exact date of my departure for Vietnam. Watsons Bay is located in South Head and was a Royal Australian Navy Base on Sydney Harbour, better known as HMAS Watson. Its name was, of course, derived from its location at Watsons Bay and generally used by the navy as a warfare training base as well as training in combat, maritime warfare and command.

The army had its personnel depot located at South Head where we would report daily to be told basically nothing and never a departure date. We would report to the orderly room and upon being told we were not leaving that day, we were left to our own devices. Naturally, we would end up going down to the local pub in Watsons Bay and sinking a few beers, often turning into sessions of heavy drinking.

Following this, we would then go into Kings Cross at night, obviously not in uniform, to enjoy the pleasures, including the sex workers, on offer. I recall walking down Chapel Street, seeing all the prostitutes lined up outside their individual flats and flouting what was on offer. The Cross was the epicentre of the sex trade as part of its night life and also known for entertaining American troops, both during World War Two and those on rest and recreation (R & R) from the Vietnam War.

On 15 April, 1968, departure day finally arrived and we were all lined up at Watsons Bay for transport by bus to Mascot Airport, before boarding the Boeing 707 for South Vietnam. The only problem was, a few of us, including fellow soldiers Rob Watson, Norm Caulfield and myself, had over quenched our thirst at the local pub and were struggling to remain upright as we boarded the bus. We sobered up very quickly when reality set in and we boarded the plane, dressed in our army green polyesters and carrying small army duffle bags, containing our worldly possessions.

The plane departed for Darwin to collect more army personnel, then onto Changi Airport, Singapore, for refuelling. It was unable to refuel at Tan Son Nhut Airport, Saigon, due to the danger of being on the tarmac for an extended period.

Interestingly, about 30 minutes from Changi Airport, we had to change into a civilian shirt, as the Singapore Government, led by Lee Kuan Yew, was initially reluctant to support the United States' involvement in the Vietnam War. Their government would not allow soldiers to be seen in uniform, even though it was only for a short stopover. I don't think we fooled anyone at the airport, as we walked around sporting very short hair, wearing GP boots and polyester green army issue pants and only a civilian shirt to try to hide our military identity.

8

Good Morning Vung Tau

As the Boeing 707 slowly began its descent into Tan Son Nhut Airport on 16 April 1968, I looked out the window and took a deep breath as the numbness set in. I was met with the ravages of war. I saw numerous bomb craters, which I thought resembled small waterholes, damaged aircraft, machine guns mounted on sandbags, ammo dumps, patrolling armed soldiers, military aircraft, bunkers and certainly a hive of activity with F-4 Phantom jets and helicopters continually landing and taking off.

I was soon to discover that the Phantom jet was being used extensively in the Vietnam War; it had a top speed of over Mach 2.2 and could carry 18,000 pounds of weapons, including air to air missiles and even napalm bombs. Unknown to me at the time, I would sadly witness the terrible aftermath of a Phantom jet napalm bombing raid.

My thoughts before we landed included, *Shit, what have I got myself into here?*, followed by, *Oh my God, I don't believe this, what a nightmare!* Yes, I was now in a war zone at the ripe old age, or should I say immature age, of just turned 21.

The airport, located near the city of Saigon, had been a major Vietnamese civil airport since the 1920s, but was now occupied by the United States as its main command and control centre and housed a number of units including marines, army and, of course, its air force. The base, subjected to prolonged attacks during the Tet offensive, was regularly hit with rockets and mortars, causing over 100 US personnel to be killed and/or wounded.

In early March 1968, it was provided with roofed aircraft shelters in addition to airborne "rocket watch" patrols to try to limit the airborne artillery attacks by the communist regime. The attacks had resulted in numerous aircraft either destroyed or severely damaged. The constant war and barrage of attacks it had been subjected to, was certainly prevalent as the plane slowly taxied and we set ourselves up for a short flight by Caribou aircraft to Vung Tau.

As I walked away from the air-conditioned aircraft with my slouch hat firmly secured on my head, the first thing that struck me was a smell which was hard to describe but could be best put as a polluted compost heap. This was followed by the impact of stifling heat that would not get below an average of 22 degrees celsius and an average high around 30 degrees celsius. A wet season would last from May to early November, with most rain falling from June to August.

We found ourselves being "welcomed" to Vietnam by other Australian soldiers who were boarding the plane after their tour of duty, telling us we would finish up in a pine box and singing Roy Orbison's hit song, doing the airwaves at the time.

'You may be a soldier but there won't be many coming home.'

We impatiently waited with our trusty duffle bags on the tarmac for nearly two hours for the plane to Vung Tau, in insufferable heat. During the frustrating wait, we watched with some trepidation as all sorts of aircraft took off and landed, including those waiting overhead, in line for their descent.

The range of helicopters, of all shapes and sizes, was endless but we boarded a U.S twin engine C-123 transport plane for the short flight to Vung Tau, my new home at the Australian Field Hospital (1AFH) as part of the 1st Australian Logistic Support Group (1 ALSG). The C-123, a specialised transport aircraft, saw extensive service during the Vietnam War and was a smaller version of the C-130 Hercules aircraft. It had the ability to land on shorter landing strips, unlike the C-130 Hercules cargo aircraft, and was manned by US air force personnel and included the two pilots and a gunner.

Prior to taking off, the American gunner had much pleasure in telling us, in the event we were attacked by the North Vietnamese Air Force, he would warn us and we would all have to unbuckle our seat belts and lay face down on the floor of the aircraft to avoid gunfire as we were attacked. I don't recall any lectures on the strength of the North Vietnamese Air Force (NVA), other than their main role was to operate within North Vietnam. Suffice to say, we took all this in as we had only just arrived in the country. As he looked to be a very experienced soldier, we took him at his word.

Sure enough, once we were airborne and 10 minutes into our flight, he looked out the window and, with some panic, gestured to one of the pilots before telling us all to hit the deck as we were being attacked. Panicking, we all scrambled to the floor of the aircraft and lay face down only to hear raucous laughter coming from the Americans.

It was a set up and I have no doubt we were not the first baby-faced soldiers to be put through the same antics. Settling back after the initial panic and looking out the window during the flight, I could see the countryside's numerous swamps, caused by flooding rivers, the rice paddies and dense undergrowth.

Without being attacked by the NVA Air Force, we safely landed at Vung Tau Airport, controlled by the United States Air Force and, not unlike Tan Son Nhut, with numerous planes and helicopters in a hive of activity. It was also the base for RAAF Transport Flight Vietnam, redesignated No 35 Squadron in June, 1966 and colloquially known by its callsign, "Wallaby". It would make daily flights to Saigon, other towns and cities in South Vietnam, remote outposts and, on several occasions, its Caribous suffered attacks causing aircrew to be wounded.

Such flights were originally by Australian Dakota aircraft for evacuating those killed in action, wounded and sick Australian military personnel. This was then followed by Hercules aircraft for transport back to Australia via RAAF Butterworth in Malaysia, then onto the RAAF Richmond Air Base in New South Wales.

We were to be transferred to 1ALSG, located on the hot, steamy and sandy south coast of Vietnam. Vung Tau, the closest beach resort approximately 100 kilometres or a two-hour drive by road or ferry from Saigon, was situated at the tip of a small peninsula, sometimes described as a thumb extending into the South China Sea. It was originally referred to as "three boats" in recognition of the trading ships activities as they unloaded their cargo at the shipping port. Eventually, it led to the name Vung Tau which means "anchorage".

It was thought the three boats reference was in recognition of the first three villages within the province of Bien Hoa, under the previous Nguyen Dynasty. Vung Tau, or colloquially known as "Vungers" but also "Cap Saint Jacques", featured both a front and back beach with numerous sand dunes. Overlooking the town was Radar Hill, situated at the top of VC Hill and used as the Australian and US radar post.

In addition, it was home to the U.S Naval Support Activity Detachment known as the Inshore Undersea Warfare Group-1-Detachment 1. Its main role was to carry out harbour patrols, using the boats from Cat Lo Naval Base, located about 10 kilometres northeast of Vung Tau and on the road to Baria and, ultimately, Nui Dat.

In 1967, the first contingent of the Royal Australian Navy's Clearance Diving team was based in Vung Tua, in order to safeguard shipping from any perceived underwater attack. Its divers had the unenviable task of patrolling the dark and murky waters of its harbour.

Vung Tau's deep waters also provided ready access to naval ships transporting troops and supplies from Australia, in particular HMAS Jeparit, which was charted by the Department of Shipping and Transport in 1966 to carry equipment including Centurion tanks, ammunition and supplies such as mail for the Australian Military Forces.

In keeping with the unrest back home on Australian shores, the Seamen's Union of Australia determined in February 1967 it would no longer provide crews to Jeparit for any further supply trips to South Vietnam, but the ship continued to operate with a combination of civilian and naval crews. Eventually, as a ship of the Royal Australian Navy, it completed 43 trips between Australia and Vietnam.

HMAS Sydney was recommissioned as a fast troop transport and in 1965, carried Australian soldiers and equipment for docking at Vung Tau port. It eventually earned the nick name as the "Vung Tau Ferry", completing 25 voyages from 1965 to 1972. HMAS Perth was involved in three deployments to the waters of the South Vietnam war zone and in 1968 replaced HMAS Hobart, which, during its 1968 tour, was mistakenly attacked with friendly fire by United States Air Force aircraft. Vung Tau also became the port of debarkation for tens of thousands of US military and a fully equipped helicopter repair facility, being the USNS Corpus Christi Bay, was moored a few miles offshore.

1ALSG was first established in tents in the sand dunes of Vung Tau in 1965 under the Australian Logistic Support Company in order to support the 1st Battalion, Royal Australian Regiment at Nui Dat. Initially, major casualties and overflow patients were treated at the United States 36 Evacuation Hospital. 32 Dental Unit was sent to South Vietnam in 1965 and first based at Bien Hoa to provide dental support for 1RAR.

1ALSG then operated out of Vung Tau in April 1966, following the setting up of Nui Dat by the 1st Australian Task Force. They initially built a number of small structures, including latrines, and it eventually became a working operational base for not only the medical and dental corps units, but also for transport, engineers and service corps.

32 Dental unit relocated to 1ALSG in June 1966 and was fully equipped with dental stores and a laboratory, followed by a contingent of the corps at Nui Dat, to provide dental care for the soldiers of 1 ATF. The initial accommodation at Vung Tau, alongside 2 Field Ambulance of the medical corps, was in tents on sand floors, but now it was tents on concrete floors.

In late 1966, and now adjacent to 8 Field Ambulance, the dental corps moved into a large purpose built Kingstrand Hut, which contained, not only two dental surgeries, but a dental technician's laboratory and the usual admin area with a tent at the front of the hut, to serve as a waiting room.

8 Field Ambulance were also in Kingstrand huts, followed three months later by galvanised Lysaght prefabricated huts, which also formed part of the hospital compound. Following the increase in 1967, to three Australian battalions together with support troops, the 33 Dental Unit was increased to five sections.

Two weeks earlier, prior to my arrival in South Vietnam in 1968, 1AFH was firmly established under commanding officer, Lieutenant Colonel Bill Watson, as the medical services, to be provided to our military, had to be further expanded. 8 Field Ambulance was relocated to Nui Dat in a revised roll with 1ATF.

1AFH also effectively replaced the 36th Evacuation Hospital to provide medical and dental services, including a triage which could take up to at least six wounded at one-time and, if necessary, could expand to 16, two to three operating theatres supported by units of pathology, pharmacy and x- ray facilities.

The hospital also contained a six-bed intensive care ward and 100 beds for medical and surgical patients. Other support units adjacent to the hospital, included a patient kitchen and mess, a sexually transmitted disease clinic, regimental aid post (RAP) and chaplain services, including the Anzac Chapel, erected by the engineers from 17 Construction Squadron. Unfortunately, there was also a mortuary and the headquarters for 33 Dental of RAADC was at the far end of the hospital adjacent to each other.

The surgical capacity was met by specialists from both the Army Reserves and the Citizens Military Force (CMF) and civilian medical specialists, who generally were under a three-month deployment. Their support teams consisted of both regular and conscripted soldiers, including those from the Royal Australian Army Nursing Corps (RAANC), New Zealand Nursing Corps (RNZNC), personnel from the Australian Red Cross Field Force and various other corps which provided drivers, chaplains and cooks.

Often going beyond the call of duty, a total of 43 nurses from our RAANC and nine from RNZNC would ultimately serve with 1AFH, caring for and assisting in surgical needs for our wounded soldiers. The Red Cross provided support to, not only patients, but also ensured a communications link for them and their families back home. In 1969, the Red Cross had a total of 67 field bases operated by over 200 dedicated personnel in South Vietnam.

1ALSG was protected by barbed wire. All soldiers were armed and entry could only be gained, other than by helicopter, through the main gate manned by military police. The base was complemented by the recently built Peter Badcoe Club, named after Major Peter Badcoe VC, and was a recreational facility. Later a pool was built opposite the sand dunes and beach and named after Harold Holt, former Australian Prime Minister.

Major Badcoe had served with the Australian Army Training Team Vietnam and was posthumously awarded the Victoria Cross for his gallantry and leadership on three occasions. The last battle cost him his life when he was killed by machine gun fire. He was also awarded the United States Silver Star and several South Vietnamese medals.

We were transported from the airport by a driver from 33 Dental, who first decided to take us for a quick tour of the township of Vung Tau, only a 10-minute drive from where we landed. I had never travelled overseas before and suddenly I found myself in a war zone, surrounded by ear deafening noises coming from overhead aircraft of all types, armed soldiers everywhere, the insufferable heat and local Vietnamese, who clearly were ravaged by a war that seemed never ending.

As we drove along the dusty road, complete with fly ridden market stalls, we saw the local sights of run down shelters with open sewers, people travelling, either on Vespa motor scooters or Lambrettas, which were motor scooters with seats in the back and locals walking, using bamboo sticks or poles while carrying heavy loads over their shoulders. The villagers would squat alongside the road, pulling their dirt-covered pants down to relieve themselves, while at the same time, yelling out, *'Uc Dai Loi,'* which was Vietnamese for Australian and giving us a friendly wave as we drove past.

The township of Vung Tau was previously renowned for being a favourite holiday resort for the French colonials and Vietnamese from Saigon, who could afford to holiday at the coastal resort close to its front beach, *Bai Truoc* and its back beach, *Bai Sau*. It now served as the favourite destination for those military personnel including Americans, Australians and other allies on rest and recreation and those on rest in country. There was also the vintage Grand Hotel built in the 1800s which was overlooked by the old French Fort and surrounded by substantial villas and many other buildings, which had definitely seen their use by date.

I would soon find out the Grand, often referred to as, "Madame T's Boom Boom Bar", was a popular release for those taking a well-earned rest. It offered over 100 bars and cafes, including dance halls, some named after American cities or other well-known towns which, without a doubt, was to attract business from the military. There were many "drinking holes" supported by very attractive young Vietnamese women who sadly, had turned to prostitution to survive during the lengthy war with North Vietnam.

It was also rumoured to be a place of rest for the Viet Cong to escape the brutality of the ever-present war and, at one stage and as early as the mid–1960s, both South Vietnam's General Nguyen Khanh and United States General William Westmoreland saw Vung Tau as a possible escape route, if it was ever needed. They were not to know at the time, however, that after the war, Vung Tau would serve as an evacuation point for literally tens of thousands of boat people trying to escape the tyrant communist rule.

The central part of the town was very active and, with Buddhism the dominant form of Vietnamese religion, it featured a number of statues and temples, including those dating back to the Nguyen lords in the 17th century when they also erected numerous Buddhist pagodas. In the centre of Vung Tau was the main central square, where, on our numerous trips to town in a Lambretta, we would all meet in the square for some fun and frivolity despite curfews and the ever patrolling military and national police. The latter were known as the "White Mice" of Vietnam because of their white uniform, hats and gloves.

On arrival at 1ALSG with the dental corps driver, we collapsed into our accommodation, which was a hut at the top of the hill overlooking the hospital and the helicopter landing zone, known as the Vampire Pad. The pad was where battle casualties were carefully unloaded to triage, not far from a, loosely described, open air picture theatre. To the back of the hospital compound was the sergeants' mess and huts and opposite, the officers' accommodation area.

Thankfully, our hut was only a short walk to the other ranks' mess and boozer which, in army lingo, meant to get as drunk as quickly as possible. Of course, I would attend it on a regular basis to quench my thirst, usually with a Four X, Courage or Fosters beer for 15 cents per can. However, you could also consume a "goffer", which was army slang for soft drink at 10 cents per can.

Next to the boozer, was the barber shop manned by our own barber, the ever-unflappable, Murray Lovatt. All the facilities, including our hut, the adjacent separate deep trench latrine and shower block were protected by sandbags in case of rocket and artillery attacks. A piece of architecture in itself, the separate latrine was known as "the pissaphone" and was a pit of unknown depth with a 44-gallon drum covered with fly wire. To say the least, it was very unhygienic and, at times, unsafe as they would collapse without warning.

The hut was very basic, consisting of about 10 army wire beds with rock hard mattresses and frames around them to hold up the mosquito nets, needed due to malaria concerns. We were required to line up each morning in our hut to be handed our anti-malaria tablet, either chloroquine or primaquine and now, as Corporal O'Neill, I was somehow designated the daily task of handing out a tablet to each soldier. Alongside every bed was a metal locker, so I followed tradition and put up a "calendar" with the number 365 and all numbers going backwards to zero on the front of my individual locker.

Each morning, the first thing I did upon waking, other than stretching and visiting the pissaphone, was to block out consecutive calendar numbers. In my case, the next morning I blocked out 365, which meant I had 364 more days to serve "in country" or, as we would all say, "364 days and a wakey", being the wake up day of leaving to return home but that was a long way off.

9

Life in a War Zone

On my first day in country and now in a war zone, I was to report to 33 Dental Unit, to be introduced to Major John Spencer, the officer in charge, who had been the commanding officer only since his arrival some weeks earlier in March, 1968. The unit was already a hive of activity as army policy dictated all serving soldiers had to be, not only medically fit but also have a dental examination at least every twelve months, whether they agreed to it or not.

Along with Corporals Watson and Caulfield and also newly arrived corps driver, George Nicholson, we were then introduced to Warrant Officer Frank Sachse, who I would effectively report to as one of the corporals. From then on, I always referred to him, not just as Frank, but also "001", being his designated rank, but also in reference to James Bond 007.

Frank 001 was a lovely man, always with a smile on his face and, in many ways, we all looked up to him as our mentor and guiding light. He had previously served in World War Two, Korea and now Vietnam, so this was his third deployment in a war zone, arriving in March 1968. Frank made it known, right from the outset, that one of his main roles, in his words, was 'to access the US system as far as dental stores and equipment were concerned,' and whatever else we could lay our hands on.

This would be by means of what he termed, "a red road freewheel convoy" from our base to Long Binh on a monthly basis. I was to personally experience that the term "red road" meant it was usually a road subject to attack by the Viet Cong, or whatever means they had at their disposal, to disrupt any convoys.

Frank told me I would not be allowed out of the base for the first three weeks, as this was part of the acclimatisation period in a war zone. I later suspected it was probably to keep us away from the perils of Vung Tau, which I was to witness firsthand a few months later.

After meeting Corporal Keith Burton, a dental technician, I then reported to the Q Store to collect my weapon and ammunition: a F1 submachine gun, together with an M1 Helmet. The weapon was now my "best friend" and was to remain with me 24 hours a day, seven days a week as we never knew when the enemy, in particular the VC, might have a crack at our army base. I would always have my army identification disc, colloquially known as "dog tags", around my neck. The dog tags had my name, my important regimental service number, my blood group, which was O Positive and my religion.

If I were on a day off and had a pass to travel into town, my weapon would be safely secured in my hut locker, but I always had my dog tags around my neck. I was also told that, not only would we be providing dental assistance to our troops, but at least one day a week and, usually on a Tuesday, we would undertake dental pain relief by way of dental civil action aid programs or "Dentcap", to the local South Vietnamese civilians, either at the unit or local villages and orphanages, if it was safe to do so.

The Dentcap program had its origins in 1966 with the first one taking place on 7 November, 1966 at Baria Oval, followed by a dispensary in Vung Tau, Long Son and Xuyen Moc. It generally included extractions of infected teeth. A similar program called Medical Civic Action Program or Medcap, was also undertaken by 1 AFH, who would also provide limited, but helpful, medical assistance to Vietnamese civilians, in particular the children in orphanages, initially at the hamlet of Nam Binh on the old main road from Vung Tau and also at Baria.

The children were the main priority with health issues such as head lice, large boils and wounds needing dressings and definitely our attention. We also provided basic vitamins and medication and, where necessary, vaccinations. Both medical and dental assistance would also be available to Vietnamese civilians and, no doubt, the local VC would parade as local villagers in order to receive free treatment.

The Medcap was the equivalent to a similar program conducted by United States military medical personnel providing aid to the South Vietnamese population. They also conducted another related program called Military Provincial Hospital Assistance where they provided hospitalised in-patient treatment for local civilians, including venereal disease suffered by young Vietnamese bar girls.

As Frank 001 had pre-empted, we would be travelling to and from the United States Army Base at Long Binh to collect, not only dental supplies, but also medical equipment and stores, as we also worked together with 1AFH regarding manpower, stores and vehicles. On an ad hoc monthly basis, we would be travelling to Saigon to carry out dental treatment to, not only army personnel, but embassy staff. In addition, Frank

001 confirmed, as a corporal, I would occasionally be required to act as the duty NCO in charge of security pickets.

Our other role, also as required, was to assist the medics with the Dustoff choppers landing on the Vampire Pad adjacent to the hospital. We would unload soldiers wounded in action, carry them straight to triage and, unfortunately, those who were killed in action, to the mortuary. Pay day would be once a fortnight when we were to line up, have our pay book entry confirmed and also collect some cash by way of military payment certificate (MPC), which was American currency devised by the U.S Military and, as paper money, would vary with denominations as little as five cents up to 20 dollars.

The MPC currency was at its peak during the Vietnam War but to prevent and deter its use by black marketers, the note style was frequently changed. We would have a "conversion day" and line up to hand over our now outdated MPC to be replaced with the latest MPC currency. This meant any old MPC was now of no value. Unfortunately, the local Vietnamese, particularly local bar owners, bar girls and brothels would have old MPC and lost their savings as they were not allowed to be part of conversion day.

I was to be the assistant to Captain Colin "Twiggy" Twelftree, who had been at the unit since August, 1967 and to say I would learn a lot from him, or "Sir", is an understatement. Colin was also a national serviceman and was very tall. He certainly towered over me. He had deferred his national service until he completed his Bachelor of Dentistry. We had a chuckle when we discussed Pucka and Healesville and had a lot in common, other than just our ranks. He was not all that happy though, when he was first conscripted as he only wanted to serve as a digger and not as a dentist. After a week of recruit training, he changed his mind and was immediately enlisted as an officer.

Colin introduced me to the dental surgery, which contained basic mechanical chairs, portable high-speed drills and associated materials to carry out tooth extractions and fillings, but generally, the bulk of the work was to maintain dental hygiene. We would work six days a week, usually from 8am to late afternoon, Monday to Saturday with Sunday being the day to relax, enjoy the beach, the Peter Badcoe Club and of course, sink a few too many beers.

On 25 April, 1968, we all gathered at the front beach to stop and reflect on the landing at Gallipoli at dawn on the same day back in 1915. The Last Post was haunting in recognition of those who had fallen before us and the symbolic support of all defence personnel. We were not to know at that time, the number of diggers serving in Vietnam who would pay the ultimate price in service to their country.

Embarrassingly though, the first three Sundays, under orders to acclimatise, I would consume too many beers at the beach barbeque, followed by a few more at the Badcoe Club and stagger back, badly sunburnt, to vomit in the hut during my sleep. The Regimental Sergeant Major for 1AFH was not impressed when he conducted a hut inspection. His role, amongst others, was to ensure that diggers maintained a high standard of hygiene and why I was never charged for my clear breach, remains a mystery.

I looked forward to our Dentcap, usually held each Tuesday when the local villagers, including children of all ages, would be either trucked into our unit or sometimes George would pick up the patients in Vung Tau, then drive them back home after their treatment. Most of the civilians were suffering from toothaches and needed to have the offending tooth extracted.

It was like an assembly line which seemed to get bigger every week and Captain Twelftree would move along the line, injecting the civilian patient to anesthetise the tooth. After he had finished, he'd return to the first person so "we" could start extracting the offending tooth or teeth and so on. It was not uncommon to see, on average, 100 teeth extracted on any given Tuesday.

When I say "we", on the odd occasion I was allowed to extract a tooth but only in situations where it was ready to fall out anyway. Due to the condition of their gums and teeth, there was no preventative or restorative dentistry, as their dental hygiene was very poor with a lot of tooth decay and betel stained teeth. The betel nut was a symbol of love and marriage in Vietnamese culture and dates back to the reign of the Hung Kings but has similar effects as caffeine and tobacco use. If used to the extreme, not only does it stain the teeth and cause damage to the gums, but it can have severe side effects, such as vomiting and diarrhoea.

As the Vietnamese population were mainly poor peasant people, they would use betel nuts to relieve toothache and probably the stresses of war, which was a constant factor in their lives. They would show their gratitude by giving us small gifts of very appealing Vietnamese food.

The Dentcap also involved travelling from Vung Tau along the main road, past the US Cat Lo Naval Base, which was situated approximately 10 kilometres (or 10 "klicks" being the army slang) from Vung Tau and then onto the Ba Ria Orphanage run by an order of Catholic nuns. The naval base initially housed the Swift Boat Squadron and River Division, together with a repair facility and housed over 600 personnel. The base also used, what became known as, "experimental Patrol Air Cushion Vehicles" or hovercraft, as part of their operations along the Mekong River.

The hovercraft was effectively used as a patrol boat because of its lack of draft which determined that it could function well in shallow and reed choked waters widespread along the Mekong River. It could also travel at high speed in the order of around 60 knots. This did not deter the VC, as they successfully sank two of the boats.

After a few months of thoroughly enjoying mingling with the local villagers at the Dentcaps and the children at Ba Ria, I sent a letter to my mother asking her to send over a parcel of clothes to be worn by the orphaned children, who were also victims of war due to losing their parents. It was about a 40-minute drive to the orphanage, approximately 20 miles from Vung Tau, on the road to Nui Dat. If the road was declared red, it was considered unsafe to travel due to VC activity, green if safe to travel and sometimes it was deemed orange, which meant you could only use the road in armed convoys.

I recall we travelled to Ba Ria Orphanage a number of times so the road was obviously green. Where possible, we would travel with 1AFH as part of their Medcap, as there was safety in numbers and we were always well armed with our trusty sub machine guns or SLRs, whilst Captain Twelftree and any other dentist would have a pistol. It must have been rather confronting for the orphanage children.

I think the view we had at the time was, being attacked by the VC while conducting the program was unlikely and would not have been a great VC propaganda exercise. I also have no doubt that some of our patients were probably innocent villagers during the day and aggressive VC at night. Ba Ria, although known as a sleepy town to buy various knick-knacks and have army greens laundered, was subject to a heavy attack by armed members of the VC's D445 battalion at the beginning of the Tet Offensive on 1 February 1968 and again on 7 February 1968.

Our dental duties also included travelling to Saigon and as one of the assistants to Twiggy. I would accompany him and also a dental technician, when rostered, to fly to Saigon from Vung Tau, usually by Caribou. The dental treatment provided was normally to our army personnel stationed in Saigon, but also included US Forces and embassy staff. On arrival at Tan Son Nhut Airport, we would be transported by army bus to our accommodation in Cholon. Usually, we would stay at the infamous Dong Khanh Hotel, whilst Twiggy's accommodation, being an officer, was usually at a Bachelor Officers Quarter, courtesy of the American military.

The ride from the airport to the hotel was interesting as it was obvious the VC were still very active following TET. The bus windows were even covered with heavy security wire to protect its passengers from grenade attack, or so they said. I always doubted the wire would have provided much protection if a VC rode past on a Lambretta scooter and lobbed a grenade. Alternatively, they could simply attach a pack of explosives in a small bag to the bus wire so, although the thinking might have been about protection, it obviously had some flaws.

We would conduct the dental assistance in Saigon at an American dental unit which was part of a three-storey building used by their military, who loaned us a dental surgery. This gave us an opportunity to see firsthand and, with some surprise, how badly managed the US dental system was. Unlike our military, if a US soldier needed dental treatment, they would have to seek it themselves as there was no requirement to not only be physically fit, but both medically and dentally fit.

The main street of Saigon was named Nguyen Hue and hosted the US Military command who would give their daily, but very optimistic, war briefing, jokingly referred to by some journalists, as the "Five O'Clock Follies". It did, however, house a roof top bar which was frequently visited by all to gaze at the bright lights of Saigon, or should I say, the constant flashes and glow of the theatre of war.

The United States Postal Exchange was also located in Saigon's Cholon district as it was in every American base, including, not only its army and marine bases, but also navy and air force. There was even one at Tan Son Nhut air base. They supplied everything from cases of bourbon, crates of Johnny Walker scotch, food, cigarettes, tape recorders, cameras and the list goes on. Due to no taxes and large subsidies, courtesy of the US government, prices were amazingly cheap. At its peak during the war, there were over 50 major exchange posts in South Vietnam.

On returning from Saigon to our unit at 1AFH, I really missed the Vietnamese food we could order and thoroughly enjoyed at the Dong Khanh Hotel. There was no comparison to what was on offer at our base. With no disrespect to our army cooks, the "etherised" or powdered eggs just didn't cut it. The army cooks were assisted by Vietnamese civilians, who did the most mundane tasks, such as potato peeling. They all worked very long hours with very little pay, trying to keep us well fed. Prawns, shrimps and baked fish were also on our menu but only when well-known dignitaries were visiting.

Despite being served preserved, rehydrated and

reconstituted meals most of the time, I don't recall any of us suffering from food poisoning, so it must have been hygienically of a very high standard, particularly in view of the tropical climate. There was also the occasional bread roll, or what we termed "hepatitis roll", at a cost of five piastres, from the local Vietnamese bakery in Vung Tau, but somehow we survived that as well.

Mind you, we always looked forward to our Sunday barbeques on the beach at Vung Tau but I was soon to find out that the Vietnam War was to become an unforgettable reality, with memories that would never leave me.

10

Reality of War

In late April, 1968, it was obvious the Vietnam War was about to intensify again. We would be woken at 3am to look out the hut window and see the night sky, many miles away, looking like a large rainbow, with flashes of light, much like lightning, but not caused by any effect of nature. It was due to the bombing of the countryside by American B-52 bombers.

The common expression was the B-52s "rained fire" in Vietnam and certainly the night sky looked like a raging fire. In 1966, the bombers had flown in excess of 5,000 missions against numerous targets in Vietnam, both South and North. In 1968, in support of US military in the Battle of Khe Sanh, they flew numerous missions dropping another 60,000 tonnes of their warheads.

They had previously dropped over 8,000 tonnes of bombs per month against the NVA on the Ho Chi Minh Trail, named after their chairman, before he stepped down from power due to ill health in 1965. The trail was a military supply route along North Vietnam through Laos and along Cambodia to South Vietnam.

We would listen to the dulcet tones of Hanoi Hannah on Radio Hanoi as she read out a list of Americans killed in action and those captured, before playing popular US antiwar songs to try and inflict homesickness on the troops. She would then describe the B-52 bombings as a complete waste of time. It is fair to say, her equivalent was probably Airman Second Class, Adrian Cronauer, a DJ working for Armed Forces Radio Service in Saigon, and for who the movie, "Good Morning Vietnam", starring Robin Williams, was largely based on.

It was against this backdrop, I was further introduced to a war zone, which I was then to experience firsthand, the trauma and after effects, following enemy contact. I had already been warned by Frank 001 we would be required to assist the Dustoffs with Bell UH-1 Iroquois helicopters, nicknamed Huey, landing at Vampire Pad. The title "Dustoff helicopters" originated in 1963 when the US Commander of Army 57 Medical Detachment, the helicopter ambulance, began to use the radio call sign "Dustoff" for his medical evacuation choppers, largely due to the dust that would billow up when the choppers landed and then took off with wounded soldiers aboard for transport to a surgical facility.

It was, in effect, a very rapid evacuation from the battlefield straight to 1AFH, usually taking 30 minutes if all went well. The wounded had already been attended to at the scene of the battle contact by infantry medics because each rifle company had its own medic. They were also a rifleman, usually armed with an SLR or Armalite and, in some cases, with an M60 with copious rounds of ammunition and at least two grenades.

Not only were they heavily armed but they also carried medical supplies, including plasma to treat the injured in the field. They had a well-earned reputation and saved many lives before the Dustoff chopper landed for evacuation of the wounded and, sadly, those killed in action. The medic was the one who arranged for the Dustoff and, where possible, to make sure the wounded digger was fit enough to be transported to 1AFH by applying morphine, plasma drips and field dressings and, in some cases, tourniquets to not only stop heavy bleeding but possibly loss of a limb.

Many of the wounded had not only suffered gunshot wounds from AK- 47 rifles used by the enemy, but terrible injuries inflicted from mines planted in villages or surrounding their jungle camps. After the VC had left their camp, our infantry was left with the problem of the mines. These included M16 mines which would jump three feet in the air before exploding, Claymore mines which could still remain in the ground and ones previously laid by our military but replanted by the VC. They also used Chinese 53 carbines and rocket propelled grenades, together with the North Vietnamese manufactured K-50 submachine gun.

The reputation of the Dustoff helicopters was extremely good in evacuating the casualties quickly to 1AFH under normal circumstances, but on the odd occasion, it was many hours before they could safely land, due to circumstances beyond their control, particularly if a firefight or contact was still occurring. We would hear stories about pilots landing under heavy fire, others hovering above the action below and winching the seriously wounded, to stories of those killed in action and taken out of the jungle in covered stretchers.

There would have been nothing more reassuring to a wounded digger than to see a Bell UH-1 Iroquois helicopter in the distance, with its distinctive Red Cross emblem painted on the chopper's front nose, side and top and about to land. The choppers were not only flown by Australian pilots, but US Dustoff pilots also assisted in evacuating our wounded soldiers from the battlefield. Each chopper would be manned with four crew and could carry up to six patients with at least one of the crew being trained in first aid.

Staff at 1AFH were like a well-oiled machine due to plenty of practice, and after receiving a radio call at the hospital's Admission and Discharge unit that a Dustoff was on its way, teams would assemble near Vampire Pad after receiving notification. The initial walkway from triage leading to the pad was made of metal strips but were later replaced with a concrete path.

There was also a dedicated telephone link between A&D and the operations and command post at Nui Dat. The information usually relayed from the chopper would include the number of casualties, types of wounds and category, number of litter cases and deceased. The siren was then activated to alert all hospital personnel at 1AFH that a Dustoff landing was imminent in order for triage and theatre to be prepared.

The rostered personnel would wait patiently with stretchers near the Vampire Pad for the choppers to land and for the wounded to be carefully lifted to triage, under the direction of senior surgical staff who would make a quick assessment of their injuries. The most serious were sent to Triage 1 and the less severely injured into Triage 2. The dilemma with which they were also faced was, many soldiers still had an assortment of weapons, including grenades with them. Usually with some assistance, the Q store staff would carefully check each weapon and render them safe for securing in the Q Store.

Being trained infantry soldiers, many of the wounded didn't want to hand over their weapons but they were carefully spoken to and assured it would be safely secured. Our chaplains would reassure them and offer prayers whilst they were being assessed.

My exposure to Dustoffs usually occurred when a siren would sound in the middle of the night. If you were rostered on, you would proceed a few minutes' walk from our hut to the Vampire Pad, to provide any necessary assistance, which usually included being a stretcher bearer for the wounded to be taken to triage. The siren would sound throughout the hospital compound and grounds and was so loud you could also hear it from the beach. Even if you were not rostered on, many of us would still go down to the hospital in case we could be of any assistance.

Not that we knew it at the time and, despite peace talks underway in Paris, the Battle of Coral- Balmoral, also known as "Mini-Tet" was about to commence on 12 May, 1968. Resulting in many casualties, it was the bloodiest engagement for Australians in Vietnam with the communists leaving the surrounding hills to target the cities and towns in South Vietnam.

What followed was a number of engagements between the 1st Australian Task Force and the North Vietnamese People's Army of Vietnam) 7th division and VC main force units. The fighting continued until 6 June, 1968 and resulted in 25 Australians killed in action, with approximately 100 wounded, during the fighting northeast of Saigon.

The intense battle close to Saigon, which was under curfew, included Viet Cong snipers in Cho Lon, who stayed with relatives and let off rounds from windows, before disappearing. This was the first occasion that Australians had been up against a regimental enemy strength and later determined as our most hazardous and sustained contact of the Vietnam War.

Hanoi Hannah broadcast a major PAVN victory, of course, but there was no doubt our Australian forces had repulsed the constant attacks with an estimated 267 enemy killed in action and many captured and made prisoners of war.

The first half of 1968 was a watershed moment for our prolonged Australian operations, including those outside of Phuoc Toy province, with the previous 18 months seeing many casualties and deaths. With 228 Australians killed in action, with an estimated 1200 wounded, that was a loss of nearly two thirds of our fighting force since January, 1967. The casualties also included three Australian reporters and an English colleague from Reuters who were shot dead by a VC officer as they attempted to enter Cho Lon, despite one of them, Michael Birch, a senior journalist with *AAP* calling out, 'Bao Chi!' meaning in Vietnamese, "journalist".

This was followed by the National Liberation Front, at a press conference in Moscow, denying the murders took place. Prime Minister Gorton did not seem overly concerned at the time at their declaration of innocence. Two poems written by Birch, *Vietnam 68* and *Saigon-1968* were subsequently published posthumously.

At 1AFH we were subjected to the constant sound of the sirens, day and night and on one particular occasion, the reality of war was to have a profound effect on me. When attending the pad to help place the wounded on board the chopper on stretchers, I can still recall the horrific sights of critically injured soldiers and the deceased lying underneath the stretchers on the chopper. One digger had been shot between the eyes and all he had was a small round hole in the middle of his forehead. When we turned him over, however, the back of his head was completely missing. Another soldier had his feet blown off and his legs stripped of flesh. These memories will always stay with me.

The surgical staff would quickly assess each patient, once their bloodied and dirty jungle greens had been removed and placed with any personal belongings in a bag for safe keeping, usually in the mortuary. The wounded were then carefully put on the resuscitation trolley. Prioritised casualties had x–rays and blood samples done, blood pressure and pulse rates were taken, then surgeons would be allocated to operate in theatre, assisted by anaesthetists and theatre technicians, with the overall management under the watchful eye of the theatre sister.

The many procedures undertaken by surgical staff included, not only amputations, but spinal repairs, repairs to major arteries, craniotomies, bowel resections and, at times, open heart massage for those in cardiac arrest. I can't speak highly enough of our medical staff who, not only saved lives, but were totally up front when, in the kindest way possible, had to inform a wounded soldier that his limb could not be saved. I remember, one unfortunate soldier would never walk again as he had both legs blown off.

Many of the battle casualties were from mine blasts, which resulted in massive haemorrhaging and it was common for the theatre floor to be blood-soaked with constant mopping up by the theatre staff. On arrival at 1AFH, 99 per cent of those wounded in action would survive, thanks to the amazing dedication and skill of all those involved, in particular, the surgeons, anaesthetists and theatre staff, and our dentists, who provided emergency dental work.

Some of the wounded suffered traumatic injuries, including gunshot wounds and shrapnel to their upper body, resulting in the loss of teeth and/or damage. One of the patients, worked on by Captain Twiggy, was injured in an armoured personnel carrier contact, causing damage to his face, gums and numerous teeth. Everything was capably stitched up and dressings were applied to the smashed and damaged teeth.

Following surgery, the critical patients would be placed in intensive care whilst those now deemed satisfactory, would be admitted to either the surgical or medical ward. The surgical ward was mainly for patients recovering from surgery and the medical ward was to treat those with health-related issues, including, but not limited to, tropical diseases, dysentery and malaria.

The unfortunate diggers killed in action would have their dog tags removed, be carefully hosed down and then placed in the mortuary in special coffins for a sad return flight home by the RAAF Aero-Medical Evacuation (Medevac) to Australian shores, together with those deemed unfit to resume active duty. Many of the severely wounded would not remember the flight as they were heavily sedated and asleep most of the way home.

In respect of our more seriously wounded soldiers who were not expected to survive, a program was put in place by the Australian Government to enable a close family member to travel on compassionate grounds to and from Vietnam. A family member would be notified in the first instance by telegram that their son or partner had been critically wounded and was not expected to live.

The duty officer, together with Q staff, had the unenviable task of attending to any severed limbs and other body parts after surgery. We would witness their burning in an incinerator called "Goodrid", situated at the rear of the hospital ward, before signing off on the record that they had been safely disposed of. The limbs and other body parts, blood-soaked jungle greens and boots, on being burnt, would result in a foul indescribable smell which drifted around the base. It was a pungent odour that would never leave me.

I was also to experience the medical ward on three separate occasions suffering, firstly, a lacerated knee which became infected, then glandular fever, followed by a mastoid in the ear, requiring a week as an inpatient where I lost two stone in weight. The ear infection was treated with crystalline penicillin injections and I vaguely remember Captain Twiggy coming to visit me to enquire about my welfare. At one stage, when I was so ill, there was talk of me being medevacked home. A specialist from the US Army in Saigon visited me and, thankfully I recovered, albeit extremely skinny.

My medical issues were nothing compared to some of those admitted at the same time, in particular very young, previously fit diggers now suffering from battle wounds. There were other soldiers in the medical ward for a variety of reasons, including serious tinea, cyst removals, circumcisions to prevent on-going tropical infections and venereal diseases, including syphilis.

During my time as an inpatient, I met a number of wounded infantrymen and one in particular had a story to tell. Private John Fountain was shot through the wrist in contact with the VC, or "Charlie": our nickname for the enemy. I had no idea how he never lost his hand. John was laying down on his side, largely protected by a small bunker, when he lobbed a grenade at the fast-approaching VC. After letting the grenade go, he, unfortunately, didn't bring his arm down quick enough.

The VC aggressor must have been a good shot because only John's hand and wrist were exposed, with his wrist subsequently receiving the bullet. John returned to active duty after being discharged but certainly kept his hands in his pockets from then on.

What also became apparent was the small number of our soldiers stationed at 1AFH, who had suffered gunshot wounds to their big toes. It was not uncommon during the night to hear gun fire and we thought it was probably a misfire, or something occurring outside the secured confines of the base. Sadly, some soldiers, deeply suffering from the effects of a war zone, would consume copious amounts of alcohol then remove their big toe by gunshot so they could be medevacked home, only to be dishonourably discharged.

The incidence of venereal disease also reared its ugly head with the high number of our soldiers, including some in our unit, (not me, I hastily add), who were infected with a sexually transmitted disease, either gonorrhoea, or in some cases, the more serious strain of syphilis. Our medics would be faced with treating the symptoms which included: anal itching, a pus-like discharge from either the penis or rectum and strained bowel movements.

In some cases, gonorrhoea had no symptoms but generally you knew if you were infected. Syphilis could result in a painless sore on the genitals, fever and sore throat and, if not treated it could disappear within a few weeks and repeatedly reappear. In its final stage, it could cause damage to the brain, nerves and even your heart.

Our soldiers would line up, either at the Regimental Aid Post or at the STD clinic each morning to be handed their daily dose of antibiotics, which, in most cases, cured them and, hopefully for some, was a lesson well learnt. Next time wear a bloody condom!

Unfortunately, one of our unit members suffered from gonorrhoea on no less than three separate occasions during his tour. On a number of mornings, before lining up for our anti-malaria tablet, he would be squeezing his penis to extract the pus before reporting for his antibiotics.

In late July 1968, the base was subjected to extreme high winds and the threat of a cyclone, so we spent two days wearing our battle helmets as we reinforced the sandbags, including ones around our huts in case the weather forecast was correct. During the late afternoon of Tuesday, 30 July, 1968, the Dustoff siren sounded. One of the stretchered wounded had been shot through his femoral artery. Thankfully, his platoon medic was able to quickly apply a tourniquet to stem the flow of blood but when he safely arrived in triage, he was still facing the amputation of his leg. I was fortunate to be invited into theatre to observe the amazing work of the surgeon who was ably supported by theatre staff.

I recall on three separate occasions, he cut a piece of vein from various parts of the soldier's body for grafting, to join the missing three inches of artery. On each occasion, on releasing the clamp, the vein would not hold and blood would literally spurt everywhere, including over everyone in theatre before the artery was clamped off again. He was given at least 25 pints of blood and the operating surgeon said he would try one more time. If the vein did not hold, he had no choice but to amputate his leg.

Luckily, miracles do happen in a war zone. The vein held and, although the soldier was not out of trouble with a chance his leg could still need amputation, at least for the time being, he had two legs as he was wheeled from theatre into the intensive care unit.

The wet and very hot season in Vietnam started around May and the rain was a constant reminder of life in a tropical country. You could normally set your watch for a downpour, as on most days at 3pm, it would bucket down. High winds on one occasion also became a real problem and we had to wear our battle helmets for two days when venturing outside.

At 4.19am local time on 2 August, 1968, a massive earthquake occurred in the Philippines in the town of Casiguran, Aurora, and was considered to be the most destructive earthquake in that country for the past 20 years. Two hundred and seventy civilians were killed and a six-storey building in Manila collapsed. A tidal wave, or tsunami, was also detected by a tide gauge in Japan and warnings were issued that it would possibly hit the south coast of Vietnam.

Sirens sounded later that morning, but this time it was not a Dustoff. To say, all hell broke loose at 1AFH, would be an understatement, as we had to evacuate all patients, regardless of their condition, this included the patient shot through the femoral artery, to a higher ground. All patients had to be quickly moved. The location selected was the sand dunes above and overlooking the base, which was the officers' lines, also known as "Officers Hill". The patients from the hospital were transported on the back of army trucks and those incapacitated had to remain in their hospital bed for transport.

Our femoral artery soldier, with his leg now in traction, was wheeled out to the Vampire Pad, loaded onto the back of a truck for transport up to the hill overlooking the South China Sea. 1ALH was completely evacuated, including all support staff. Hundreds sat at the top of the hill, with a number on stretchers, inside the officers' huts and mess, all waiting for the tidal wave. It would be fair to say the Aussie dark sense of humour was about the only thing that kept us sane, which included jokes that we should get our surf boards to ride the tidal wave to Saigon.

One wounded South Vietnamese interpreter, on being asked if this has ever happened before, said, with tongue in cheek, that the last tidal wave to hit the south coast of Vietnam finished with the waters receding at Ba Ria, a good 30 kilometres from the base on the way to Nui Dat.

You had to feel sorry for the soldiers wounded in battle, as the poor buggers thought they had survived the VC, only to be drowned by a tidal wave. Fortunately, it never eventuated and, after what felt like an eternity, we all moved back down to 1ALH, taking all the patients with us again on the back of army trucks.

Shortly after the non-event of the tidal wave, on 6 August, 1968, 1AFH was visited by Prime Minister John Gorton, a former fighter pilot during the Second World War. Mr Gorton had previously announced in February, 1968 that Australia would not increase its troop commitment to Vietnam, but three months later, there was an amendment to the National Service Act, to include a two-year jail term for draft resisters.

Mr Gorton came into our unit with a warm smile on his face. At this stage, while our involvement in the Vietnam War was still very active, he had finally started withdrawing some of our troops, but that was mainly due to the constant public dissent in Australia. The patient we were treating during Gorton's visit was, in fact, Barry Pearce, a medic, and Mr Gorton asked him how long he had been in Vietnam and, 'Was the dentist doing a good job?'

Funnily enough, Barry left after his treatment and went back to the triage area of the hospital, only to be again visited by "All the way with JG", as we now fondly referred to him. He asked Barry, 'Haven't we met before, son?' obviously thinking he must have been sent to our unit to pretend that we were busy. Full credit though to Mr Gorton, as when he was told by his minder that they were behind schedule, he abruptly told him they would not be leaving the base until he had spoken with every patient and medic.

On a warm sunny day in late August, 1968, Frank 001 confirmed I would be one of the "shotguns" travelling in the "red road convoy" to the United States Army logistics and command centre at Long Binh, situated at Bien Hoa, 25 miles northeast of Saigon and about at least a five hour drive from 1AFH at Vung Tau. The road was declared orange at the time. The convoy would consist of 10 to 15 vehicles, including army trucks and land rovers, and was to collect numerous stores and supplies, not just our medical and dental needs.

My main role, with other armed soldiers, in addition to gunshot duties, would be to ensure the needed supplies were what had been ordered by 001. Our main supply line was usually met by the Royal Australian Navy, courtesy of the aircraft carrier, HMAS Sydney, for not just our needs but the overall war effort in South Vietnam. From time to time, we still needed to arrange for additional supplies, especially when unionists, supported by the Waterside Workers Federation and backed by the Australian Council of Trade Unions would go on strike in Australia in opposition to the war.

Very intrigued that I would be one of the armed shotguns, I realised I needed to ensure my trusty F1 submachine gun was operating efficiently. I must admit, notwithstanding we were in a war zone, I had somehow ignored looking after my weapon and certainly hadn't been cleaning it. Upon checking it that day at a firing range just outside the base, I soon found it would not fire any bullets as it kept jamming. Being rather gullible, I went down to the Quartermasters store (Q store) and saw the sergeant who I had the "pleasure" of meeting at jungle training at Holsworthy.

The Q store staff not only had the task of running their store, but the overall day to day efficient operation of the hospital, such as supplying items like soap, pyjamas, bed linen, food plates, boots, toilet paper and a myriad of other supplies. This also included weapons and ammunition.

Their other unenviable role was preparing soldiers killed in action for transport back home, which included placing bandages over gaping wounds, then washing and cleaning their bodies, putting them in a body bag in a refrigerated section before moving them to the main mortuary in Saigon for the sad journey back to Australia. Q store staff would also be required to escort the deceased to the Saigon mortuary, a massive complex located at the Tan Son Nhut airbase. Unfortunately, it was always full as it also included US service personnel killed in action.

It was against this background that I politely asked the Q store sergeant for a shotgun, as I was in a convoy to Long Binh the next morning and my F1 wouldn't function. In no uncertain terms, he told me to stop being a smart arse, gave me an M16 Armalite with two magazines and then ordered me out of his Q Store as I was rightly "pissing him off".

The road to Long Binh was a long and arduous journey. After we left 1AFH in the early hours of the next morning, I was sitting as shotgun in a Landrover with my recently acquired Armalite, battle flak jacket and helmet, worn in case the orange road turned to red. On a number of occasions, we were greeted along the road by numerous Vietnamese villagers with their children wearing big smiles on their faces, waving and yelling, 'Oc-Dai-Loi number one,' meaning, 'Australian very good'.

We would wave back, throwing them lollies and other small gifts as we continued our journey, which included crossing a temporary and dangerous looking portable bridge over the Mekong River.

Some hours later, we arrived at the Long Binh Post which, in effect, was like a city and, at its peak, housed in the order of 60,000 personnel. After a short lunch in an American mess, we were taken for a tour while our trucks were being loaded for the return to Vung Tau later that afternoon. It was an amazing place! There were American Postal Exchanges, dental clinics, restaurants, snack bars, swimming pools, post offices, tennis and basketball courts and even a golf driving range, to name a few of the numerous amenities. There was even a Chase Manhattan Bank branch.

It was also an army base, unofficially known as the "Long Binh Junction", with its own army prison, titled the Long Binh jail. Both had the initials "LBJ" and were perhaps influenced by the initials of American President, L.B. Johnson. It was, in effect, the central command post for the United States military, to centralise its logistics and communications with the security of its armed forces.

It contained, not only the 199th Light Infantry Brigade, but numerous other units including the 44th medical brigade, the 93rd and 24th Evacuation Hospitals and it was the first stop for newly arrived US personnel in country before they were permanently assigned to other units in South Vietnam.

In February, 1967, the Viet Cong, in a sustained attack, destroyed its ammunition supply and it was, of course, part of the February 1968 TET offensive, which then resulted in the urgent erection of a perimeter post system, consisting of 19,200 metres of double row triple concertina fence, together with 1900 metres of access road, including multiple firing bunkers.

Fully loaded with our supplies, we departed the post for our journey back to Vung Tau, only to be stopped, due to no access across the Mekong River. The bridge that I first thought was a shaky portable, had been blown up. From all reports, this was a common occurrence and, it seemed, the very friendly local villagers who warmly greeted us with the title of number one, may have had other occupations, particularly at night, namely as "Charlie".

By this stage, we were obviously concerned that our orange road was now red but, thankfully, the Americans arrived in force, with overhead gunships as we waited for another bridge to be flown in, after putting a defensive perimeter around our convoy. Amazingly, about 30 minutes later, a Chinook helicopter arrived with a portable bridge slung below it. It slowly placed the bridge across the river, allowing us to get the hell out of the area and continue our journey.

It was obvious the Americans had a lot of practice in erecting portable bridges over many parts of the Mekong River and while this was all happening, there was not one villager in sight cheering us on as number one Australians. If they were present but in hiding, they would have been yelling out 'Uc-Dai-Loi number ten' meaning we're now considered 'very bad' Australians.

My initial nervous venture to Long Binh was short-lived. A few days later, Frank 001 kindly informed me, not only would I be flying to Long Binh from Vung Tau via Nui Dat, but I would be spending a day helping with supplies for drop offs to our fire support bases (FSBs) as part of my learning experience and courtesy of the Americans flying Chinook helicopters.

The FSBs were to enable battalions to be deployed in the field and not always at a static location, but some could simply be mobilised and moved from one location to another. For example, during the Mini-Tet in May 1968, the 1st Australian Task Force deployed two battalions to a location 20 kilometres north of Bien Hoa City, not only to disrupt North Vietnamese battalions, but also the Viet Cong trying to withdraw from Saigon and their base complex at Bien Hoa.

A number of FSBs were also set up in order to utilise artillery and mortars which would provide a level of protection to our battalions, particularly 1RAR and 3RAR. They were considered "fortresses without walls" but were protected by barbed wire, claymore mines and gun pits.

Our FSBs were sometimes named after a girlfriend or a wife back home. FSB Coral, located approximately seven kilometres from the town of Tan Uyen and 80 kilometres from Nui Dat, was subjected to an intense enemy attack, including rockets on 12 May, 1968. Eleven Australians were killed and 28 wounded. The attacking force lost more than 52 by a body count left behind. This was followed by a further attack on 16 May and 22 May, 1968, including on FSB Balmoral, with a further five diggers killed. The losses of the North Vietnamese army were believed to be much higher and in the order of 300 killed in action.

Other FSBs were named Julia and Virginia with one even named Giraffe, which may have been after a girlfriend with very long legs. In March 1967, there was also an FSB permanently located on a circular hill known as the Horseshoe, approximately eight kilometres southeast of Nui Dat and north of Dat Do. A month later, approximately 22,000 mines were laid over 11 kilometres from the Horseshoe down to Dat Do, then along the coast to the fishing village of Lang Phouc Hai, about 16 kilometres from Vung Tau.

It was against this background in late August, 1968, when I boarded a US CH–47 Chinook at Vung Tau Air Base for the short trip to Luscombe Airfield at Nui Dat. It was loaded with numerous supplies and freight for distribution to a number of FSBs and then onto Long Binh. I had seen many Chinook helicopters flying over but this was my first time on board, and as a crew member.

They were mainly utilised for troop transfers, resupplying field operations with fuel and ammunition and, when needed, for casualty evacuations. It could lift a variety of complex underslung items of freight such as a M113 Armoured Personnel Carrier (APC) and, of course, portable bridges, as we had witnessed on the trip back from Long Binh.

The Chinook was armed with usually one single 7.62mm M 60 machine gun on either side of the chopper and had devices fitted to make sure the gunners didn't fire into its twin rotor blades. It also had dust filters fitted to ensure engine reliability. At its peak during the Vietnam War, there were 22 units in operation, totalling 750 helicopters, of which 200 were either lost in action or due to wartime accidents while on field operations. The Australian government had previously assessed the Chinook helicopter as suitable for its needs and ordered twelve of the choppers, but the order was cancelled because it would be well into the 1970s before delivery could be made.

During the Vietnam War, the US Army kindly loaned Chinooks for our use, as and when required, while we concentrated on the expansion of our Caribous and Bell UH-1 Iroquois tactical transport helicopters. The fighting had again escalated around this time with NVA and Viet Cong carrying out numerous attacks on the allies, rocket attacks on Saigon and house to house fighting in Tay Ninh, a town situated near the Cambodian border but only 50 miles from Saigon. This occurred despite President Johnson previously suggesting he would cease bombing North Vietnam, provided Hanoi also took some reciprocal action. The action they took was on 23 August, 1968 when the NVA continued with heavy and sustained rocket and artillery attacks on numerous South Vietnamese cities, military installations, including the airfield at Da Nang and the cities of Hue and Quang Tri, some 600 kilometres from Saigon.

The flight to Nui Dat was short and uneventful luckily and, after further loading, we departed for one of the first FSBs to unload urgently needed food, ammunition and other supplies. On the way, one of the American gunners decided to test his M60 machine gun and, without warning, fired numerous bursts into the jungle undergrowth below. I immediately thought for some reason we were under attack but his explanation was that he was bored on his fifth tour of Vietnam and he needed a release.

I had no idea of what was below or if the rounds fired indiscriminately had hit any poor, innocent and unsuspecting villager who just happened to be walking along, minding their own business. I suspect the gunner, despite being a jovial chap, may have experienced too many tours and was affected by the tropical heat and had gone a bit "troppo".

Following a number of drop offs in the middle of nowhere, the Chinook suddenly lost all power without warning. I thought my tour of duty was about to come to an unpleasant and abrupt end but the chopper slowly made a descent to the ground below, landing quite softly, with all of us hanging onto a cargo net and me onto my Armalite rifle. This unplanned landing in the jungle of South Vietnam occurred, either as a result of loss of power in one or both engines or some concern over the main drive gearbox temperatures or pressures.

The procedure followed by our very experienced pilots, was to lower the collective pitch, maintain a specific airspeed and then convert the engine rotor blades into air driven brakes known as autorotation. This also allowed the pilots to utilise the stored energy in the rotating blades as the aircraft approached the ground. Then, by lifting the collective pitch and nose of the chopper, it decreased the air speed, allowing it to settle very gently onto the ground.

Despite the soft landing, it was obvious the chopper and its crew were a sitting target for any marauding VC in the area. Very quietly, we put a guarded perimeter around the chopper, while some of the crew started very discretely unloading the remaining cargo and dismantling the M60 machine guns.

After what seemed like an eternity, another Chinook suddenly appeared from out of nowhere, landing approximately 100 metres from our downed chopper. After reloading onto that chopper without incident, we began our journey back to Nui Dat and finally Vung Tau. That Chinook may still be stuck there, no doubt sinking in the middle of the jungle, however, I suspect the Americans would have recovered it at some stage.

My experience in Vietnam, although having a profound impact on me with memories I can never erase, the exposure to death and mayhem was nothing compared to what many of our infantry soldiers and medics were exposed to and they still suffer profoundly to this day.

In many ways, I was fortunate to experience both sides of a war and, as my father said before I left, I would have a tour that would forever remain unforgettable, including the fun and frivolity of a war zone.

11

Fun and Frivolity

For the first four months of my tour, I behaved myself with the occasional drink at our Sunday barbeques on the beach, before staggering across to the Peter Badcoe Club to enjoy whatever was on offer. I had the options of going to the club, listening and watching the local Vietnamese bands with their very attractive girls gyrating in their very short miniskirts on the side of the stage, or going to the outdoor theatre adjacent to the Vampire Pad. There were also visiting groups of Australian pop singers, including Pat Carroll and Yvonne Barrett. I must admit, I had a bit of crush on Yvonne who was an absolute delight, not to mention also extremely attractive. Personalities such as Ian Turpie, Denise Drysdale and Tommy Hanlon Jnr were also among the government-sponsored entertainers to visit the Australian troops in Vietnam.

After consuming too many beers on one particular occasion, we all ventured across to watch the entertainment when one so-called mate challenged me to throw a half pound of melting Western Star butter, left over from our barbeque, at a dancer. Not being one to knock back a challenge, I stood up and let fly, hitting the poor unsuspecting dancer on the side of her shoulder, much to the delight of all and sundry, except for the military police, who happened to be keeping a watchful eye on the audience.

I was dragged to the office and, if it wasn't for my grinning mates joined by numerous other participants who came to the door chanting, 'Let him go, let him go,' I would have been charged and spending a night in the brig.

Drinking also took place in our boozer listening to Barry Navin, a much-liked medic, strumming his guitar in the background, with everyone consuming cheap copious amounts of Victoria Bitter or Four X cans. Our favourite game was to stack the empty cans to see how high you could place them without them crashing to the ground.

Medic, Grantley Payze, was very good at stacking the cans and I would take great delight in waiting until his stack reached the top of the boozer before knocking them over. To say Grantley was not amused was an understatement and, on more than one occasion, he threatened to punch the living daylights out of me, which I definitely deserved.

The easy availability of alcohol did not seem to worry the army brass, despite the fact that, full of grog, we would all return back to our huts which also stored our weapons complete with ammunition. There were incidents called "fragging", one of which sadly took place at Nui Dat on 23 November, 1969 with the murder of Lieutenant Robert Convery of the 9th Battalion Royal Australian Regiment. A grenade was placed in his tent after a night of heavy drinking in the lines. Private Peter Allen was convicted of murder and served 11 years imprisonment.

The availability of grog and a weapon became all the more real after one of our Sunday afternoon escapades when our driver, George Nicholson, grabbed his F1 machine gun. He staggered off towards the front gate with his clothes falling off him, slurring that he was going into Vungers to sort out a few "noggies" or "slopes", being slang for Vietnamese. George was promptly arrested and spent the night in the company of the military police.

How he wasn't charged, I had no idea. One MP involved in this incident played football for Essendon and was also a conscript. I told him I was an avid bomber supporter so maybe that convinced him not to lay any charges.

The day-to-day stressful environment of a war zone with the constant Dustoffs flying overhead, listening to Hanoi Hannah, missing home and receiving only the occasional letter, was taking its toll on us. Grog was really the only outlet. There was no such thing as mobile phones or internet and emails, so all you had to remind you of your loved ones and to keep up to date with local news, were the letters of love and support from home and the occasional odd newspaper which were many weeks old. I wasn't good at returning the favour and in one letter from my father, he reminded me that it might be appropriate if I wrote to my sister Susan to remind her she had a brother.

Our letters from home would soon become less frequent as the Waterside Workers Federation, opposing the Vietnam War, became involved and placed a number of postal strikes and embargoes on Australian soldiers serving in Vietnam. A "Punch a Postie" slogan soon found its way around the base, initially emanating from Nui Dat, encouraging us to "Sock it to 'em, Diggers" when we got back.

Whilst the war was vehemently opposed, it was not our fault that we found ourselves in a much despised conflict as conscripts, such attitude being maintained well after the war ended.

Of course, there was the attraction of the very enticing local bar girls overseen by a much older "Mama- San" (Madam). I initially managed to stay away from them offering their favours in Vung Tau, which was, in many ways, the equivalent of Kings Cross in Sydney. Using a land rover, we would go sightseeing into the town but if off duty, wearing plain clothes and full of beer, usually on a Sunday afternoon, we would hire a Lambretta and a driver, who was always patiently waiting outside the main gate of 1ALSG for the short trip into town. Curfew was around 8pm.

When we drunkenly arrived at the main centre square, we would all jump out and take off in different directions, without paying the driver. When I think about it now, it was pathetic conduct, given the locals were all struggling to financially survive with no thanks to the war.

On some occasions, we would travel into Vung Tau on an army bus which would collect its passengers at the main gate of 1ALSG. We soon avoided that mode of travel as it usually finished in a punch up due to us being full of grog when alighting from the bus. On one occasion I was hammered, not only from alcohol, but from another soldier who didn't take kindly to me being a smart arse and mouthing off.

The local bar girls were certainly an attraction, standing outside their local place of work, offering their services and wanting you to buy them a Saigon Tea, which was a highly diluted whisky in a shot glass. For the first four months I didn't give in to them. Sometimes the tea would be just clear water with a slight mint taste. The young bar girls, or Saigon Tea girls, were all very young, either married to locals or had Vietnamese or American boyfriends.

Their job as prostitutes was to offer a "boom boom",

meaning sexual favours. They'd tell the young drunken soldier how handsome he was and continue to entice him to buy them more watered-down drinks with the profits going to the bar owner. In my case, they started referring to me as 'baby face Uc-dai-loi' to attract my attention and accept their offerings.

If I refused to buy a Saigon Tea, which would be around the equivalent of two Military Payment Certificates or the equivalent in piastres, they would chant back to me:

Uc- dai -loi, Cheap Charlie, Uc- dai -loi, Cheap Charlie,
He no buy me Saigon Tea, He no give me MPC,
Saigon Tea costs many many P, Mama – San go crook at me,
Uc- dai -loi, he Cheap Charlie. Uc- dai -loi, he Cheap Charlie.

I was soon to learn an expanded version of this melody when staying at the Dong Khanh Hotel in Cho Lon, and my four months of being a Vung Tau virgin was about to come to an abrupt end.

A couple of my soldier colleagues, who shall remain nameless, had by now experienced the sexual favours of the local Vietnamese girls to the degree that they were in a "relationship" with them, for want of a better word. Unfortunately, one had suffered VD during the course of their relationship on two separate occasions, but somehow that did not deter him. They were very concerned about my welfare and lack of enjoying the fruits of the local girls, so invited me to spend the night with them in the back streets of Vung Tau at the home of one of the girls.

The offer was reluctantly taken up and, despite curfew at 8pm, we stayed overnight. I ventured down to what can only be described as a shanty, to be welcomed in the pitch darkness by a very sweet sounding and attractive Vietnamese girl, or so I thought. I paid my 20 piastres to have sex with her and as I struggled to put on a condom, she turned on a hurricane lamp.

I took one look and decided she was downright ugly, with quite a few teeth missing, so with my tail between my legs, so to speak, I scampered back to my mate's girlfriend's slightly better shanty. Much to my mate's amusement, he opened the door to the sight of me naked with a condom half hanging off.

The story doesn't end there because some hours later, I woke up. Thought, *What the heck,* and went back to the shanty to complete my first Vietnam sexual experience. We returned to base next morning in our land rover as though we were simply on duty and without any issue from the soldiers on duty at the 1ALSG main gate.

The fun in a war zone improved a few degrees after that, especially on our future trips to Saigon and staying in Cho Lon. The Dong Khanh Hotel had a lot to offer, including accommodation and meals. It also had a number of floors where you could be entertained by the bar girls.

I became very friendly with one whose name was Tiger Lily and she was certainly a vast improvement on my Vung Tau experience. The hotel had a sauna room, massages on offer and the girls would take great pleasure walking on our backs, with of course, the occasional crotch rub, as we merrily consumed more beers.

Much to my delight, Tiger Lily would often stay the night and, although we had a relationship, of sorts, it was more about sex for me, while for her, it was the money she earnt. The Saigon Teas were still a marketable commodity as was looking out the top floor window at 3am in the morning to watch the fireworks, in other words, the VC, making their presence felt on the outskirts of Saigon, including the B-52s dropping bombs in the distance.

On one of those early morning escapades, Captain Twiggy, who had stayed overnight and certainly behaved himself, took a US Major to task. Being quite pissed, the Major was giving everyone a hard time and acting like a complete dickhead. He would tell everyone how good he was as he held the rank of a senior officer in the US army. I knew Twiggy could look after himself and I was proven correct when he made short work of the disgruntled and now battered major.

In one of my many moments with a few too many Vietnamese beers, known as "Ba Muoi Bas", on board, I also made a fool of myself when I grabbed a very young bar girl, threw her across my shoulders and marched off towards my room with her giggling or perhaps she was screaming for help. I soon put her down when I was surrounded by some very young, but fit-looking Vietnamese chaps who also worked at the hotel. They were known as "Vietnamese cowboys", the equivalent of what we know as nightclub bouncers. Twiggy wasn't impressed with my conduct and he gave me a well-deserved dressing down.

Tiger Lily, who was pregnant, but I hastily add not with my child, also wasn't impressed by my drunken escapade. This then led to a further adaptation of "Cheap Charlie" which was sung by the bar girls, including the ones at the Dong Khanh Hotel:

Uc- dai -loi, cheap Charlie, Uc- dai -loi, cheap Charlie,
He give baby san to me, He go home across the sea,
Baby san costs many many P, Uc- dai -loi he leave baby san with me,
Uc- dai -loi, he cheap Charlie. Uc- dai -loi, he cheap Charlie.

Our entertainment was not just confined to the local bar girls. Volleyball and the occasional football game also kept us busy, as did swimming, surfing the waves and sailing on the South China sea in small boats known as bobcats and corsairs. The bobcat was like a small dinghy with one sail and usually manned by two people. We certainly enjoyed sailing, despite being constantly reminded by the noise from helicopters and F-4 Phantom jet fighters flying over, that we were in a war zone.

One such reminder came when running along the beach quietly enjoying myself. A fighter bomber flew past and frightened the living daylights out of me. I never heard them coming, due to their sheer speed until they were right on me. The pilot, obviously, was quite amused and let me know by doing a superb victory roll.

Swimming definitely had its hazards. On one occasion in the water, I stepped on something which had great delight in biting my foot. A painkilling injection, followed by the usual consumption of beers, was required to quell the pain. Sunbaking was also a favourite past time and, being fair skinned, I tanned very easily. One day though, while lying on the beach, listening to a broadcast of Essendon v Carlton grand final being broadcast over loudspeakers, I ended up very sunburnt. That, of course, paled into insignificance when Essendon lost to Carlton by a meagre three points in front of 116,000 spectators at the Melbourne Cricket Ground.

I had never played volleyball before but Alan "Barry" Pearce, also known as AB, one of the medics from radiology, talked me into it. I wasn't even what you would call a better than handy player, with the ball continually going over the top of my head due to my lack of height and scoring for the opposition. Volleyball competitions between a number of units were a regular occurrence, as were games of rugby union.

I was definitely more suited to Aussie Rules. A competition called the "Vietnam Football League" had been established within the first 12 months of the Australian base being set up. The matches were usually played at a very small square oval soccer ground in Vung Tau. Due to the size of the area, each side only had 14 players with no flanks. The soccer goal posts were extended and we installed temporary behind posts on each side.

It was fair to say the games were played with some vigour, especially when we played the navy or airforce teams. An ambulance was always in attendance. The Americans watching the game could not believe how we played without any padding, unlike their grid iron. The other problem we had was keeping the local Vietnamese from running onto the oval while our games were underway.

The only injury I suffered was a lacerated knee, which became infected through my own fault as I didn't attend to it at the time. It landed me in hospital for a few days where they extracted the core pus from my knee, much to the amusement of the medics. One of our players suffered a badly broken nose, but surgeon Colonel Don Beard had great delight in clicking it back into place, despite saying he would probably need surgery. The good colonel even operated on the same soldier for a bullet to the head on two separate occasions, once when he was surgeon in Korea and again at 1AFH.

We had some really good players, AB and me included. My now good mate, Grantley Payze, played for West Torrens back home and was related to Travis Payze, who played 127 games for St Kilda in the Victorian Football League. Our training usually consisted of the normal football drills, including running along the sand dunes adjacent to the Peter Badcoe Club. After the game, it was back to the boozer, downing celebratory beers, including Courage beer, with the distinctive Red Rooster emblem, and chanting, 'Up the old red rooster and more piss.' This was the catch cry used by the Royal Australian Engineers and we borrowed it. The origin of such a verse went back many years prior, as a military drinking song in the Second World War.

After six months of my tour of duty, I took some rest and recreation to at least give me a brief respite from the war and the fun and games we all got up to. I decided to return home for the short seven days leave as my fiancé's sister was getting married and we were invited to the wedding. I did have a choice of spending my time in Bangkok, or even Hong Kong, but to me, the wedding was more important and the thought of seven days in another Asian country and its attractions was not very appealing.

I had heard a number of stories from soldiers who spent their R & R in Bangkok and it was really another version of either Vung Tau or our Saigon trips, continually on the grog and becoming too friendly with the local bar girls. In addition, on returning from Bangkok, many guys suddenly found themselves reporting to the hospital suffering from a venereal disease.

Many American soldiers chose to go to Sydney for their R & R, even though our government had a number of concerns as to how they would be treated, due to the unpopular war, and whether the African Americans would be subject to racial taunts. Their other concern was the possibility of an increase in sexually transmitted diseases, but profit before concerns apparently was more important.

Despite the opposition, generally our people treated the American soldiers very well and around 300,000 US military personnel visited Australia for their well-earned R & R between 1967 and 1971. My visit, which I enjoyed, went very quickly and despite my communist sympathiser auntie demanding I not return, I was soon back at 1AFH.

It wasn't long before a couple of incidents would see me eventually transferred to Nui Dat on the orders of Major John Spencer, our commanding officer. The first nail in my coffin was when our unit was invited to spend some quality time with the US Naval Support Activity Detachment at Radar Hill. It was their way of thanking us for looking after their teeth.

This was used as the Australian and US Radar post, which was situated at the top of VC Hill overlooking Vung Tau. Along with Rob Watson and Norm Caulfield, plus a few others from our unit, we were driven to the unit's post by our driver George, who returned to our base after dropping us off.

The idea was to make our own way back by 8pm curfew, courtesy of one of our host's drivers. Of course, we didn't worry about getting back to base as we enjoyed the beers and food on offer. The beer, even worse than Australian Resch's, was in fact Budweiser and Schlitz, but despite me drinking to excess, I remained sober. This type of beer was much like a light alcohol drink and, for whatever reason, had no effect on me.

However, the navy boys, who certainly were not the greatest beer drinkers, had consumed copious amounts. Around 9pm, they had either gone back to their beds or were asleep around the tables with flies buzzing over the leftover food. The issue we now had was to either stay the night and return next morning to our base, as I had managed to successfully do once before, or borrow a vehicle from their transport compound. Common sense would suggest staying overnight and then arrange a lift the next morning but we all decided to leave then, making our own way back, by borrowing a US military vehicle.

Their transport compound was not guarded and the vehicles were all left with keys in them, so I selected a very clean US military truck with the big American white star on each door. Obviously, the truck was a left-hand drive and with me as the nominated driver, I somehow got the truck started and headed for the main gate of the naval unit. What I didn't foresee was a guard on duty at the gate. He waved me down and came up to my window.

In my very best American slang I said, 'I am just driving these here Aussies back to their camp.'

Without hesitation, he lifted the boom gate and waved us through and off we drove. Radar Hill is very steep and I had no idea how I managed to drive down that dirt road. If we'd finished up over the edge, it was curtains for all of us, as it was a very long way to the bottom.

Miraculously, I manoeuvred the truck off Radar Hill and started heading towards 1ALSG. Along the way, we saw what appeared to be a soldier hitchhiking along the road just out of Vung Tau. Despite it being way past curfew, he didn't seem to have a worry in the world, so I pulled up alongside and offered him a lift. He was an American sailor returning to the Cat Lo Naval base approximately six kilometres further on.

At this point, I determined that my American slang voice would probably not work at our main gate, so I said to our new passenger, 'Seeing you're going back to Cat Lo, would you like a truck?'

Without hesitation, he answered he would love a truck so we swapped seats and he drove on the proviso that he would first take us back to 1ALSG, preferably to our unit hut. I suddenly became guilt ridden as, not only had I effectively stolen a US Army vehicle, but had now implicated the unsuspecting sailor. Then again, he did say he would love a truck.

Arriving at the 1ALSG main gate, the sentry, on seeing it was a star-spangled banner US truck, simply waved us through and our now smiling driver took us to the top of the hill just outside our hut. We all thanked him profusely and off he drove in his newly acquired US truck, courtesy of the American military.

It would be fair to say, the proverbial hit the fan next morning and I was called in to have a short word with a grumpy Major Spencer, who had been informed of, or knew a little bit about the shenanigans that occurred overnight. I, of course, pleaded my innocence and attempted to explain, to a degree, exactly what happened, all to no avail. The poor, unsuspecting sailor had now been arrested by the military police and, as he was dragged off to the brig screaming, he kept saying that some Australians had 'given him a truck'.

The upside was the Americans recovered their truck undamaged, but we were not invited back to their base. This incident was the first recorded black mark against my name and one more was to follow with the arrival of our new warrant officer, Jack "Shocker" Goodwin.

Unfortunately, on 22 October, 1968, Frank 001 was medevacked home due to illness. His replacement, who arrived on 25 November, 1968, was Shocker. Frank would be sorely missed as he was looked up to by all Australian conscripts as a father figure. For his exemplary service in three theatres of war, he was awarded four medals for World War 2, two for Korea and three for Vietnam, together with a Cadet Medal and a US Commendation Medal. In recognition of his service to his country, he was subsequently awarded an Order of Australia medal (OAM). Frank was a brilliant and much-loved man.

On the other hand, it seemed Shocker, who was regular army, was given this nickname after he allegedly bit off a budgerigar's head and spat it out, in the boozer back home, or so the story went.

When we were attending to some Vietnamese villagers on our normal Tuesday Dentcap, Shocker, on his arrival, took exception to the way we were treating one of our patients. He told Captain Twiggy what he should be doing. Mind you, the infamous Shocker had only been in country a mere two hours, but here he was telling all and sundry how to go about their business. He also had a problem with some of our haircuts, particularly mine. He deemed them not to be short back and sides, so we all had to get a haircut to his satisfaction. To say he was the exact opposite of Frank 001 was an understatement.

Unfortunately, I had the honour of travelling with Shocker to Saigon on one of our regular visits. To make it worse, we were sharing a room at the Dong Khanh Hotel in Cho Lon. I returned to my room quite early, without Tiger Lily, I might add, and upon turning on the light, I was zapped by an electric shock. Obviously, it was faulty, as well as dangerous.

l was in bed when Shocker came into the room and, lo and behold, he turned on the light, was zapped and shocked, worse than I was, much to my laughter and amusement. Shocker was not impressed and, on arrival back at 1ALSG, he ordered me to get another haircut, then informed me I would be the duty corporal in charge of the radio and security picket, commencing on the Friday night through to Sunday.

I dutifully worked the radio security picket without incident, but with little or no sleep, so I determined that I would take the Monday off and simply just laze around on the beach and consume a few beers. What I didn't do, though, was tell anyone what I was doing, or get permission for obvious reasons. On my return to the hut that night and worse for wear, I was told Shocker was looking for me and that I would be charged with being absent without leave. In a war zone, this is a very serious charge and rightly so. It was fair to say I was in a lot of trouble.

The following morning I was marched in by Shocker with Rob and Norm as "guards" on either side of me. I was presented before Major Spencer, who again was not impressed. The charge was read out and I was asked to explain myself, which I attempted to do. However, although the good Major was not amused, he did sympathise with me and said that in view of my medical issues, in particular the glandular fever and ear infection, he felt it was better if I was transferred to Nui Dat as soon as possible.

I also got the distinct impression the major might have had an inkling there was some ill feeling between myself and Shocker, which was an understatement. On being marched out by the escort guards, I had a smile on my face, knowing I would soon be out of the confined space and noise of 1ALSG and well away from Shocker.

Prior to my departure in a land rover to Nui Dat, I did get to enjoy a lazy day on the HMAS Perth docked in Vung Tau harbour. It was on its second deployment after departing from Sydney to replace HMAS Hobart. The navy sailors took us on a tour of their warship followed by our assistance with consuming large cans of Foster's beer. My recollection is that their ration was one large can a day, but they would allow their allocation to accumulate and then have one big booze up.

One of my last days at 1AFH was spent enjoying the Christmas Day tradition of being waited on in our mess by the officers and senior NCOs. There was excellent service from Captain Twiggy, even though I made him return a few times with extra portions from the kitchen. Our Christmas day meal was amazing, with a menu of turkey, ham, fresh vegetables and mugs of hot coffee laced with rum. The traditional cigar followed and, although I didn't smoke, I thought what the heck. I don't recall Shocker ever taking part of the service as a waiter. Probably just as well.

The fun and frivolity of a war zone was about to end but before it did, the much despised Shocker and I had a punch up behind the boozer. Not a good look to say the least, as I was only a pissed corporal taking on a pissed warrant officer. My recollection is, and I will stick to this story, I belted the crap out of him. Nui Dat, here I come.

12

The Dat

Nui Dat, meaning "small hill" was considered an excellent location for the establishment of the Australian Task Force base. It was selected by Lieutenant General John Wilton in early 1966 and erected mainly by soldiers from the 1st and 5th Battalions, Royal Australian Regiment, together with assistance from members of the United States 173rd Airborne. The surrounding area of Nui Dat, known as the Dat, was a well disguised stronghold for the Viet Cong. The Dat was seen as a priority and ideal base for numerous counter-insurgency warfare operations to be carried out by our forces in Phouc Tuy province.

It was well known that the military situation in the province had largely been ignored by the South Vietnamese government, without any control for many years. The roads were only suited to single lane traffic and the Buddhist and Catholic population, of around 104,000 people, was mainly living in Ba Ria, Long Dien, Hoa Long and Dat Do.

However, before Nui Dat could be built, it required the forcible relocation, without any compensation, of all the Vietnamese inhabitants living within a four-kilometre radius of the proposed camp, obviously for security reasons.

This required their resettlement and included the villages at Long Tan and Long Phouc, with a population of over 1,000 villagers. Operation Hardihood was carried out by the 1st and 5th battalions of the Royal Australian Regiments and the relocation to nearby Hoa Long, Binh Ba, Dat Do and Long Dien, included not only the villagers and their possessions, but also their livestock. The operation was completed in July, 1966.

The village of Long Phouc was destroyed as part of the operation, causing great resentment from the Viet Cong supporters. The landmines which were laid, ultimately became weapons to be used against our soldiers. Plans were also put in place for barrier minefields to try and disrupt the important VC supply route, with approximately 20,000 M- 16 "jumping jack" mines located between two wire fences for 10 kilometres from Dat Do, as far as the coast. When detonated, these mines would jump at least a metre into the air. The M-16 mine was capable of killing and maiming anyone unfortunate enough to be in its wide radius and, on average, there were at last six casualties for each detonation.

The mines, however, proved ineffective as the VC quite easily breached the barrier fences and again, reused them against both our troops and the South Vietnamese Army. This became known as the "Dat Do mine store". There were many accidents involving injuries and deaths when laying the mines. In essence, the laying of these mines was considered to be the one of the biggest mistakes made by our senior military commanders during the Vietnam War.

In addition, a herbicide, known as Agent Orange, was used up until 1970 to effectively destroy and control the jungle vegetation and undergrowth. Roadways and paddy fields within the designated radius and throughout Phouc Tuy province, including around the base camp perimeter of Nui Dat, were being sprayed from low flying C-12 aircraft, or from helicopters. The use of the chemical resulted in millions of Vietnamese and our own veterans, suffering from debilitating illnesses as a consequence of exposure. Birth defects in children, leukemia and various kinds of cancers were just some of the after-effects of Agent Orange.

Conditions for the new compact army base were very basic with our troops sleeping in the open, initially, then on stretchers in World War Two tents. Over time, access roads were provided, followed by essential buildings and installations. The defence of the base was paramount. It was surrounded by concertina wire, claymore mines and elevated bunkers manned around the perimeter of the base. The vegetation, including rubber plantations, were removed and destroyed, allowing at least a small arms range where each soldier had their own fighting pit.

Overall, the area was very flat, with open farmlands and numerous rice paddies. Even after the relocation of the villagers, the area would still be dominated by the VC, along with part-time guerrillas and regular main force NVA soldiers, with their network of tunnels and underneath bunkers, especially around the area of the village of Long Phouc.

The network of tunnels, located in the Cu Chi districts, was used by the VC, not only as a hiding spot during contacts but also as communication and supply routes. The Cu Chi tunnels, which contained weapon caches, hospitals and food, were also the living quarters of the NVA and VC. The tunnels were often referred to as the "Black Echo" by our infantry soldiers tasked with searching the ever winding tunnels with u-turns.

These soldiers, known as "tunnel rats" or, as called by the

enemy, "sewer rats", faced very dark tunnels, infested with vermin, including rats, snakes and scorpions, not to mention numerous booby traps left behind by the enemy. A tunnel rat would enter with only a small revolver, bayonet, flashlight and explosives to either destroy the tunnel, locate intelligence and, if necessary, kill or capture the enemy found within.

The soldiers chosen to be tunnel rats were small in stature, enabling them to fit more easily into a selected space. Sadly, after the war ended, many suffered from the effects of Agent Orange which had leaked into the tunnels causing polluted airways.

The initial operations conducted by our battalions, including 6th Royal Australian Regiment (6RAR), were primarily focused on securing the new task force base but two significant operations, codenamed "Enoggera" and "Hobart" resulted in a number of VC camps being destroyed, 36 enemy killed in action and a large quantity of weapons and supplies found. All that was left of Long Phouc was its pagodas and churches. What was to follow in the early days of Nui Dat labelled "Operation Smithfield", later became known as the Battle of Long Tan.

Access by air to the Nui Dat base was courtesy of the Luscombe airfield, built in late 1966 by 1 Field Squadron, Royal Australian Engineers (RAE) and named after Captain Bryan Luscombe, who was killed in action during the Korean War. As fixed wing aircraft could only land at the Vung Tau airfield, the plan was for the Luscombe airfield to be of a limited Caribou standard, with a large landing and take-off area for helicopters, together with other facilities. They selected a natural cleared location between SAS Hill and the task force rubber plantation, with the now accessible chopper area known as Kangaroo Pad.

The development of the airfield continued until December 1968, with parking areas and a further extension of the runway now permanently sealed. It ultimately became known as the front door of 1ATF, initially welcoming and then saying goodbye to our soldiers. One of its features was the area known as "Eagle Farm", which was used as a helipad. It had a rubber signpost with arrows pointing to a number of overseas destinations including Singapore, Auckland and, of course, Sydney.

The airfield also accommodated a large amphitheatre with a concert stage known as the "Luscombe Bowl", or sometimes nicknamed the "Dust Bowl" because of the ever-present red dust. It could hold over 1,000 troops who would be entertained by visiting groups, dancing girls, comedians and well-known singers. These included Johnny O'Keefe and Dinah Lee, the latter singing *These Boots Were Made for Walking* or *We Gotta Get Out of This Place*. Lorrae Desmond also serenaded our troops with memories of home by singing *Leaving On a Jet Plane*.

Despite the hot, steamy and monsoonal weather, the concerts were certainly a distraction from the war with each soldier sitting on a chair with his trusty weapon by his side and drinking the never-ending supply of cold, canned beer, waiting excitedly to be entertained. Before Luscombe Bowl was built, the concerts were normally held on the back of a flatbed truck or on hastily built canvas stages.

The majority of our combat soldiers were stationed at Nui Dat and, in effect, saw very little of the base, as our counter insurgency operations saw them out in the field for many weeks at a time. They would only return to the Dat to rest for a few days, before leaving again for contact with the enemy.

If they were out for at least six weeks "jungle bashing",

then they would be allowed two days rest in country (R & C), usually spent in Vung Tau. They certainly deserved the rest as, not only were they subjected to close contact with the enemy, but carried on average, an 80-pound load consisting of water, rations, weapon and ammunition, including a light anti-tank device capable of firing rocket propelled grenades.

Nui Dat was not only to be the home of the infantry soldiers, nicknamed grunts, but also such regiments as the Special Air Service (SAS), Artillery and Armoured and Engineers. Our infantry was also joined by New Zealand units in 1967 and, in March, 1968, they were integrated with our battalions at 1ATF to become known as ANZAC Battalions.

Further reinforcements were desperately needed to combat the escalating war. A third infantry battalion arrived at the Dat in December 1967, reinforced with a squadron of Centurion tanks with Iroquois choppers in early 1968, bringing our total troop strength to in excess of 8,000 personnel, which, by this time, doubled our combat forces.

Infantry companies were also supported by what was known as "War Dog Operatives", which were dog tracker teams. The dogs were housed in well-built kennels constructed by our engineers and they included concrete runs, drainage and wash points for each dog. The dog team would be picked up by huey choppers or armoured personnel carriers and transported to areas of interest, with the task of locating not only the enemy, but also camp sites, bunkers, weapons and explosive caches.

3SAS squadron was first deployed to South Vietnam in April, 1966 and their elite three SAS sabre squadrons rotated yearly. By 1968, New Zealand special forces were attached to each of our SAS squadrons. Their traditional role was long range reconnaissance patrols to determine the strengths of the enemy and to provide intelligence for use by a follow up infantry battalion.

Their soldiers would also be utilised in ambushes and, where possible, to capture and interrogate a prisoner to further gain valuable intelligence. Their reputation was formidable.

Over a period of five years, a total of 580 soldiers served with SAS and they carried out 1,175 patrols, reinforcing their status as an elite unit of the Australian Army with their motto "Who Dares Wins". They inflicted heavy casualties on the enemy, killing 492 with 11 VC taken prisoner and they had the highest kill ratio of all Australian military units in South Vietnam. Their losses were two killed, 28 wounded and one missing in action. Their US equivalent was the Green Berets of which 20,000 were deployed to Vietnam for the duration of the war.

The North Vietnamese and Viet Cong also had an elite unit, known as Sappers, who were considered to be a dangerous and feared assault force, much like our SAS. They would cover their bodies in charcoal and grease and stealthily approach remote allied outposts, silently entering through the barbed wire, before throwing their grenades and explosives contained in satchels. They were called sappers from the French word "saper" meaning to "weaken or undermine", which in today's terms now refers to combat engineers.

The Armoured Regiment was the senior regiment of the Royal Australian Armoured Corps (1st Armoured Regiment) and was first deployed to South Vietnam in May 1965. In February, 1968, C squadron was sent to Vietnam with a total of 20 Centurion tanks to link up with the 3rd Cavalry Unit, who were equipped with the M113 A1 Armoured Personnel Carrier. For the remainder of the war, the regiment proved highly effective in providing close support to our infantry battalions, including the clearing of the never-ending Viet Cong tunnels and bunker systems.

Although always vulnerable to anti-tank weapons and mines, Centurion tanks were able to move through the countryside more easily than expected, with a decisive firepower having a telling impact on the battlefield. C Squadron received a Unit Citation for Gallantry and the regiment was awarded battle honours for combat at Coral–Balmoral and Hat Dich in 1968, and Binh Ba in 1969.

The 17th Construction Squadron, together with the Royal Australian Engineers, was involved in a wide range of engineering tasks and was first deployed to the construction of 1ALSG at Vung Tau with 8 Troop. This was followed by 1ATF being based at Nui Dat in August 1966, with elements of the squadron involved in its defence during an attack the day before the Battle of Long Tan. Other initial operations included the clearing of undergrowth with 5RAR, improving base defence, opening key routes, providing land for the growing of crops and houses for resettled villagers.

Engineers also actively involved in Operation Cooktown Orchid in April, 1968 were being exposed to land mines and booby traps, followed by small arms fire as they cleared undergrowth bush near the Long Hai hills. 9 Troop supplied floating bridges after many were blown up by the VC. They were involved in the building of an 118-foot bridge over the Song Da river. Overall, RAE had 12 officers and 334 other ranks serving in Vietnam at the height of the involvement of the regiment.

Earlier in 1965, it was determined to reinforce our infantry battalion with the 1st Regiment, Royal Australian Regiment

(1st Field Regiment) and in order of deployment battle, with 101st Field Battery followed by the 105th Field Battery, Royal Australian Artillery. This was to provide further fire support and included engagement to assist D Company, 6RAR in the Battle of Long Tan, firing over 3,000 rounds from their M102 105 mm L5 Pack Howitzer guns. I was soon to become acquainted with the constant fire support provided by 105th Field Battery at Nui Dat, when it returned for its second deployment in February 1969.

Nui Dat was also the garrison headquarters for the 1st Australian Civil Affairs Unit (1ACAU) whose main task was to coordinate our army's contribution, together with the US Military, known as the Allied Pacification Program to operate in Phouc Tuy Province. 1RAR had conducted various civil aid projects since 1965 but there was no dedicated capability for civil affairs assistance to the Vietnamese people to win their support.

Under Captain Bob Rooney, who was attached to 1ATF, warrant officers from the Australian Army Training Team Vietnam initially conducted a number of civil aid projects with various US attachments, but they were still considered ad hoc and overall, difficult to operationally maintain.

In June, 1967, 1ACAU, funded in part by the Southeast Asian Treaty Organisation and our Department of External Affairs, became integral to our military operations, particularly during village cordon off and search operations. 1ACAU was also involved in the Phouc Tuy resettlement of its population. The unit also had a detachment at the headquarters of Australian Force Vietnam in Saigon and its commanding officer liaised closely with the commander of 1ATF in respect of its daily operations.

The detachments also included units specialising in, not only medical and dental but also, engineering, education and agriculture. The medical and dental civic action programs were largely supervised by 1ACAU, but the Medcaps and Dentcaps could also be conducted without involvement by 1ACAU.

Its liaison detachment also had Australian officers able to speak the Vietnamese language. Interacting on a daily basis with the civilian population, they were able to provide English language tuition and determine where support was needed, including and not limited to, where new schools could be built. They effectively became the eyes and ears and sounding out members of 1ACAU, as the local villagers accepted them, even to the degree where they would deliver mail from and return with presents for, the Viet Cong who were now in prisoner-of-war camps.

They also became involved in what was known as the Chieu Hoi Open Arms Program, an initiative launched by the South Vietnamese government to promote the defection by the Viet Cong and their supporter base, to the South, away from the North Vietnamese Communist Government. The allied propaganda program consisted of leaflets, usually dropped over enemy territory by either artillery shells or low flying aircraft. They included such slogans as:

> *"There is nowhere to run, nowhere to hide. Tanks will find you. Beware Viet Cong. Rally now under the Chieu Hoi program."*

By the end of 1967, over 75,000 had defected but whether they were genuine is somewhat debatable. Some, now known as "Hoi Chanh Vien", loosely translated as "members who returned to the righteous side", integrated into a unit known as the "Kit Carson Scouts" and joined in combat in areas from which they had previously defected. They were even awarded US military honours, including the Silver Star.

To complete my last few months in Vietnam and, as an assistant to Captain Michael Wenden, I travelled to the Dat in our usual armed convoy along Route 2, being the main highway from Vung Tau and past my favourite orphanage at Ba Ria. We drove through the armed base gates and past SAS Hill to my tent in the quarters of 4th Royal Australian Regiment(4RAR), which was one of three battalions now stationed at Nui Dat.

By now, the base accommodated over 5,000 soldiers and it was protected by a barbed wire perimeter in excess of 12 kilometres. It was still surrounded by rubber trees and, as I was to subsequently find out, infested with snakes and scorpions. My new accommodation, albeit a tent and certainly different from our hut at Vung Tau, was like living in a small village, surrounded by a canteen and boozer, mess, post office and store.

Our chlorinated shower facilities were now canvas bags, replacing the old buckets. Many of us would listen to the dulcet tones emanating from either radio broadcasts or cheap stereo equipment purchased from the local US Army American Post Exchanges. Our chairs, loosely described as furniture, were still very basic and mainly made from artillery and mortar boxes. I think we had it very easy though, compared to when our troops originally set up camp at Nui Dat.

My day was fairly regimented, beginning with flag raising as we were now in the area of an infantry battalion, followed with the mandatory anti-malaria pills and breakfast at 7.30am before starting the day's work. The latter was providing necessary dental treatment to our soldiers, and also Dentcaps to various villages with 1ACAU, interspersed with the occasional trip to Saigon.

Lunch usually consisted of cold meats and salads and knock off time was around 4.30pm, then it was straight to the boozer for some quenching ales, followed by a hot or cold meal. I recall the battalions were limited to one can, sometimes two cans, per day if they were lucky, but of course their number of available cans increased immensely, particularly when they were away from the base for weeks at a time.

My first two nights were spent in a bunker with sleeves rolled down to prevent mozzie bites and with my recently issued Armalite rifle by my side. I listened to the deafening intermittent artillery and mortar rounds being fired at regular intervals in support of our field operations and what was thought to be an attack by Viet Cong on the base. We were later advised that a booby mine trap on the outside of the wire appeared to have been detonated by an animal.

What also became very apparent in my first few days, was the never-ending noise from the constant landings and take-offs by Caribou aircraft and Iroquois helicopters at Luscombe airfield. At this point, I made sure my Armalite was not like my useless F1 and took it to the base firing range, just to make sure. I found it to be very light as it weighed less than seven pounds. Fully loaded, it held 20 rounds but on advice from an infantry soldier, I only had 15 rounds in each magazine, in order to avoid any jamming if I had to use it.

The Caribou, also known as CV-2 Caribou, was a Canadian designed aircraft with the capability of a short take-off and landing and was largely utilised in South Vietnam for short haul resupply missions. I considered myself lucky to hitch a ride in one from Nui Dat to Tan Son Nhut and return, for one of our infamous Saigon visits.

However, on its return to Luscombe Airfield in terrible weather and drenching rain, it landed sideways, known as a "ground loop", although we nearly finished belly up at the end of the strip. I have no idea how we all survived without it rolling over and, after my experience with the Chinook, I honestly thought my days were numbered.

On 15 February, 1969, a seven-day TET ceasefire, declared by the Viet Cong, commenced. At this point in time, the allied troop numbers in South Vietnam had reached an all-time high of just over 1.6 million. The TET ceasefire ended on 22 February, 1969 and communist forces continued with their attacks, firing rocket and mortar rounds into Saigon and numerous other allied positions throughout South Vietnam. During this period, two battalions from 1 ATF, who had left Nui Dat in late December 1968, were still involved in heavy fighting against suspected communist bases in the provinces of Hat Dich, Bien Hoa and Long Khan.

The Battle of Hat Dich commenced on 3 December, 1968. Over almost two and half months, our battalions from 1RAR, 4RAR and 9RAR, together with our New Zealand counterparts, conducted numerous sweeps, supported by tanks and calvary throughout Hat Dich under the codename "Operation Goodwood". This was against suspected enemy bases of the People's Army of Vietnam and the VC and included sustained patrols in Western Phouc Tuy and Long Khan provinces, including Bien Hoa. Such sweeps, as a part of an allied operation, which had commenced earlier in June 1968, were known as Operation Toan Thanjg II (Complete Victory) and were conducted by US and ARVN forces.

Overall, Operation Goodwood lasted 78 days and was considered to be the longest of all province combat operations undertaken by our battalions. There were heavy PAVN and VC casualties, in the order of an estimated 285 killed in action with 17 captured while allied losses totalled 53. Operation Complete Victory saw an estimated 25,000 enemy killed in action, whilst US losses were around 1790.

It was an easy life at the base in comparison to what was happening outside the wire, included Corporal O'Neill driving around in an army land rover because at this stage we had no designated driver. Despite not having an army driver's licence, I took it upon myself to drive the good Captain Wenden to different parts of the base whenever he requested. When he enquired if I had a licence, my gallivanting in the land rover all over the Dat came to an abrupt end.

Although I was lucky, he didn't charge me, unlike Shocker Goodwin, some of the soldiers from 4RAR were not so lucky. Countless times we would witness various "grunts" from 4RAR being marched in before the commanding officer to be found guilty, no doubt, on some spurious charge. Some were sentenced to time in the brig with military police as companions. The reason we all knew they had been found guilty was courtesy of the Regiment's Sergeant Major who, on marching them out to spend some time "resting in country", would scream out at the top of his lungs, 'Guilty!' and then repeat it again and again, but each time at a louder volume.

I suppose some were lucky not to be sentenced with "time to reflect" at the prisoner of war compound, located near their incarceration and gleefully known as the "Nui Dat Rest Centre-Home for Wayward VC". The attraction was that it offered bed and breakfast, bodyguards and running water. At the entrance, there was a picture of a kangaroo wearing a bowler hat and carrying a jug of water as the POW was frog marched into the compound.

For a period of time, there was a large sign signifying that it was for "Club members only" and welcoming those unfortunates to the "Nui Dat Playboy Club - Exclusively for VC and NVA". The Australian humour was certainly alive and well. We needed something to keep a smile on our faces, given what was happening outside the base on a daily basis.

Once again, cricket, like our football games at Vung Tau, became a joyous pastime. Games were played close to the wire and even at the Eagle Farm Helipad. They were interrupted from time to time due to the audacity of choppers landing and disturbing the match. I played in one game and went back to my "Wally Grout" keeping days. As a reference, Wally played 51 tests for Australia behind the stumps. However, one of the RAAF batters smashed the ball for six outside the wire. It was the only ball we had. Due to the hidden mines protecting the base, there were no volunteers brave enough or perhaps, stupid enough, to venture outside the wire to retrieve the ball. Hence the game came to an abrupt end.

My time in South Vietnam was fast drawing to a much eagerly anticipated return home but one more confronting episode was to take place. It would again remind me of the reality of war and the suffering of those innocent villagers and their children, who through no fault of their own, lived their lives in constant fear and trepidation.

13

Winning Hearts and Minds

The on-going daily struggle to win the hearts and minds of the mostly rural South Vietnamese population was also called, for want of a better term, "pacification". Such a term can mean, to be a social process to obtain peace by way of a treaty and, on the other hand, can also be a means to establish or relinquish power and control over a divided nation due to the insurgents' forces.

In 1966 in Hawaii, US President Johnson, at a meeting with the South Vietnamese government, pushed to get the "Gospel of Pacification" established into the minds of the South Vietnamese people, based on the combination of security followed by the isolation and weakening of the insurgents. Finally, such a strategic process would then be applied throughout Vietnam to defeat what, at this point, was a largely indecisive war.

In May 1967, a program titled "Civil Operations and Revolutionary Development Support" (CORDS) was established and it included military personnel and civilians from both governments, with an initial base of around 5,000 staff. By 1968, it was established in 44 different South Vietnam provinces with over 8,000 personnel. It was divided into effectively two parts, namely civilian for community development and military to oversee security concerns. The latter also focusing on operations in opposition to the Viet Cong.

Although there was an emphasis on winning the hearts, minds and support of local villagers with rural aid, education and health initiatives, a controversial program was initially orchestrated and coordinated by the US Central Intelligence Agency. Known as "Phoenix", it was an ugly attempt to destroy the political infrastructure of the VC still firmly established in most of the provinces of South Vietnam.

The program, carried out under specially enacted legislation, commenced in 1967 with 700 American advisers, US Special Operations Forces and similar operatives from the Australian Army Training Team. Their task was to, not only identify members of what was considered to be local support of the VC infrastructure but where possible, to capture, torture, imprison and carry out numerous executions where necessary. Those captured were then taken to a local interrogation centre to gain information and intelligence on any VC area activities.

The CIA lost responsibility in 1969 and CORDS now had the overall control of the program, whose statistics later revealed that Phoenix had effectively "neutralised" 81,000 suspected of being part of the VC infrastructure. There were 23,350 killed, with 87 per cent of that number considered to be part of normal military activity. The remaining 13 per cent were assassinated with some, allegedly, thrown out of choppers. The rest were either captured or surrendered to be part of the Chieu Hoi program.

The Phoenix program, carried out by loosely termed "death squads", certainly didn't win the hearts and minds of the local population as it was deemed to be a civilian assassination program. It utilised torture and various coercive methods to suppress, what were later determined to be, innocent villagers who were certainly not involved in any combat operations.

On the other hand, while not convincing many of its effect, because of the methods the program employed, it did suppress the political and revolutionary impact of the VC, to a degree. Following immense criticism and publicity, the program was suspended but a similar one, known as Plan F-6, continued under the control of the South Vietnamese government.

The VC, in any event, certainly didn't win the hearts and minds of some of the local population. On one occasion in 1968, they planted jumping jack mines to punish various hamlets for their suspected liaison with allied units. The mines were detonated by an innocent farmer and blew up a group of school children as they walked by. In another incident, they disembowelled the pregnant wife of a local village chief, made him look at her body and dead foetus, before they brutally clubbed him to death.

With their prime targets being village chiefs, teachers and officials, many assassinations took place at the village of Suoi Nghe, built by the 1st Australian Task Force. This relocation village, with designated parcels of land to grow food, was newly constructed and housed Vietnamese civilians in corrugated iron houses. This was as a result of the villages being previously forced to hand over much of their locally produced food to the VC, who obviously acted in retaliation.

An operation titled "Speedy Express" was a further misguided attempt to pacify areas along the Mekong Delta during the early months of 1969. As a result of indiscriminate firepower and wanton killings, there were around 6,000 South

Vietnamese civilian deaths. The justification was that it also resulted in the deaths of over 10,000 PAVN and VC.

The United States also had a special operations force which was a long-range reconnaissance patrol unit politely named, "Tiger Force". It gained notoriety as it had committed extensive war crimes against the Vietnamese civilian population.

The US military also had a policy that was known as "free-fire zones" which meant that any civilian found in a designated zone was deemed an easy target and considered to be the enemy. If, for example, you ran away from a chopper about to land before it unloaded troops, you were considered an enemy combatant and killed at will. This alone caused widespread dissent amongst Vietnamese civilians and approximately 95 US soldiers were court-martialled during the war, for the unlawful killing of innocent Vietnamese civilians.

The South Korean military actively participated in Vietnam from 1965, sending 350,000 troops from, not only its army, but also from its navy and air force. Its involvement suffered immense criticisms, particularly in respect to alleged massacres, atrocities of civilians and, notably, when deployed to Tuy Hoa valley, resulting in further undermining the ever-increasing deterioration of the relationship with the locals.

To its credit and in a further allied attempt to win the hearts and minds of the local population, the military assisted with the building of schools, bridges and roads in Bien Hoa. Their medical teams also ably assisted in the medical treatment of some 30,000 South Vietnamese.

The yearly cost of the war to the United States by 1969 was now around $25 billion, which even included a reduction of some $3 billion. On 20 January, 1969, Richard Nixon was elected President of the United States. His successful election campaign was predicated on the fact that he would end the involvement of the US in the Vietnam conflict within 12 months. Nixon started a campaign titled "Vietnamisation", which effectively meant the ARVN would slowly become responsible for the primary defence of South Vietnam against the NVA enemy.

This Nixon policy involved the equipping and training of the ARVN forces in order to allow for the slow but regular withdrawal of the US military. The American commanders had formed the view that the ARVN could be improved to a degree that the war could be "de-Americanised" and the containment of communism was no longer a top priority.

At the same time, however, the Nixon government was involved in high level talks with the Soviet Union and China. This bi-lateral relationship was seen as a much higher priority than the problems of South Vietnam and the communist North.

Knowing the US would slowly withdraw from its country, leaving it to fend on its own, it could hardly be seen as strengthening the relationship and winning the support of the South Vietnamese people. This became obvious when the South Vietnamese government increased its conscription of every available male for combat service.

Nixon, however, tried to offset any suggestion of dwindling support for the South Vietnamese people by increasing the use of long-range B-52D heavy bombers and targeting selected NVA camps in Cambodia. They were loosely described as "Menu bombings". These camps were seen as strategic resupply bases and training facilities used by the NVA before they recommenced combat missions in South Vietnam.

At the same time, the Paris negotiations with the NVA

to try to peacefully end the war, continued. However, the communists only had one agenda that they would accept and that was solely on their terms. This included, not only a political settlement, but the complete withdrawal of all allied forces and no further foreign interference. This again did nothing to pacify the hearts and minds of the South Vietnamese.

In an attempt perhaps, not to win the hearts and minds of our servicemen, but to convince them to lay down their arms and return home, the Baria VC Liberation forces circulated a typewritten message throughout Nui Dat. It was titled, 'Aussie Go Home'. The opening paragraph stated:

> *"Why do you come here to kill our people and do harm to the Vietnam revolutionary movement…since stationing (sic) at Nui Dat… you have committed untold crimes to our compatriots."*

Despite this crude attempt to convince our troops they were committing untold acts of genocide, the strategy of winning the hearts and minds of the local villagers throughout Phouc Tuy Province, was diligently undertaken. There was much dedication from those who served with and assisted, 1ACAU in its almost daily field operations, including the Medcap and Dentcap programs. Many additional Vietnamese civilians were provided with treatment in other programs, such as the United States Military Provincial Health Program (MILPHAP), including hospitalisation as needed.

These programs were seen as a way to improve, not only the popularity of the Australian military, but also their American and South Vietnamese allies. It was considered a means of improving the existing medical and dental infrastructure, which clearly lacked sufficient resources to provide humanitarian assistance overall. Conversely, it was sometimes found the views of the Village Chief Medical Officer were not taken into account, thereby undermining and resulting in the loss of face of their local physicians with the villagers.

On average, Australian army personnel would visit 15 villages per week, not only to carry out medical and dental tasks, but to distribute food, clothing and household goods, construct houses and windmills, school and community buildings. They even provided English lessons and conducted sporting activities. The windmills were first made in Australia and then instilled throughout the province. Such was the dedication of our 17th Construction Squadron from the Royal Australian Engineers; they trained local Vietnamese youths as apprentices and supported them with cash and materials from Australia.

The task of assisting with the medical and dental health of the local population was confined to treating mainly minor issues, in particular skin ailments, cases of malnutrition and, as necessary, the extraction of rotting teeth. In the more serious cases, the unit's medical officer would determine whether the patient needed to be driven and sometimes flown, to 1AFH at Vung Tau for more personalised medical attention.

This was very evident following the recapture of Ba Ria by Australian infantry from 3RAR, together with a section of 2RAR infantry battalion, following the February 1968 TET offensive, when members of 1ACAU determined that three wounded villagers would need to be flown to 1AFH for urgent treatment.

The Ba Ria Hospital, which had been taken by the VC, had effectively been destroyed and much of its equipment was damaged beyond repair. The local Ba Ria High School was now a temporary home for the villagers living on the perimeter of the town. While our troops were actively involved in providing rations for the local Vietnamese Refugees Relief Organisation, engineers from 1ACAU were busy addressing the sanitation problem for the now estimated 2,000 refugees sheltering at the school.

It was the usual practice of 1ACAU to consult with the local population on the type of projects they considered essential and, at the same time, give them a sense of security, albeit on a temporary basis. On the other hand, such civilian assistance was considered, by some back home in Australia, as propaganda rubbish delivered by the Australian Army to gain support for a very unpopular war.

In addition, although the civic action projects were commendable, they were compromised by the reality of the war and, perhaps to a degree, in not understanding the local cultural needs and the lack of support for what was seen as a corrupt and unpopular South Vietnamese government.

It was evident, given the nature of the tasks undertaken by personnel from 1ACAU, and their close and regular interaction with villages in Phouc Tuy as part of their operational tasks, they were exposed to contact with the marauding VC. In fact, early on, a few of their members were wounded in action suffering minor gunshot wounds at Hoi My, just south of Dat Do. This exposure was to become very evident on Tuesday, 18 March, 1969, at the village of Ngai Giao.

14

Attack on the Village of Ngai Giao

In the early hours of Tuesday, 18 March, 1969, Captain Michael Wenden, Corporal Bruce Menzies and I hastily loaded all our dental supplies in the back of our land rover. We were to be part of a detachment with the 1ACAU medical team, led by Major Ray Atkinson and accompanied by Vietnamese interpreters, to carry out a medical and dental civil aid program, travelling to Ap Suoi Nghe, Binh Ba and the village of Ngai Giao.

Binh Ba was approximately five kilometres north of Nui Dat, with the village of Ngai Giao a further five miles along the Route Two dusty red road of Phouc Tuy province. The resettlement village of Ap Suoi Nghe, only three miles north of the task force at Nui Dat, would be our first stopover.

All heavily armed with a variety of weapons, Bruce and I had our Armalite rifles with at least three magazines each and Captain Wenden was satisfied with his 9mm pistol strapped to his side. Our weapons were more of a safeguard as generally, civil aid programs were treated with some respect and not usually subject to contact by enemy fire. Major Atkinson was similarly armed and supported by a number of other assistants, including medical officers.

Approximately 1200 Vietnamese families were resettled to Ap Suoi Nghe by the 2nd and 7th Battalions as part of Operation Ainslie in September, 1967 in a further effort to deny the supply route of the Viet Cong, who would also terrorise the villagers for food and safe sanctuary. Their original huts and straw houses were first destroyed by engineers from 1 Field Squadron but with the assistance of the owners, they were then relocated to houses in various stages of construction at the resettlement village.

Binh Ba had a population of 3,000 villagers who were mainly farmers and rubber plantation workers and were well known to our troops. The first tour of 5RAR had them stationed in the village to deter VC tax collectors and squads, who thought nothing of it to assassinate the villagers, particularly their chiefs. The Galea rubber factory was located at Binh Ba and previous civil aid programs had been carried out at these villages, in particular at Ngai Giao.

When we were at Binh Ba, an urgent radio communication advised of heavy fighting between South Vietnamese soldiers and a company of VC, near the village of Ngai Giao. There were many casualties, including two village chiefs killed by decapitation. We were advised that the VC may try to attack Binh Ba and it would definitely be in our interests to seek safety at the South Vietnamese Army compound situated two miles from the village.

On arrival at the compound, it was already under fire and being shelled by heavy mortar attacks, most likely Soviet-designed rocket propelled grenades. After making it through the front gates, we went straight to a building at the rear of the compound because it appeared to be better shelter from the incoming rounds. Two young Vietnamese children were lying on the floor of the building and it was obvious they had been severely wounded during the attack by the VC. They were immediately attended to by our medical team, while the mortars continued to land in the compound.

I decided to have better look at what was going on, so climbed a 30-foot tower lookout being manned by a South Vietnamese soldier. On reaching the top, I could see the VC about 200 yards off and it looked like they were running along the treetops. Heavy mortar fire was now heading in their direction, so I decided to fire off at least one angry shot. As I brought my rifle up, the gunner alongside me opened up with numerous bursts from his submachine gun, which was most likely a Smith and Wesson M76.

Determining that he would be subject to incoming rounds, I clambered down the ladder and from about 15 feet, with bursts of gun fire still happening, I jumped off, landing heavily on the ground but still managing to hold onto my gun.

I then crawled into a sandbagged bunker, only to find a number of American advisers inside, happily smoking away, surrounded by, what looked like, a 44-gallon drum of petrol. I did not hesitate to get the hell out and determined the safest option was the building at the rear of the compound where the wounded children were located. The firefight was not letting up and, almost without warning, two Phantom jet fighters suddenly appeared above the village.

The Phantom American fighter–bomber was used extensively during the Vietnam War, particularly in firefights with enemy MIG fighter aircraft over the skies of Hanoi and in dropping napalm on villages throughout the Mekong Delta.

The aircraft was a tandem two-seater with twin engines and considered an all-weather, long range, supersonic fighter-bomber. Manned by one pilot, sometimes with a back seat crew member, it had a top speed of Mach 2.2. It was capable of carrying in excess of 18,000 pounds of weapons, including air to air missiles and various bombs, such as napalm.

Napalm was originally used as flamethrowers to burn sections of the jungle in Vietnam and to clear out bunkers, trenches and tunnels. It was also used by US navy riverboats on the Mekong River and, in the event the flame did not kill on impact, the fire it created sucked out the air, causing its victims to suffocate.

Although dropping napalm bombs from jet fighters didn't have the same accuracy, it would still engulf an area of at least 2,000 square yards, thereby causing many civilian deaths. The napalm itself was a substance mixture of plastic polystyrene, hydrocarbon benzene and, of course, gasoline. When ignited, it would literally stick to anything, including human flesh and burn for up to 10 minutes.

The first Phantom jet flew over the top of the village, radioed his partner aircraft, who then zeroed in and dropped its napalm cannister, which tumbled head over head before hitting the ground. It appeared to be bouncing along before exploding and igniting, destroying everything in its path. The other Phantom jet followed the same trajectory and again, the cannister rolled over through the air before exploding into a massive fireball, no doubt killing all those unfortunates who happened to be below in the village.

The Phantoms were then followed by two Huey helicopter gunships, known as "Çobras", depending on their role. They were originally designed for medical evacuations and used in

Vietnam but once they were equipped with rocket and grenade launchers, together with 7.62-millimetre machine guns, also known as "mini guns", they could unleash a barrage of rounds with their tremendous fire power. After raking fire around what was once was the village of Ngai Giao but now a smoking ruin, the hueys departed as quickly as they arrived. A stony silence followed with no further gun fire.

We immediately left the compound and headed straight towards the village to render what assistance we could. After alighting from our land rover, I slowly walked along a track that led to the smouldering ruins. I was in complete shock at what had just transpired and then further impacted by what I was about to witness. I was followed by a cameraman from the Australian Broadcasting Commission, who arrived not long after the gunfight had ceased. He filmed me walking very slowly towards a dead VC who was lying on his back and dressed in their distinctive black but now blue pyjamas or shirt and trousers, with a blue and back red "flag" attached to his left pocket.

What I saw next would sadly remain in my memories as the most unimaginable sight I could ever face. Under burnt rubble and what was once a much-loved home, I found the bodies of a family, including, what appeared to be, two children who had been incinerated. It was obvious there was nothing we could do for them, so we sadly left the bodies to be recovered by their grieving family members.

I then saw six Vietnamese women and a dog, raking through the charred remains. It was obvious they were in a state of shock. I suspect they had left their village at the first indication of a pending attack by the VC, only to return to discover the smouldering ruins that were once their homes and village.

There were also a number of wounded Vietnamese villagers who somehow had survived what had been unleashed on them by both the VC and the aircraft above. They were being treated by Major Ray Atkinson for eventual evacuation to our hospital at Vung Tau. At this point, the South Vietnamese forces were about to search what was left of the village and countryside for any remaining VC trying to flee and avoid capture.

They asked us to go with them in case medical aid was needed but a decision was made that it was not safe to do so as the area may contain, not only wounded, but very angry VC and, no doubt, land mines left behind or laid on purpose. Any wounded soldiers who were found and needing treatment, would be transferred out of danger enabling medical assistance to be provided by our medical team.

We were soon joined by a platoon of very merry American soldiers, who were ambling along in single file with transistor radios plugged into their ears and obviously not for military purposes. We could hear them approaching from a fair distance away, so it was obvious they were unconcerned about any VC left in the area. I was not sure why they were even at the village, as they soon wandered off on their jovial way.

The wounded Vietnamese were then placed on the back of our land rovers for transportation to an area south of the village and earlier secured by our infantry. This was followed by immediate evacuation by helicopter to Vung Tau. The concern was, given the possibility there were still VC in the area, it was more prudent to evacuate the wounded to a secured area but away from the destroyed village. We drove the patients to their pending transport and saw them safely loaded onto the chopper and flown to our hospital at Vung Tau.

Our arrival back at Nui Dat was certainly met with some

relief and that evening we sank quite a few beers in our boozer. Later, in our tents and still in shock, we reflected sadly on the day that had unfolded. Drinking in our tent was against army rules but we all did it without any repercussions. With our loaded weapons, our "best friends" beside us, there could have been huge problems due to soldiers getting so drunk. They could decide to do something really stupid such as "fragging".

The following morning, a Saigon Army radio bulletin, which gave daily briefings on enemy contacts overnight, stated that, 'at least 66 VC had been killed at the village of Ngai Giao, which was destroyed during heavy fighting between South Vietnamese soldiers and the estimated company strength of Viet Cong.'

We were all simply flabbergasted.

We knew the burnt out and now destroyed village was most likely caused by the napalm or certainly made worse by the bombing after the attack by the VC. Furthermore, the alleged body count of enemy killed in action was most likely either inflated, or simply over estimated. This confirmed our suspicions that a number of the innocent villagers were also included in the body count and most likely seen as collateral damage.

It was obvious the number killed during the heavy fighting and added to the body count, were innocent villagers and their children. Somehow, that all became caught up in the US controlled bulletin, with its propaganda to try and demonstrate that the war was being won and the policy of Pacification and Vietnamisation was an overall success. Interestingly, as part of the radio bulletin that same morning, it was also announced the US Secretary of Defense, Melvin Laird, had requested an additional $126 million in order to further increase the capability of the South Vietnamese forces to replace the US troops.

15

Leaving Vietnam in One Wakey

With only two weeks left of my 12-month tour of duty before leaving for home, I was eligible for five days rest and recreation. To say I needed the break after the trauma of Ngai Giao, was an understatement and Vung Tau was my obvious choice. I was lucky enough to be able to catch the short flight from Nui Dat by chopper and decided to spend most of my time on the beach relaxing and improving my suntan. The time spent there would also be with the usual sojourns into Vungers with a few others, getting on the booze and no doubt "terrorising" the local bar girls, much to the disgust of their mama-san.

On the day before I left to return to the Dat, with only a couple of "wakeys" to go, after returning to 1ALSG from the local bars, I stumbled past the Anzac Chapel to witness one of our soldiers from another unit, urinating up against the wall of the church. Unfortunately, this was not only in full view of me, but also military police who happened to be driving past. The offending miscreant was immediately placed into custody and my name was taken down as a witness. Thinking I would hear nothing more of it, I returned to Nui Dat the following morning to await the flight from Luscombe Airfield to Saigon, which was leaving in two days' time on the morning of 16 April, 1969.

Much to my disappointment, I was called in to the tent of the commanding officer to be told I was required as a witness to the soldier caught up against the chapel, so I had to return to 1ALSG forthwith. The only available transport was a land rover, so off I went, past Ba Ria and on the way to Vung Tau. With two days left in country and hoping to remain in my tent in the relative safety of Nui Dat, I found myself travelling in a convoy along the dusty road I knew so well. Suddenly, without warning, two rifle shots were heard in the distance. Thinking they were aimed at our vehicle, I hit the floor with a thud and lay there thinking, *I seriously don't believe this!*

Eventually, I got up from the floor of the land rover as we arrived at 1ALSG. I was marched in before the colonel who was hearing the charge as laid and he immediately asked me what I had witnessed. I truthfully pleaded drunkenness, which was reflected in my evidence, or lack thereof, and relying on the Sergeant Schultz mantra, 'I see nothing, I hear nothing, I know nothing'.

To say he was not happy was an understatement. As I continued to plead, I couldn't remember what I had allegedly witnessed. When the colonel told me I was a disgrace, then ordered me to leave the building, I felt like I had been on trial but I marched out, wearing a huge smile on my face. I never found out what happened to the digger as charged but it was probably exposure and bringing the army into disrepute!

Prior to returning to Nui Dat, Rob Watson asked me if I would stay on for a few weeks to be his best man as he was getting married to a local Vietnamese lady called Bea. As much as I liked Rob, I politely refused, as there was no way I was staying in country for one more day, let alone a few weeks. To his credit, after marrying Bea, Rob returned to Australia in early May, 1969 and she followed him two years later. They even adopted a young Vietnamese child.

On the morning of 16 April, 1969, I was waiting in line to board the Qantas Boeing 707 at Tan Son Nhut Air Base, when I saw my good mate from schoolboy days and playing cricket and football together. Ross Clark was alighting from the same plane and we were about to pass each other, when we both got a surprise and shock. We hugged and I wished him well as he was about to start his 12-month tour of active service. I don't recall reminding him though, of the six I belted from his bowling across the road and into a neighbour's window.

Ross was a sapper with 1 Troop 1st Field Squadron, Royal Australian Engineers and would serve in Vietnam as a combat engineer. Little did we both know then that the next time we would see each other, would be when Ross was medevacked home eight months later.

I boarded the plane alongside a number of other departing soldiers, including my affable mate, AB Pearce. After what seemed to be a very short time, no doubt I slept most of the flight home, in between visiting the cockpit of the plane as we flew over Borneo, we arrived at Mascot Airport at Sydney in the early hours of the following morning.

The flight time was approximately eight hours with a distance of 7,000 kilometres without a stopover, although we did travel over Darwin and certainly not by way of Singapore, unlike our flight one year earlier. Overall, during the Australian involvement in the Vietnam War, Qantas, also known as Skippy Airlines, flew a total of 600 charter flights to and from South

Vietnam and later became known as the Skippy Squadron Vietnam 1965-1972, in recognition of the flight crew.

My flight to Essendon Airport was not for a few hours, so AB and I went for a stroll around Kings Cross at 4am in the morning, only to be confronted by military police. They were quite annoyed that we were walking the streets in our army uniform and especially without our slouch hats on the top of our heads. I thought, 'Here we go again!' assuming they were out looking for arrest numbers on their patrol sheet to justify their existence.

I made some spurious comment to them that, 'at least we had served in Vietnam,' which pissed them off even more. The very amicable AB somehow convinced them that on just returning from a war zone, surely we should be given some slack. They somewhat begrudgingly agreed to let us go.

On my arrival at Essendon, I was greeted by my family and fiancée and, despite a mix up with our bags, with mine somehow finishing up in Moe, I was glad to be back on Australian soil. My sister, however, commented that I absolutely stank and despite many subsequent showers and baths, she said the smell of obviously, what was Vietnam, stayed with me for many months.

When visited by Peter Paul, an old high school mate, he commented on the American army shirt I was wearing and asked me where I got it. My smart-arse reply was, 'From a dead yank soldier', an answer I am not proud of. Understandably, he was not impressed, immediately walked away and never spoke to me again until some years later, when he was appointed President of the Victorian Primary School Principals Association.

In my defence at this misguided attempt at humour, I did

not speak to any of my family about what I had witnessed in Vietnam for many years and certainly made no comment when I returned home. However, my mother did tell me many years later, I was not the same person on my return that she waved off at Spencer Street railway station when I left for Vietnam.

Waiting for me at home was a letter from the Victorian Public Service, advising me I had been promoted in my absence, to the position of Purchasing Officer (Transport) with Victoria Police. Although I was very happy to be promoted, I didn't think it was purely on merit, as the policy then was to give priority to any conscripts serving in Vietnam in respect of employment vacancies.

I could have signed on for a further three years with the Australian Army, but that thought never entered my head as I was "done and dusted" and wanted only to return to civilian life. I still had nearly three months to serve as I was not due to be discharged from army service until 9 July, 1969. My father was very annoyed with me while I was on leave because I didn't find alternative employment for nearly three months until my discharge. I virtually spent that time doing nothing apart from enjoying counter lunches most days and putting on three stone in weight.

Pending my discharge, I had further arguments with my father about the length of my hair. I had decided to grow my short back and sides in a further attempt to cover up my receding hair line. The unkempt length of hair was quite obvious when I put on my uniform to report to the Watsonia army base two days before discharge. Dad, or should I say "Shocker the second", said I looked like a hippie and there was no way he would allow me to report for discharge in my army uniform looking like a ratbag.

After a visit to the barbers, I arrived at Watsonia in full uniform and looking spic and span, much to my disgust. All the other conscripts ready for discharge and in uniform, looked like they hadn't seen a barber for a very long time. Some even sported luxurious beards. This resulted in me being selected as the only one suitable to do a picket, while the others all went to the local Heidelberg pub, pending discharge.

On Wednesday, 9 July, 1969, I ceased to be a soldier in the Australian Army and my Certificate of Discharge reminded me of my total effective service in Australia of 365 days and outside Australia of 365 days. The general remarks column made no comment to my AWOL matter, but it did contain a standard warning in respect of the Official Secrets Act, rendering you liable to prosecution in the event of disclosure of information obtained that 'might be useful to the enemy' after leaving Her Majesty's Service.

It was obvious the army wanted to have the last say but happily, despite some reservations, I was about to return to civilian life as a public servant with Victoria Police.

17 Dental Unit, Puckapunyal Army Base.
(Rob Watson far left, bottom row with me alongside him)

Major John Spencer and Captain Colin Twelftree at 33 Dental Unit.
Courtesy of 1st (Aust) Field Hospital Assoc. Image by Robin Watson.

My good mate, Corporal Robin Watson.
Courtesy of 1st (Aust) Field Hospital Assoc. Image from Robin Watson's collection.

Dent Cap at local village.
Courtesy of 1st (Aust) Field Hospital Assoc. Image by Roger Nation.

1st (Aust) Field Hospital double bunks ward for malaria epidemic.
Courtesy of 1st (Aust) Field Hospital Assoc. Image by Murray Lovatt.

Removing the wounded from a Huey chopper on the dust off landing pad
at 1st (Aust) Field Hospital, Vung Tau.
Courtesy of 1st (Aust) Field Hospital Assoc. Image by Ian Dann.

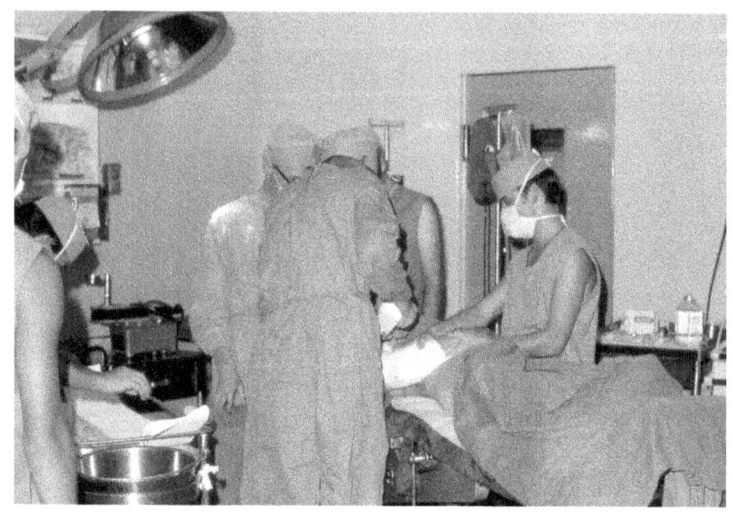

1st (Aust) Field Hospital operating theatre.
Courtesy of 1st (Aust) Field Hospital Assoc. Image by David Wittner.

Harold Holt pool, Peter Badcoe Club, (Sept 1968) named in honour of
Australian Prime Minister, Harold Holt.
Courtesy of 1st (Aust) Field Hospital Assoc. Image by A.B. Pearce.

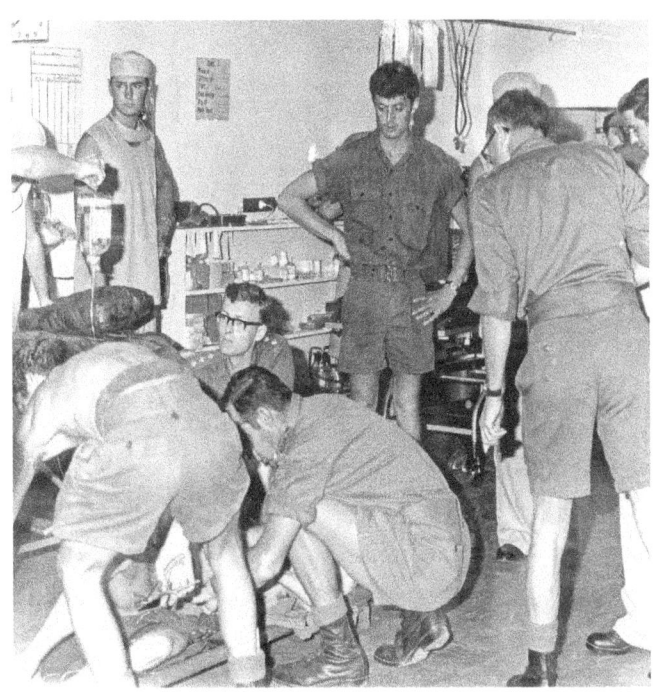

Triage, 1st (Aust) Field Hospital.
Courtesy of 1st (Aust) Field Hospital Assoc. Image by William A Dodds

SOLDIERS OF AUSTRALIA!
UNITE AGAINST PMG STRIKES!
PUNCH A POSTIE ON RTA
SOCK IT TO 'EM DIGGERS!

Encouraged Diggers to punch a postie on returning home. (I didn't)
Courtesy of 1st (Aust) Field Hospital Assoc. Image by Margaret Young.

Always good for a few beers and a concert at the Peter Badcoe Club, Vung Tau.

Bev Harrell was easy on the eye and her singing was superb at the Peter Badcoe Club.

Boat launching area at Vung Tau Beach.

Fun and frivolities at Vung Tau Beach.

Children with their ABC books at the Baria Orphanage.

The kids from Baria Orphanage loved getting attention from us.

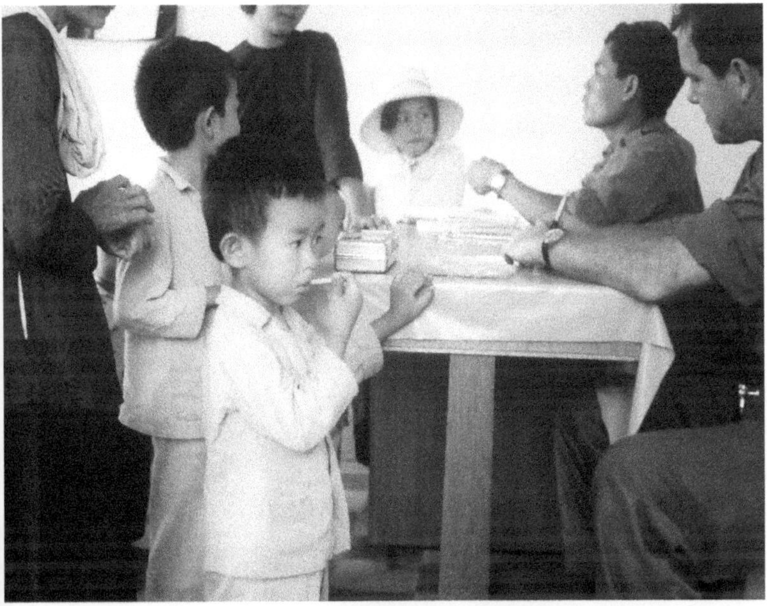

Dent Cap at Baria Orphanage.

Vung Tau Firing Range, where I still couldn't hit the target.

Shotgun Escort from Vung Tau to Long Binh.

Long Binh USA Army Base.

An ice cream truck at Long Binh was the last thing you'd expect to see!

Lunch at Long Binh.

2nd from right. USA Navy Patrol boat on the Mekong River.

Home, sweet home, my hut at Nui Dat.

Left: No matter where you go, there's always the laundry, even in Nui Dat.
Right: Taking a break from the laundry.

Resting after all that laundry!

My batting definitely improved as I got older.

Nui Dat chopper pad with SAS Hill in background.

The lock up, Nui Dat.

Luscombe Airfield, Nui Dat.

Chopper pad at Nui Dat.

Huey Dust off pad, Nui Dat.

The M60, a belt fed automatic machine gun, has a cyclic rate of fire around 500 to 650 rounds per min. (RPM)

The Armalite (M16) was light, had a rapid rate of fire but continually jammed.

Nui Dat.

Watching the attack on village of Ngai Giao from the ARVN Compound (Army of Republic of Vietnam).

The aftermath of napalm attack on Ngai Giao.

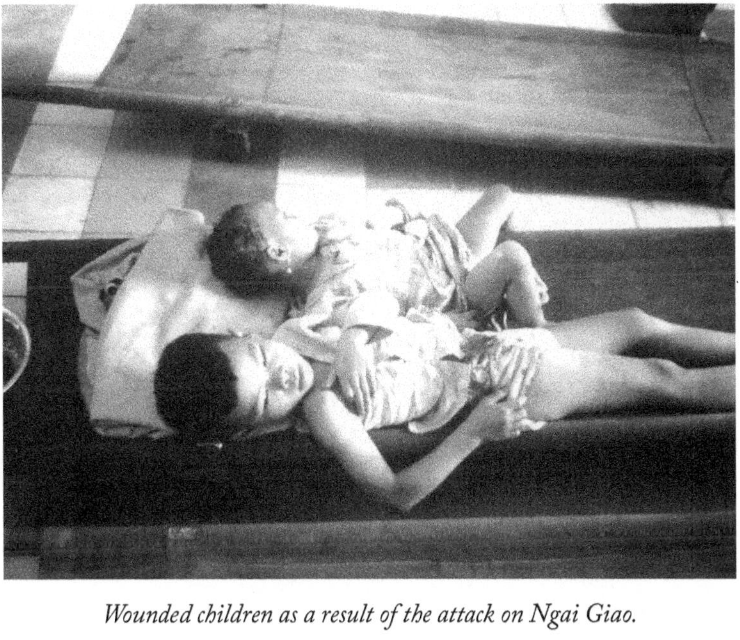

Wounded children as a result of the attack on Ngai Giao.

Sadly, not much remained after the napalm attack.

Accidentally meeting former Vietcong soldiers on a 2006 Vietnam tour resulted in tears, hugs and an amazing feeling of peace.

With my good mate, A.B. Pearce (Alan) at Callsign Vampire's reunion in WA, 2007.

It was an honour to be asked to speak on USS Intrepid on Anzac Day, 2016 during a cricket tour in USA.

16

Allied Withdrawal from Vietnam

The Battle of Binh Bah during Operation Hammer in early June, 1969, was probably the last effective victory for our Australian Forces in South Vietnam, prior to the withdrawal of our military. Troops from the 5th Battalion, Royal Australian Regiment, together with the 1st Armoured Regiment and supported by artillery and helicopter gunships, were involved in a vicious fire fight, including house to house fighting, against elements of both the People's Army of Vietnam, the Viet Cong, including a guerrilla squad from Ngai Giao.

The village of Binh Bah was effectively destroyed and a large number of civilians were unavoidably killed during the three days of heavy fighting. This battle effectively brought large scale contacts to an end, notwithstanding our units would still be involved in fighting PAVN and VC main force units, but certainly not on the scale witnessed at Binh Bah. The enemy suffered heavy losses, in the order of 107 killed, six wounded and eight captured, whereas we had 10 wounded and lost one soldier, Private Wayne Teeling, who was killed in action. Private Teeling was a conscript who had only been in country for one month when he was mortally wounded.

During February and March 1970, the Long Hai hills still remained a secure refuge for the VC. Supported by tanks and armoured personnel carriers, 8th Royal Australian Regiment (8RAR) commenced Operation Hammersley, involving ambushes and patrols to flush out the enemy who were now well concealed in heavy fortified bunkers. Overall, in excess of 70 Australian soldiers were killed or wounded during the operation and, on one day alone in February 1970, eight of our soldiers were killed by mines that had been laid in the area.

As a result of the US strategy of Pacification and Vietnamisation by negotiation, President Nixon now proposed a phased withdrawal of all allied troops within 12 months. This was ultimately greeted by one of a number of anti -war moratoriums, particularly in Australia, with 200,000 marching in protest in most of our capital cities in May, 1970 and demanding our involvement come to an end. This was followed by another anti-war rally on 18 September, 1970 with a further 100,000 Australian dissenters resulting in over 300 being arrested.

The withdrawal of Australian troops effectively started from November, 1970 with 8RAR not being replaced at the conclusion of its tour. This left about 6,000 Australian soldiers down from 8,000, with now only two infantry battalions at Nui Dat, but still effectively supported by our armoured regiment, together with artillery and air fire support.

By April, 1971, the majority of communist forces were temporarily rendered ineffective in Phouc Tuy province being cleared of local VC, giving our government further confidence to continue with its strategic slow withdrawal, including further combat soldiers. On 6 June, 1971, Operation Overlord saw the last major joint initiative with the US military when 3rd Battalion, Royal Australian Regiment was involved in attacking a heavy, fortified base camp at Long Khanh manned by the PAVN and VC, resulting in three Australians killed in action with six wounded and the loss of an Iroquois chopper during the fire fight.

On 30 June, 1971, a third and final demonstration took place with an estimated 110,000 protesters throughout Australia, voicing their opposition to the Vietnam War and demanding it end. On Wednesday, 18 August, 1971, Prime Minister Billy McMahon announced to the Australian people that our Vietnam War combat operations would finally end by October, 1971. This meant the majority of Australian troops would be withdrawn from South Vietnam by Christmas, leaving only a small contingent of training advisers, who were subsequently withdrawn in December, 1972.

A similar announcement was made by the New Zealand government, who had already halved the number of their combat troops, followed by South Korea who ceased all operations and left South Vietnam three months later.

The last major battle fought by our forces, including 4th Royal Australian Regiment, was at Nui Le on 21 September, 1971, involved another attack on Ngai Giao. Our losses of five killed, including three bodies not recovered and thirty wounded, could have been much higher if it was not for the assistance of US Phantom and A37 Dragonfly jets dropping napalm and air to surface missiles on the enemy, mainly from the 33rd Regiment of the North Vietnamese Army.

On 16 October, 1971, our forces gave effective control of Nui Dat to the South Vietnamese military with our last main infantry battalion 4RAR, apart from D Company, sailing for home on HMAS Sydney on 9 December, 1971. D Company, together with elements of the Armoured Corp, relocated to 1ALSG at Vung Tau to provide security, pending the withdrawal and closure of the base.

In respect of the closure of 1AFH, the most pressing and complex task was to determine what supplies and equipment would be returned home to Australia and what could be left behind to be used by the South Vietnamese. The equipment, in particular, had to be thoroughly cleaned and messes had to be closed. The boozers, of course, had much attention and from all reports, a number of "Farewell to Country" functions took place, obviously to eliminate any remaining stock.

The hospital ceased to operate from 24 November, 1971 but up to that time, it continued to carry out elective surgery until 4 November, then ceased all surgical operations from 11 November, 1971. Medical evacuations back home were completed on 15 November, 1971, with the main personnel leaving 10 days later with those remaining, including 8 Field Ambulance, finally departing for Australia on 16 December, 1971, followed by the security detachment from 4RAR in March 1972.

Two Vietnamese hospitals in Vung Tau were the recipients of numerous medical supplies, which were warmly received by the commanding officer of their medical infirmary. Some selected medical supplies, subject to expiry or temperature changes, that could not be returned to Australia, were also sent to the Bien Hoa Hospital for use by our Australian civilian medical unit.

On 20 December, 1972, our remaining Australian Training Team advisers left South Vietnam, ending their active service which began on 31 July, 1962, with 67 servicemen arriving by Hercules transport at the Richmond RAAF base, New South Wales. National Service conscription was also abolished and the seven men, still imprisoned as conscientious objectors, were finally freed. Prime Minister Whitlam said the release of the men was undoubtedly a 'historic decision ending peacetime conscription in Australia for all time.'

All combat operations involving Australian Forces were officially at an end on 11 January, 1973, following the announcement by the Australian Governor General, Paul Hasluck and Prime Minister Gough Whitlam. The only Australian military that remained behind was a small detachment guarding our embassy in Saigon, but they finally departed from South Vietnam on 1 July, 1973, which meant this was the first time our armed forces were not engaged in any world conflict since 1939.

On 23 January, 1973, at the Paris Peace Accord, governments of the United States, South Vietnam, North Vietnam, also on behalf of the Viet Cong, announced that a cease fire would commence at 0800 hours on 28 January, 1973. This effectively ended any further US involvement in what turned out to be the longest war in America's chequered history and bringing an end to their draftee conscription. Sadly, an American colonel became the last US soldier killed in action at AnLoc in the South Vietnam Binh Long Province, eleven hours before the truce came into effect.

The accord also provided for the return of American Prisoners of War with most being held at the prison known as the "Hanoi Hilton" in North Vietnam. These POWs consisted mainly of enlisted airman officers, although there was a smattering of army personnel and civilians also being held at one of the 12 other prisons. Operation Homecoming in February, 1973 initially saw the release of 142 US POWs, followed by a further 445 eventually leaving Vietnam and returning home.

It was quite obvious the North Vietnamese government had only one further objective on their mind. It was the complete liberation and control of North and South Vietnam and the conflict between the two respective governments continued unabated.

On 24 March, 1975, the Ho Chi Minh Campaign began for the liberation of the south as, by this stage, the communists had effectively rebuilt their military forces and logistics for one last decisive and final offensive.

17

End of the Vietnam War Postscript

The rapid advance of the North Vietnamese Army was no surprise following the departure of United States combat units two years earlier, although the Central Intelligence Agency considered that South Vietnam could survive until at least May, 1975, following the end of the dry season. However, by 30 March, 1975, Hue and Danang had been taken by the communist forces, with many civilians killed in the mayhem when trying to escape from the towns, local airports and beaches.

At this point in time, the CIA were now of the firm view that only the resumption of B-52 strikes on Hanoi would stop the advance to Saigon. On 17 April, 1975, Phnom Penh in Cambodia fell to the Khmer Rouge and Australia had now decided to close its embassy in Saigon.

The Australian Government sent RAAF transport aircraft to Saigon in order to assist in evacuating refugees who were trying to escape from the ever-advancing Ho Chi Minh campaign by communist forces. Up until 25 April, 1969, daily flights by our air force became a constant reminder of what fate was about to fall. The humanitarian evacuation also included several hundred Vietnamese orphans and Australian Embassy staff. Unfortunately and despite an undertaking by Prime Minister Gough Whitlam, 130 South Vietnamese staff, who had previously worked at the embassy, were abandoned and left to suffer at the whim of the advancing communist forces.

The American evacuation efforts were also not without their problems when, during Operation Babylift, involving South Vietnamese orphans, the transport plane crashed after take-off with 100 young children lost in the inferno. The final evacuations during Operation New Life and Frequent Wind saw over 117,000 Vietnamese refugees safely evacuated. This was followed by the largest helicopter evacuation ever witnessed when over 19 hours, commencing on 29 April, 1969, 81 helicopters were involved in the evacuation of over 7,000 Americans and Vietnamese to offshore aircraft carriers.

Some days earlier, US President Gerald Ford had announced to the world that as far as he and his country were concerned, the Vietnam War was at an end. Probably with a tongue in cheek comment, he also said the United States could now somehow, 'regain a sense of pride that existed before the Vietnam War.'

I don't think many of his fellow country men and women would have shared the same view. At dawn on Sunday, 30 April, 1975, after a three-year fight now left solely to the South Vietnamese and which had by now also enveloped neighbouring Cambodia and Laos, Saigon fell with little resistance. South Vietnam was totally in communist control and was being renamed Ho Chi Minh City. The toll on all nations involved in the Vietnam War was simply mind boggling and very distressing, not to mention the loss of lives and the cost.

Overall, in the order of 60,000 Australian soldiers served in Vietnam from 1962-1972. This number included 15,381 national service conscripts with 210 killed in action and 1279 wounded, with many of those losing their life afterwards due to ambushes, booby traps, land mines and rocket propelled grenades. As a result of the Vietnam War, sadly a total of 523 Australians died, including 25 killed accidentally, and over 3,000 wounded. Six Australians, initially listed as missing in action, were eventually located, with the last of their remains being returned home in 2009. The overall estimated cost of our involvement in the war was $218 million.

Our sole servicewoman casualty, Lieutenant Barbara Black, served as a nursing sister at Vung Tau with the First Australian Field Hospital, Royal Australian Army Nursing Corps in 1968-69. During her service in Vietnam, Barbara was diagnosed with leukaemia but there was no cure at the time. On returning home, she fell pregnant. Prior to the birth of her child and, despite her terminal illness, she vigorously and successfully lobbied the Australian Government to amend a child entitlement benefit under the *Veterans Entitlement Act 1971* (Cth) (as amended), which was previously only available to children of male veterans. Despite passing away in Australia, her death was still considered a casualty of war and rightly so. Vale Barbara Frances Black F35135.

My mate, Ross Clark, was medevacked home from Vietnam in late 1969, at a time when his troop was suffering extremely high casualty rates. Ross, at only 24 years of age, tragically died of a brain tumour at the Heidelberg Repatriation Hospital on 25 January, 1971. I visited him in hospital the day before he died and asked how he was feeling. His reply was a muttered, 'Shithouse.' Ross is also proudly named on the Australian War Memorial Roll of Honour. Vale Ross Tasman Clark 3793971.

Australian civilians totalling 210 also went to South Vietnam. This included medical staff and the Red Cross. Sadly, the first Australian woman to be killed during the Vietnam Way was popular singer, Cathy Wayne. Cathy was performing at a concert in Da Nang in July, 1969, when she was shot accidentally, allegedly by an American soldier, who only served a pathetic two years imprisonment for her death.

Some eight million Americans, with an average age of only 19, served in the military from 1964 to 1973. Those killed in action totalled 47,253, with another 10,449 dying from unrelated to combat causes. Those wounded totalled 313,616 and it was roughly estimated that the total cost to the United States was a massive $150 billion.

South Vietnam listed 185,528 killed in action with just over 500,000 wounded. Winning the civilians' hearts and minds took a massive blow with 415,000 estimated to have died and nearly one million wounded. New Zealand lost 37 soldiers with 187 wounded, whereas the toll to South Korea was much higher, with just over 5,000 killed and nearly 11,000 wounded.

In a widely held view, the exact toll of the Vietnam War on all sides varies greatly. The best that can be said is all up, allied forces suffered in the order of an estimated 282,000 deaths, whereas PAVN/VC casualties were estimated at anywhere between 444,00 to 666,000 and total civilian deaths for both the North and South has been put roughly in some quarters as low as 415,000, but as high as 627,000. Overall, this does not take into account the number of refugees who also suffered, with the loss of loved ones and the country of their birth.

In a further attempt to determine Vietnam War facts, it has been estimated that the total number of helicopters involved during the conflict was in the order of 12,000, of which 4,865 were shot down. The number of Dustoffs has been estimated in excess of 500,000 and the defoliants sprayed was believed to be at least 19 million (US) gallons. The loss of Dustoff pilots and crew totalling 88 killed in action, is evidence alone of how dangerous their task was.

It was also estimated and, despite some evidence, the Medcap and Dentcap programs had an altruistic purpose during the Vietnam War, such as winning hearts and minds. Over 40 million Vietnamese civilians received medical and dental care at an estimated cost to the allied governments, somewhere between $500 to $700 million. This, however, does demonstrate the programs did serve a humanitarian purpose.

Any way you look at it and, given the total estimated deaths as a consequence of the Vietnam War, what a sad waste of valuable lives. No doubt today, post war still continues to have an on-going terrible impact on both North and South Vietnam, not to mention those who survived its trauma.

Our survivors, of course, included those who served in the Vietnam War between 1962 and 1972. Initially, Australian battalions, on returning from Vietnam, were welcomed home with parades through the streets of major cities, in particular, Sydney. The Australian public though, generally had little sympathy and our veterans, on many occasions, were treated with disdain with many believing it was not a "real" war. Their treatment included social exclusion, even being prevented from joining the Returned & Services League of Australia and initially, marching in Anzac Day parades.

Despite our soldiers serving with distinction in a war zone, they were even unmercifully shunned by Second World War veterans as they were considered to be unworthy recipients to carry on the Anzac title and tradition. Many of our veterans, myself included, didn't wear their well-deserved medals for many years, for fear of being chastised and told they were not earned like other veterans in previous wars.

Due to my own personal experiences in Vietnam, which was nothing compared to many of our veterans, and the events that occurred when I returned home, I never spoke about the war or even told people I had served in Vietnam, until many years later.

My good friend, Jack Higgins, served as a national serviceman with distinction with A Company, 7th Battalion Royal Australian Regiment (7RAR), especially during Operation Ballarat and the Battle of Suoi Chau Pah in which six Australians were killed and 20 wounded in a battle lasting over several hours. The enemy loss was in the order of 33, believed killed or wounded, with seven bodies recovered.

To this day, Jack vividly remembers the VC bodies and those of our own soldiers killed in action, lined up waiting for evacuation to the morgue at Vung Tau. One of those bodies was the enemy officer he had fatally shot before the officer could discharge his pistol, which was pointed at Jack. On returning home, Jack's service also left him with memories best forgotten but always there. He said:

> *"Our homecoming was less than enthusiastic for many reasons, including leaving our mates behind, returning home to be reviled, arriving in civvies, certainly no fanfare and immediately being placed on leave. Even the RSL rejected us as we were not considered real*

soldiers. The press was scathing and it was our family who bore the worst of our situation. Our discharge from the army was quick with a pay out and down the local pub for the never-ending drink, which would stay with me for many years, with many crippling flashbacks and survivor guilt only deadened with the consumption of alcohol and prescription drugs."

I recall being at the Bundoora Hotel where I was quietly having a meal with my family when the DJ suddenly announced my welcome home as a Vietnam veteran. I suspect my mother, in her wisdom, thought it would be a great way to celebrate my arrival home with a welcome to country and told the DJ. What followed next was dead silence in the hotel lounge room from all and sundry, with only my family clapping my welcome home. I sat there cringing.

It was obvious the images, resulting from the Vietnam War, had a profound impact, in particular the image of a nine-year-old Vietnamese girl running away after being burned by napalm, dropped by South Vietnamese aircraft on June 8, 1972. She was subsequently referred to as the "Napalm Girl". The summary execution with a pistol shot to the head of a Viet Cong member by a South Vietnamese commander in the streets of Saigon and the My Lai massacre, also certainly swayed public opinion and increased the already growing dissent on what was seen as an unjust war.

With regards to the Napalm Girl, President Nixon's comments, stating he doubted the authenticity of this memorable photograph, carried no weight as it won a Pulitzer Prize. It was further evidence that, in some ways, our leaders didn't see the war as horrific and authentic as it actually was. The young girl became an international symbol of a very unpopular war and arguably assisted in ending it.

What was totally forgotten is that many of us were sent to Vietnam at the whim of a politician. Sadly, we really had no say in it. We were associated with and seen as supporting, what was in effect, the mind set policies of the United States of America against the never-ending perceived threat of rising communism, or the "yellow peril", throughout Southeast Asia. The words of Robert Menzies saying that the 'takeover of South Vietnam would be a direct military threat to Australia', were simply deceitful.

The long-term health effects were extensive. Seventy-four per cent of our Australian Vietnam veterans were classified by the Department of Veteran Affairs (DVA), as now suffering from a health issue, due to serving in Vietnam. The DVA provides our veterans with a gold card, which covers clinically required treatments for all medical conditions and also a wide range of services and support for those 70 years old or over. Disability compensation payments and service pensions also apply to our veterans who meet the defined criteria.

Apart from physical issues, other health problems, such as chemical exposure from the defoliant Agent Orange used in the Vietnam War and including psychological trauma, mental disorders and hearing loss, are also now prevalent. Other health issues now detected include and are not limited to: back pain, hypertension and heart disease. Following the Vietnam War, it is also a tragedy that many of our veterans have committed suicide. To what extent is not known.

The exposure to herbicides is particularly prevalent and has not only been linked to fertility issues and birth defects, such as cleft palate and lip, but also numerous types of cancer.

Overall, it has been estimated that around 19 million gallons of herbicide were sprayed by aircraft in South Vietnam, mainly in Military Region Three, where our Australian forces were based.

In a widely criticised decision, which was rejected by the Vietnam Veterans Association of Australia (VVAA), a 1985 Royal Commission somehow formed a conclusion that Agent Orange was not the cause of higher rates of cancers, birth abnormalities and suicides amongst Vietnam veterans. They concluded the issues were more likely due to post traumatic stress disorder and the poor reception given to our soldiers on returning from Vietnam. However, its findings were contradictory as it also recognised that certain types of chemicals may cause cancer and that any nexus to illness in veterans was 'unlikely but not fanciful'.

The DVA, in its major study, was more widely accepted as they suggested that our veterans' health was very much affected by their service in Vietnam due to the exposure to chemicals, including Agent Orange. A US class action, joined by 4,000 Australian veterans, was also settled resulting in seven chemical companies paying $180 million in an out of court settlement to Vietnam veterans, known as the Agent Orange legal settlement.

Fortunately, our veterans have not reported any long-term effects from drugs, particularly heroin, which was more associated with US Vietnam veterans. What has been seen though, is excessive alcohol use stemming from the "beer culture" ingrained in many of us when we were serving in the Australian army, particularly in Vietnam. I now recognise I was one of many veterans who consumed, not only too many grogs in Vietnam, but certainly on returning home from the war.

My exposure in Vietnam, to the availability and use of drugs, was nil. I can honestly say I never saw any drug use by our soldiers during my 12 months tour of duty. I do, however, accept that drugs existed and were most likely freely available, but somehow the majority of Australian soldiers escaped its clutches. Sadly, allegedly, many American soldiers didn't and perhaps it explains, with certainly no disrespect, the jovial mood of the US Army platoon at the village of Ngai Giao.

The Vietnam War did result in our veterans forming strong bonds and looking out for each other. This led to the Vietnam Veterans Counselling Service formed in 1982. The service, now called Open Arms, has provided free mental health counselling support sessions to our veterans, including me when I was having a number of issues with a stress related illness. I spent a few days on retreat in the Warburton Ranges, which certainly helped.

The Australian attitude towards its Vietnam veterans also witnessed a notable change when, on 3 October, 1987, a "Welcome Home" parade in Sydney saw 25,000 veterans proudly marching to the rapturous support and cheers of several hundred thousand people looking on, in gratitude for their service to their country. Five years later, on the same day and month in 1992, the Vietnam Forces War Memorial was constructed and dedicated to Vietnam veterans and is now firmly cemented on Anzac Parade in Canberra.

In 2014, the Vietnam Veterans Family Study was undertaken by the Australian government, examining the physical and mental health, including the social impact on partners and children of Vietnam veterans. Over 27,000 participated in the study and it was determined, families of veterans in active service were more likely to suffer an emotional toll, together with physical and social issues, compared to those families who had a loved one serve but not in active service.

Regrettably, a number of our veterans committed suicide and on 8 July, 2021, a Royal Commission into Defence and Veteran Suicide was established. Its Terms of Reference included and was not limited to, an inquiry into 'systematic issues and any common themes among defence and veteran deaths by suicide… analysis of contributing risk factors relevant to defence and veteran death by suicide'.

As a nation, there is still a lot to be learned, particularly in respect to providing all the necessary resources and support services for our veterans. We need to adopt a proud and dignified tradition, to ensure our future serving members are never again treated with such anger and disrespect as our Vietnam veterans were. The RSL, with over 150,000 members and 1,135 branches, now plays an important role in supporting our veterans and their families. Not only providing support, advocacy and camaraderie but also an RSL Veteran's employment program with free career support services.

The Australian Veterans Children Assistance Trust (AVCAT), established in 2003 as a national charity, which followed the Australian Vietnam War Veterans Trust (AVWT), distributed a share of the proceeds as cash payments from the Agent Orange legal settlement to our veterans and their dependants. The main focus of the AVWT was to provide for 'the increased number of widows who can then be expected to seek assistance for themselves and the education and care of their children'. AVCAT also supervised the Long Tan bursaries on behalf of the DVA, together with scholarships sponsored by various ex-service organisations and other individual donors.

Many of our veterans have returned to South Vietnam and I was one, along with a number of others, who attended the 40th Anniversary at the Long Tan Memorial Service on

18 August, 2006. It was held to remember those who died in the Battle of Long Tan in 1966, and this day, now known as Vietnam Veterans Day, commemorates all the battles involving Australians in Vietnam. It is a day to say 'thank you' to those who served.

I have an incredible memory of my visit to South Vietnam with many members of 1AFH and their partners that will stay in my mind forever. We were doing a bit of sightseeing at a temple when we came across a tour group of Vietnamese men. Our guide, after speaking to theirs, told us the men were a group of former VC soldiers and, without anyone uttering a word, we and the VC started shaking hands, smiling, nodding at one another.

And then came the hugs.

It was an incredible moment in time that touched everyone there and quite a few of us shed tears. It actually felt like we had come full circle and peace now reigned in all our hearts.

Understandably, a number of our veterans won't ever return to Vietnam as the memories are just too painful. I was also given the honour of speaking at the Anzac Day Service held on the USS Intrepid in New York as part of our National Day of Remembrance. I paid tribute to our fallen diggers including, of course, with much sadness, my mate Ross.

Luckily, some Vietnam veterans have not suffered as badly from the trauma of war and have easily adapted back to their civilian life. Also, to their credit, over 1,000 Vietnam veterans have now been interviewed and their memories stored in the Australians at War Archive. I was also interviewed and received a letter from the Archive's Project Director thanking me for my time and memories. It said:

In the years and decades to come, school children,

> *teachers, academics, film makers, historians and the ordinary people of this country will read and view these interviews and gain both knowledge and understanding of 'the way it was' when you were there.*

Some Vietnam veterans have gone on to become very successful businessmen, achieved recognition as politicians and others have restarted their careers after serving in Vietnam. One fine example is Dr Colin Twelftree, who returned to Vietnam after the war as a dentist with the Australian Vietnam Volunteers Resource Group (AVVRG). He also established a practice in the village of Long Tan.

Colin and his wife adopted a two-week-old orphan immediately following the fall of Saigon and now they are very proud grandparents to a part Vietnamese grandchild.

Another veteran who served with distinction was decorated Vietnam veteran, General Peter Cosgrove. He was awarded the Military Cross for his heroic actions in Vietnam in October, 1969, then went on to be appointed as Governor-General of Australia, where he once again served with distinction.

My achievements later in life are nothing compared to Colin Twelftree and General Cosgrove. I returned to Victoria Police in July, 1969, and in 1974 I commenced a new position, initially as Security Control Officer and then Manager, of the Victorian Education Department Security Services Group. For the next 19 years, I would be actively involved in the prevention and detection of school crime. Shortly after my appointment, journalist Michael Wilkinson, penned a headline in the Herald Newspaper article, 'A Vietnam veteran for a close-to-home war'. Of course, I did not know it at the time, but how right he was.

18

Police Department 1969 -1974

My return to the Victoria Police Department on Monday, 14 July, 1969 was met with some reluctance, despite being promoted in my absence. I now held a 'C' class position as Transport Purchasing Officer with the Supply Branch, reporting to Len Richter. At this point in my life, I was still somewhat confused about my career path. I continued having thoughts of joining Victoria Police as a sworn officer and not as the unsworn member that I was.

I was now eligible, as the height requirement of five foot nine inches had just been abolished and I honestly believed my army service would assist in making a successful application. The Chief Commissioner of Police was Noel Wilby who was in charge of over 4,700 police officers. Other changes included the establishment of a Crime Prevention Bureau and the police wireless patrols were now known as Crime Car Squads.

I still may have had visions of becoming a pilot after my experiences in Vietnam and watched with great interest, along with an estimated 530 million viewers worldwide, as astronaut, Neil Armstrong, together with pilot, Buzz Aldrin, landed on the

Moon on Sunday, 20 July, 1969. I will never forget his famous words when he stepped onto the moon's lunar surface and said, 'That's one small step for man, one giant leap for mankind.'

Armstrong had previously served in the Korean War, flying F9 Panther jets and, for his moon walk, was subsequently awarded the Presidential Medal of Freedom.

I decided firstly to see how I fitted into my new role at Police Supply Branch. It mainly involved the purchase of select motor vehicles for the force, together with various other supporting supplies to maintain an effective transport branch. The type of vehicles varied and included Falcon GTs, which were mainly used by the Police Traffic Branch, often referred to as "Candy Cars". As part of my duties, I frequently visited the police garage located across the road from the Russell Street Police Headquarters and run by Inspector Bob Mason.

I was also involved in assisting with ordering necessary supplies and equipment for the newly established small crime intelligence unit, which was independent of the Homicide Squad and headed by Detective Sergeant Phil Walliss and his deputy, Sergeant Ken Moss. Because of his investigative skills, Phil was seconded from the Homicide Squad, whereas Ken previously worked with police radio maintenance, giving him the necessary technical skills needed for covert surveillance methods.

The small intelligence unit was a consequence of the Cusack Report into organised crime. The report also recommended that Victoria Police establish an Extortion Squad to go after what was known as the "Honoured Society", in other words, the Mafia, and was to be ably supported by the intelligence unit.

The unit was located in the basement of the newly constructed building at the rear of the Russell Street Police Headquarters, as were the CIB and Information Bureau. The Police Association and its well-stocked club bar, as I was to discover in later years, was at the front of the new building, facing McKenzie Street. The association was in fact the Police Union and was formed in 1917 as a consequence of low wages and extremely poor working conditions suffered by Victorian police officers.

What followed was the Victorian Police strike in 1923, resulting in the *Police Pensions Act 1923* (Vic) which gave rise to better wages and conditions for police. By the mid-1960s, following a number of allegations against police, the association became more actively involved in providing legal assistance for its members, thanks to then Association Secretary, Bill Crowley.

In 1970, Colonel Sir Eric St Johnson was appointed by the Victorian Liberal government, led by Henry Bolte, to examine the administration and organisation of Victoria Police and to make recommendations on how the efficiency of our police force could be improved. Although he referred to police corruption in seven paragraphs of his report, he did comment favourably on the low number of disciplinary matters, given the size of Victoria Police.

His 186 recommendations on the restructure under Chief Commissioner Reg Jackson, resulted in a further three assistant commissioners being appointed in the new positions of Operations, Personnel and Services. This was to further offset what St Johnson believed to be a very low level of supervision by senior officers.

Mick Miller was in charge of operations and his excellent credentials included active service in the Australian army as part of the 1st Armoured Car Squadron in the occupation of Japan in 1945. He was also the first Australian police officer to graduate in 1967 from the FBI Academy and would eventually be appointed as Chief Commissioner of Police in 1977. Not long after his appointment and in keeping with the Cusack recommendations for a fully equipped Bureau of Criminal Intelligence, he enlarged the intelligence unit. He was also responsible for the new Special Operations Group, the introduction of Neighbourhood Watch and a revamped Detective Training School.

Further recommendations made by St Johnson were accepted and the rank of First Constable was abolished. New ranks of Senior Sergeant, Inspector Grade One and Two, Chief Inspector and Chief Superintendents were created. One of his interesting recommendations was that promotion should be on merit, not simply on the basis of seniority. At this point, the total number of police were in the order of 5,170, ably supported by numerous unsworn members or public servants in various administrative positions.

On 15 October 1970, many of these police were needed when 35 construction workers died after a 360-foot span from the unfinished West Gate Bridge collapsed. The span, weighing almost 2,000-tonnes, fell into the Yarra River below, causing the Victorian government to declare a disaster, urgently needing the assistance of numerous emergency workers, including police, fire and ambulance units. The Royal Commission immediately set up by the Premier, Sir Henry Bolte, ultimately blamed the construction design and what they termed, 'the foolhardy attempts to rectify a construction failure.'

My love of boxing had not dissipated and on 8 March, 1971, the Fight of the Century for the World Heavyweight championship took place at Madison Square Garden in New York between Joe Frazier and Muhammad Ali. Frazier won in a unanimous points decision, only to be knocked out by George Foreman in two rounds 22 months later. Ali went on to defeat Frazier in the "Thriller in Manilla", to regain the title of world champion.

From time to time, as Acting Stores Control Officer, I was also required to carry out duties at the Police General Store located at the St Kilda Road Depot. I recall the Consorting Squad was located on the ground floor of police headquarters and as I walked through the building on a daily basis, I would often see many well-known detectives, including Paul Higgins and Brian 'Skull' Murphy.

Higgins was known as a handy Australian Rules footballer, playing a couple of games with South Melbourne in 1965. He also liked playing snooker in the billiard room, situated on the ground floor, where I played against him a few times. He was an amicable sort of chap but unfortunately, some years later, he was charged with corruption and subsequently sentenced to seven years in jail.

The role of the consorters was to effectively monitor well known criminal identities and groups to prevent and deter them from their criminal escapades. The Skull, always a smile on his face, or perhaps it was a scowl, was subsequently charged with manslaughter, following the arrest and death in custody of Neil Collingburn in March, 1971.

Collingburn had been arrested in possession of property believed to be stolen when he was taken to Russell Street Police Headquarters. It was then alleged he had the crap belted out of him, including his head bashed into a steel locker by the Skull and another police officer, Carl Stillman. They both vehemently denied the allegation and were subsequently found not guilty in a jury trial in March, 1972.

The Collingburn death resulted in the first police ombudsman being appointed in September, 1971, retired Stipendiary Magistrate, Allan O'Connell, whose prime task was to investigate complaints against police by members of the public. The term Stipendiary Magistrate was because they were paid for the duties like a stipend, usually sitting in the lower criminal court and normally adjudicating on matters such as drink driving, other traffic offences and assault, but they could only impose prison terms of one year. His appointment was however welcomed by the Victorian Council of Civil Liberties, who had been advocating for a police ombudsman for the previous five years.

By now, I was a married man. I had married Marjorie in 1969 and had our first daughter, Karen, in 1970, followed by Alison in 1973. To make ends meet, I also worked part time at a petrol station. I did, however, qualify for a war service loan and had moved into a new home in Bundoora. The Commonwealth government established a War Services Home Scheme (WSHS) in 1919 under the *Defence Services Home Act 1918* (Cth). It was a repatriation activity to erect homes for returned soldiers, provide loans to purchase them and to recognise their service to our country. These loans, now known as Defence Service Homes, also included a comprehensive home building insurance offer for former Australian Defence Force members with at least one day of service. Peacekeepers, reservists and widows/widowers of ADF members were also eligible.

I never spoke about my time in Vietnam and the larrikin streak in me probably helped me put on a good face to all and sundry, that I was no different to who I was before my nasho service. I always ran a book on the Victorian Football League Brownlow medal and, I might add, I never made a loss, leaving many punters, including various police members, very disappointed.

Another public servant, Shane McKew, who played 33 VFL games with South Melbourne and worked in the accounts branch on the second floor of police headquarters, was also a victim of my humour. I telephoned him one afternoon after I found out he had not been selected due to an injury. I pretended I was Alf Brown, a well-known sports reporter with the Herald newspaper, enquired after his health and, to this day, I suspect he still thinks it was Alf who telephoned him.

I was still confused about my goals in life and whether I wanted to continue as a public servant in an administrative role. I would religiously go over the Victorian Public Service Gazette on a regular basis, desperately looking for any vacancies that might be available in other government departments. One vacancy that came up was a position as a clerk at C1 level in the Motor Registration Branch, which was now situated in Lygon Street, Carlton. My limited interest only stemmed from the fact I was playing football on a Sunday with the MRB in the Public Service Competition.

I was even selected as a squad member for the Victorian Public Service Team, but much to my disappointment, I failed to make the cut. I suspect my lack of match fitness didn't help. The captain was Laurie Fowler, who worked for the premier's department and was playing for Richmond at the time. Laurie is well remembered for literally flattening John Nicholls, captain of Carlton, in the 1973 VFL Grand Final and avenging their loss to Carlton in the previous grand final in 1972.

My unwavering support of the Essendon Football Club by this time had waned and it may have been due to their loss in the 1968 grand final. Although I didn't like to admit it, I had now changed my allegiance to the Collingwood Football Club. I suspect it was because my former school mate, Len Thompson, was playing for them at the time and our sojourn to Victoria Park, with a few mates, was a regular occurrence. The park then, was the third largest of the local VFL suburban grounds and, in those days, we could take our own beer with us.

By the last quarter in the outer, we'd use our empty cans to stand on to have a better view of the game. I only ever got into one fight watching the football and that was with a St Kilda supporter. It was over the king hit of Collingwood player, John Greening, by Jimmy O'Dea of St Kilda. Greening only played a few more games with Collingwood as he was never the same player after that incident.

My love of sport continued unabated and I successfully captained the Victoria Police cricket team to win the public service premiership in 1973, in a very strong competition. One player, we had trouble with in restricting his scoring ability, was Paul Hibbert, a left-handed opening batsman. He went on to play one test for Australia in 1977 against India and played a total of 78 first class games. Our premiership team was ably assisted by Des Healey, a public servant with the Criminal Investigation Branch (CIB). Des was a well-known former Collingwood footballer, having played 149 VFL games but, in addition, a very good cricketer, playing 52 district cricket games, also with Collingwood.

I only played one season under Des at Preston Cricket Club but found, after playing on matting wickets for many years, my lack of experience on turf wickets was, to say, in the least, "wanting". Indeed, in my first game at Preston Oval in Cramer Street, it was a sticky wicket after overnight rain and I literally had no idea how to bat. It was an embarrassment. I was out, leg before wicket, for a duck in about the third over of the match, having only faced this one ball.

Our senior coach was Jack Potter, who played 104 first class matches with a highest score of 221. One day at training, he observed me bowling leg spinners and suggested I might be better off doing that instead of keeping. Jack went on to be the inaugural head coach of the Australian Cricket Academy and was one who was instrumental in the development of Shane Warne. Maybe I should have stuck with my leggies.

One of Des' favourite pastimes was having a few beers, literally before the game and I vaguely remember playing against Ringwood and missing an easy stumping. My days as a wicketkeeper were numbered after that and just before a semi-final against Box Hill, I was replaced. I still managed to keep my spot as a batsman but was now batting down the order. Lasting only one season, I then returned to playing with East Preston Cricket Club in the Jika competition, only to be put in hospital by a very quick opening bowler by the name of Alan Quaife, the captain of Sumner Colts.

Alan dropped one short on the matting wicket and I tried to hook it but didn't move my feet. My elder daughter was so distressed, she asked her mum if that meant she would 'get a new dad'. I woke up in PANCH hospital in Preston with a very sore head and cut lip that had to be sutured. Alan was a lovely man and was most upset at what happened. He was also a very good footballer, having played for Fitzroy Football Club in the VFL.

I also captained the Victorian Public Service Cricket team in Sydney when we played the New South Wales Public Service. The only highlight, after being washed out before lunch, was visiting Frank 001 at his dental surgery where he politely reminded me, although I had always promised, I failed to invite him to my wedding some years earlier. I felt bloody awful but simply forgot. Interestingly though, we never spoke about Vietnam at all.

My premiership ambitions were, however, met with East Preston Cricket Club in the Jika competition and Prahran Police, winning a premiership in the mid-wicket cricket competition against University High. We had some very good players, including serving police officers: Rex Hunt, Terry Lorkin, Ian "Bluey" Fountain and Inspector Brian Harding.

I remember one game we played against the Metropolitan Fire Brigade (MFB) at South Melbourne Cricket ground, when I opened the batting with Rex. What an innings he played! He scored a hundred to my measly few runs and he would also bring his lovely and very attractive wife, Lynne, to our games. AFL legend, Tommy Hafey, always referred to Lynne as "the eighth wonder of the world" and at our games, she would sometimes sunbake in her bikini, making it very hard for us to concentrate.

The mid-wicket competition, played on turf wickets, had some excellent players, including John Dugdale, a well-known North Melbourne VFL player, playing 248 games and also captaining the club. The competition also comprised a team known as the Plastic Eleven. They certainly weren't plastic, as their team had a number of test and state level players. Ian Botham played a few games for them but was dropped at one stage because he wasn't much good.

Botham, of course, went on to become one of the greatest all-rounders for England. One of the Plastic Eleven's inaugural members was Colin Lovitt QC and, although he wasn't much good at cricket, he certainly became one of Australia's most eminent barristers, appearing in over 200 murder trials, including obtaining a "not guilty" verdict on a murder charge when representing Mark "Chopper" Read.

On 6 October, 1972, two armed men, plasterers by occupation, named Edwin Eastwood and Robert Boland, would certainly need the counsel of Mr Lovitt, if he was available, when they entered Faraday Primary School, kidnapped a teacher and six students and held them for ransom in the bush at Woodend. They demanded $1,0000,000 to set them free. Their escapade was always bound to fail. Minister for Education, Lindsay Thompson, was to hand over the ransom and was driven to the scene by Police Assistant Commissioner, Bill Crowley, with an armed, Mick Miller, concealed in the car under a blanket.

The ransom was never collected. Eastwood and Boland abandoned the now distraught victims but were arrested by heavily armed police, following a manhunt. Eastwood was sentenced to 15 years imprisonment with a non-parole period of 10 years and Boland copped 17 years with 12 years, before being eligible for parole.

I didn't not know it at the time, but I would cross paths with Eastwood after he escaped from Geelong prison and carried out a similar kidnap in 1976, when I was promoted to a new position in the Education Department. Once again, the kidnapping involved Eastwood and Lindsay Thompson as Minister of Education. Mr Thompson had previously served in World War Two in the Australian army and was awarded a bravery medal for his exemplary conduct during the 1972 kidnapping.

In 1973, Victoria Police began to conduct helicopter tests to determine whether a Police Air Wing would be a useful addition in combating crime. I was still Transport Purchasing

Officer but was no longer required to work at the St Kilda Road police depot. A new rank of commander had been established and the Glen Waverley Police Academy was about to be used for recruit training. I, again, looked at whether I should try to join Victoria Police but, for a number of reasons, I abandoned that idea, thanks to a certain police inspector and due to my own careless drunken escapade, but I digress.

By this stage and, while police were looking at the use of helicopters, the Police Aero Club was, in fact, being used on restricted police duties. They leased two twin-engine Aero Commander planes, which were mainly utilised as transport for various police officers throughout the state. This clearly demonstrated the potential use of aircraft and, in particular, helicopters for police operations. Such operations now included policewomen working in the CIB and Mobile Traffic, plus a full squad of recruits who were mainly trainee policewomen.

At the end of 1973, the authorised strength of our police force was 6,000 members, 700 police cadets and supported by at least 300 public servants in various roles, including Supply, Accounts, Personnel and the Central Correspondence Bureau. A number of other unsworn members also worked at, not only Russell Street, but various other branches as required. The Director of Administration, reporting to Chief Commissioner Jackson, was Ash Rundle, ably assisted by Don McPherson.

The use of public servants in police line ups had not changed, with the only difference being the lines ups were mainly conducted on the vacant sixth floor of the new building at the rear of Russell Street. For whatever reason, I was still chosen to be part of line-ups and on Tuesday, 26 March, 1974, I stood alongside two males in custody for armed robbery. The men were Barry Quinn and his alleged accomplice, Robin

West. Quinn was shorter than me but was placed right beside me, due to our similar build and hair style.

Homicide detectives then brought in a witness who was asked to look along the line of men to see if he could recognise the person, or persons, who robbed him at gunpoint. He then would walk up to him and tap him on the shoulder. The witness was wearing his left arm in a sling, as apparently, he had been wounded during the robbery allegedly committed by Quinn and West. The well-built male witness walked along the line, stopped in front of me, then took one step to my left and let go with a round-arm right hook, knocking Quinn to the floor.

I just stood there in sheer amazement before police quickly escorted the witness away. As he was leaving, a bloody faced Quinn screamed words to the effect, 'You think you were tough when you had a snooker cue in your hand, you fucking, weak prick!'.

I found out later from investigating police that when Quinn and West attempted to rob a snooker parlour, they burst in, telling everyone to stop playing and hand over their wallets. Our witness just kept playing and told them both to piss off. Quinn, or West, then shot him in the arm as he was trying to hit them with the snooker cue. That witness was one tough cookie in my mind and I doubt he would have been charged by police with assault. As much as they were shocked with what took place, a couple of boys in blue had smirks on their faces.

West was subsequently charged with a number of armed robberies, including wounding with intent to murder, whereas Quinn was charged and convicted of the botched armed robbery and murder of two men at the Car–O-Tel motel in St Kilda. As the saying goes, 'live by the sword; die by the sword' and Quinn received his judgement from a fellow convicted murderer, called Alex "The Barbecue King" Tsakmakis in H Division at Pentridge Prison.

Tsakmakis was convicted of the murder of Bruce Walker, allegedly over a dispute regarding the ownership of a motor vehicle. He needed funds to pay for his upcoming trial and somehow, he was out on bail when he shot two owners of a Tattslotto Agency in Hawthorn. Luckily, they survived. Tsakmakis later boasted to all and sundry that he was responsible for not only the shooting deaths of three Melbourne jewellers on St Patrick's Day 1978, but also for the mysterious disappearance of celebrated chef and owner of the Olinda Cuckoo restaurant, Willie Koeppen.

Quinn, being the joker he was, thought he would torment Tsakmakis over the rape of a former girlfriend of his. For revenge, Tsakmakis decided to pour industrial glue over Quinn, then flicked lit matches at him until he went up in flames. I often wonder whether Quinn said to him, 'you fucking, weak prick' as he was about to meet his maker. You have to give Quinn credit for his stubbornness though. Even as he lay dying in his hospital bed, he refused to comment when questioned by detectives about who set him on fire.

Tsakmakis, on the other hand, also didn't last long on this earth. Craig Minogue, jailed for the Russell Street bombing in 1986, brought a quick end to his life by hitting him with a pillow slip filled with weights. The excuse offered from Minogue, which most likely had merit was, 'It was either him or me.'

Promotion was still on my mind, as I was now blessed with two daughters and working separate jobs was starting to take its toll. In early July, 1974, there were two chapters in my life that would result in a total change in direction, although a number of years apart. The first one was when I met Michelle, a lovely young girl who had worked at Supply Branch for three months. She always wore a warm jacket to work but on this particular day, decided to take it off for the first time.

I could not help but notice her certain "attributes". I always found her to be very attractive and now, she went even further up the scale, probably a 9.5 out of 10. I didn't want to give her a perfect score but that would change many years down the track. My male co-workers had also noticed the removal of Michelle's jacket, which eventuated in her being the main topic of conversation at our lunch at the local that day.

The other chapter in my life began with the advertisement in the Victoria Public Service Gazette for the C1 classified position of Security Control Officer with the Victorian Education Department. I determined that perhaps this was the direction I was meant to take. I also considered, if I was to be successful in my application, I certainly needed to, not only present well, but have a thorough knowledge of crime in schools and to have some ideas on how best to tackle what was clearly becoming a pressing problem. There had been increasing publicity around schools being burgled and, in a number of instances, set on fire, causing untold damage.

19

Crime in Schools
An Overview

Prior to completing my application for the position of School Security Control Officer, I realised I needed to, not only have a thorough knowledge of school crime in Victoria, but some idea on how to implement a policy to make schools safe and secure. It was obvious from the publicity given to school crime, in particular major attacks of arson, that I needed to impress in the interview, by talking about a method of prevention and detection of would-be offenders intent on stealing school assets and, in many instances, causing major damage.

It became apparent in my research that the design of school buildings had shifted from the late 19th century with intricate designs looking like Scottish churches in appearance, to several now resembling a type of 'H' pattern design built with a light timber construction. There were, of course, many schools still with old brick buildings and numerous window areas that could be easily accessed, by either smashing the glass or simply jemmying open a door to gain entry.

What I also found, by perusing the police crime statistics and in my discussions with an officer from the Crime

Prevention Bureau, entry was being gained on a regular basis by removing louvre-style windows, situated above the main timber classrooms, from the roof area. There were other schools in a variety of shapes and sizes and many were now being equipped with valuable equipment, particularly in libraries and science blocks.

Once entry was gained, the offender(s) would systematically move through the school, reaping their rewards by going from classroom to classroom, then eventually to the school administration area. They would steal any equipment they could find and, unfortunately, many of the schools left cash on the premises, making them an ongoing target for repeated entries.

In a number of instances, not only would property and cash be removed, but the crook(s) were prone to leave behind evidence of their entry by splashing paint, destroying teachers' property, kicking over tables, chairs and lockers and, in many instances, setting the school buildings on fire.

The offending was most likely committed by young males who were students either attended the same or surrounding schools. On the other hand, school crime was not solely committed by existing students with a grudge against their school and acting in revenge against particular teachers who may have imposed corporal punishment or even the education system in general. Older, adult professional burglars saw schools as an easy target and were more likely to enter a school in the dead of night.

In many instances, they would simply try every door in the school and, lo and behold, would find one open. They would be extremely quiet to avoid detection and take whatever could be sold for cash at a later date. What also became apparent was, a number of schools were being subjected to repeated burglaries, some within days of each other. It was also possible that even this type of offender could set a fire to disguise their original crime.

Arson was a real issue. It appeared, when I was applying for the role in 1974, a number of schools had been the subject of an attack by a pyromaniac with a compulsion to set fires, either due to tension or sexual arousal. The research indicated in some instances, certain individuals had a total disregard for the safety of anyone unfortunate enough to be caught in their path and, after using alcohol and or drugs, they would set fire to the buildings.

There was some evidence that distressed youngsters would light a fire as a signal for a call for help. Academics and psychologists stated this type of arsonist was unhappy at home and wanted to be removed from that environment. One case put forward was "Tony", who believed he was disliked by his adoptive parents. He went on to light several million dollars' worth of fires before he was apprehended.

Another possible reason for school arson was that juveniles might see their school as a safety net, where they could break in and sleep the night. It was also very evident that arson was normally committed by boys, rather than girls and the latter were more likely to go down a path of sexual promiscuity.

Schools being vacant at night, poorly lit and set back from the road, would also be seen as a means to satisfy their craving to not only light the fire, but watch it burn. This type of offending was common and the arsonist would be able to meet the craving by watching, perhaps from a distance or mingling with locals, who were observing the fire brigade fighting the flames.

During a spate of fires in 1972 and 1973, one well known

arsonist was responsible for destroying 14 public buildings, including eleven schools. His degree of pyromania was such that during one attempt, he fell from a high security fence, fracturing his leg. He completed his dirty work by setting fire to the school, causing $500,000 damage, dragged himself back to his vehicle and then drove to hospital for treatment. On his release from hospital, he continued to carry out arson attacks before he was subsequently arrested and convicted.

The end result of all this arson was schoolteachers, students and the local community would be left disillusioned, frustrated and simply devastated by the attack on their schools. Not only was school crime a real social problem but it was costing the taxpayer millions of dollars each year in rebuilding and replacing equipment, either lost in a fire, stolen or damaged.

The loss of school records, personal papers, set assignments and exams, was also heart breaking for teachers, temporarily losing their place of employment, as well as for students who not only lost their exam papers, their school or many of its buildings but also their sense of security. Many primary schools had pets, such as guinea pigs and fish in some classrooms. One cannot imagine the impact these losses had, particularly on the very young students, following a fire.

The problem was not only confined to Victoria. A number of Australian states reported on average, a loss in dollar terms to the equivalent of five fully equipped schools per year due to theft, vandalism and arson. In the majority of instances, school crimes were reported to police, but it appeared in the Victorian education system there was most likely no mandatory reporting of crime to the department. The publicity given to school arson, in particular, was a regular news item, either in the daily newspapers or on television and, without a doubt, further fuelling the offending.

My task was to convince the interviewing panel how the problem could be best met by way of prevention, to reduce the instance of crime and arson in our schools. The statistics indicated that some schools were more vulnerable than others based on demographics, social factors and design.

In other words, a school situated in a more affluent suburb was less likely to be burgled, compared to schools in the northern or western suburbs, for example. The design of schools seemed to also play a part with the small, older and more compact type, less prone to a forced entry.

Prevention methods based on overseas studies suggested such methods as increased external lighting, security rooms to store valuable equipment, high security fencing and patrols at night by armed guards, were the answers. The department could consider installing smoke detectors and even fire sprinkler systems in schools but, of course, the money to provide such fire detection systems may be cost prohibitive.

The problem faced in providing effective security management, was not to turn our schools into fortresses. Despite many of our schools having live-in caretakers, they could not be on hand 24 hours a day, seven days a week. Many of these schools were still subject to high incidents of crime after normal school hours and certainly during a weekend period.

The penalties for committing a crime in our schools provided that, pursuant to section 197 of the *Crimes Act 1958* (Vic), a felon could be sentenced to a term of imprisonment for destroying or damaging property including by arson, whilst s.76 also provided for a term of imprisonment for committing a burglary, by entering a building as a trespasser with intent. Section 9 of the *Summary Offences Act 1966* (Vic), also provided as a maximum, a term of imprisonment up to six months for wilfully damaging property under the value of $5,000.

On completing my research, I attended an interview at the Education Department situated at the rear of the Treasury Buildings in Spring Street, Melbourne. I was interviewed by Neville Barwick, the department's Assistant Director–General (Building), together with Neville Rohan and Barry Carr from the department's building branch. Somehow, I convinced them I was the person to solve the problem of escalating school crime.

My title as School Security Control Officer was a new position, although the department did have a Safety and Security Officer, Don Woodcock. He would now only be responsible for safety programs in schools. Obviously, the problem of school crime in Victorian schools needed more focused and specialised day to day attention and I looked forward, with some trepidation, to my commencement date of Monday, 19 August, 1974.

Prior to leaving for my new position, I spent the remaining two months teaching my replacement and discussing my new role with Detective Sergeant Phil Walliss of the Bureau of Criminal Intelligence (BCI). Phil assured me he would support me in any way possible. I was very grateful to have a person like him, a highly experienced police officer, to fall back on, as my new position, no doubt, would have many moments of difficulty.

My last day with the police department was spent celebrating a little bit too much: first at the John Curtin Hotel in Lygon Street, Carlton, then with Phil and members of the

BCI at the police association. Once again, I didn't know what I was in for over the next 19 years.

20

School Security

From 1 January, 1974 and prior to my appointment, there had been a total of 27 school fires. The majority caused damage in the order of $1 million and were determined to be deliberately lit. In the preceding four years, school fires in Victoria were at an all-time high so it was quite obvious from the outset that I was tasked with an enormous problem. It would take a number of years to keep such occurrences to an acceptable level, if indeed there was such a level.

A fire at Koo Wee Rup High School on 30 June, 1974 caused damage estimated at $250,000, although its cause was determined as accidental. I would later determine that any school fire had to be considered deliberate, unless there was compelling evidence that it was not arson. On 13 August, 1974, six days before I commenced in the new role of School Security Control Officer, Murrumbeena High School was set alight with damage estimated to be in the order of $300,000. It was a large fire destroying a number of classrooms.

On my first day on the job and perusing the police school crime statistics, apart from a plethora of arson, burglaries and wilful damage being reported, it was obvious that a better system of mandatory reporting was needed in the first instance.

This was certainly no criticism of police and the department but it was obvious that a lot of the incidents of school crime, most likely forced entries, without the loss of property and minor wilful damage, were not being reported.

This type of reporting would allow me to first determine what schools were prone to forced entry and potential arson, then to consider what preventative measures could be implemented. My research at the time also suggested some offenders tended to escalate their type of crime. An example was offenders initially smashing a few windows, to then, over time, forcibly entering a building, causing internal damage, followed by escalating the crime by setting fire to the school.

With the help of Mark Swift, a very young public servant in his new role as my assistant, I introduced mandatory reporting of crime by school principals. We designed a criminal offence report form which was to come into operation on 1 July, 1975. It not only included details of the school but listed five main areas where the offences were committed. Some were in administration, library, canteen and assembly hall, to name a few. We wanted to know about any break and enter, break and steal, wilful damage, arson or any other type of crime that was committed. The forms were initially used in selected schools to see if they would be appropriate and, what changes, if any, were necessary.

What became apparent though, was the high incidence of bomb hoaxes received by schools, no doubt from disgruntled students and others who had nothing better to do to pass the time away. The problem was, all hoaxes had to be treated seriously and, on each occasion, a school would have to be evacuated until it was determined to be a hoax.

The report form was quite basic but it would advise us of

the date of an estimated time of the offending, give particular details of any damage to the building and /or property and a description of the stolen goods. The plan was then to collate all the forms into areas, for example, northern or western region. This would enable us to determine which schools were targets of repeated offences and also if there were any apparent trends emerging that needed further and better preventative methods.

In addition to Mark and I collating all the offences, I would be the primary point of call to attend any major school crime incidents, in particular arson. My afterhours telephone number was provided to D24, the police communication hub at Russell Street Police Headquarters and the Metropolitan Fire Brigade control room.

By attending the crime scene, it would enable me to liaise with each respective school principal to determine what assistance was needed from the department and what preventative measures should be put in place. By witnessing firsthand, the devastation being committed against our schools, I could gain a better understanding of the way forward to reduce the level of offending and, more importantly, how to protect our schools.

These preventive measures could include local security and police patrols or, with schools facing repeated attacks, local audible alarms to at least scare off any would-be intruders. Funding from the federal government, as well as the Commonwealth, had already been provided for alarm systems to be installed in schools in their separate library building. The alarms at this point were not being monitored. They had been installed to react to any unauthorised entry and hopefully the internal and external siren would deter the would-be offender. The Commonwealth libraries also contained computer rooms with, not only computers but televisions and video cassette recorders that would be very attractive to any potential thief.

Once we began collating the crime reports from the schools, we could then determine if several further preventative measures, such as patrols, could be effective. It allowed us to consider increasing the number of alarmed schools, not just their libraries. At this point, I started to think the already installed alarms should be monitored by a private security control room. This would alert us to any illegal entry and the possibility of any fire being lit. The use of audible sirens seemed to be a good method in deterring the offender from stealing more property and causing extensive damage.

In the first four months of my appointment, I attended or was advised of, a total of 16 school fires. One was a major fire on 12 December, 1974 at Hadfield High School, causing an estimated $220,000 damage. This school was situated in the northern suburbs and was particularly prone to forced entry and vandalism. The fire was one of many as department records indicated a total of 46 school fires for the year to date. Thirty were deemed to be deliberate, with 11 offenders charged, seven listed as accidental and the cause was unknown in nine fires. The total damage bill was estimated at well over $1 million dollars but I had my suspicions that of the 16 fires deemed possibly not arson, some of these were, in fact, deliberately lit.

On 3 January, 1975, an offender had set fire for the third time to Shepparton Technical School. Fortunately, on this occasion, it only caused around $5,000 in damage. The offender was local 20-year-old Raymond James Saville, who had a prior history of offending, dating back to 1973. Saville would become agitated during inclement weather and, on this occasion, while on Christmas leave from a local youth detention centre and in his pyjamas, he rode his bicycle to the school during a storm to light the fire.

On learning of the fire, the local police immediately knowing it would be Saville, went to his house and found him in his wet pyjamas in bed. He was subsequently sentenced to four years jail in 1976. I didn't know it at the time, but he would be one of many rogues that I would encounter in due course.

Fawkner State School was effectively destroyed by fire on 5 January, 1975, followed by Wodonga High School two weeks later on 19 January, 1975. I attended both fires and at least for these two, witnesses were able to provide police with descriptions. Police Artist, John Rogers, drew sketches, now known as facial composites, of a possible offender seen leaving each school as the fire took hold. The only problem with each drawing was the suspect looked like your everyday youth, with no distinguishable features and, therefore, were never apprehended.

The suspect for Fawkner Primary School was described as, 'about 16, long blonde hair, medium build and around 5 feet 10 inches'.

The miscreant wanted for the Wodonga High School arson was said to be, 'about 14 to 16, a pale complexion with shoulder length blonde hair'.

Looking at both drawings, they appeared remarkably similar and if the incidents had been at schools not far apart, we would have thought we were after the same offender.

The drawings were circulated in the school community, including nearby schools, local milk bars and food outlets. Peter Fitzgerald, a journalist with the Melbourne Herald, tried to assist in capturing the individuals with an article in late January 1975. The headline was "The School Destroyers" and the story featured a copy of our recently introduced criminal offence report form. Unfortunately, the two offenders were never apprehended and, for all we knew, may have gone on to light other school fires.

I did, however, meet with arson squad detectives at Wodonga High School when we examined the classroom and administration offices damaged by the fire. The principal advised us that in the previous three weeks, the school had been broken into on three separate occasions. At this point, I started to form a good working relationship with members of the arson squad, in particular, Detective Sergeant Howard Cornish and Senior Detective Jimmy Coulson. Both men were extremely good coppers and Howard would go on to be awarded with the Order of Australia Medal, not for his exemplary police service, but for his service to music through brass bands, including the police band. He was also a former national serviceman in the 1950s, even then playing in an army band.

My concern about offending escalating to setting fires, seemed, at this point, to carry some weight. The crime rate in schools continued to increase with a further five fires, including Glenroy High School with damages around $65,000. In the early hours of 23 April, 1975, I was contacted by both D24 and the MFB reporting a large fire at Footscray High School. It effectively destroyed the administration block, 12 classrooms and the library, causing damage estimated to be $1 million.

I remained at the scene for some time and, after speaking with detectives from Footscray Criminal Investigation Branch, I made some enquires of my own of any possible suspects. My charter was the prevention of school crime against buildings and property and I didn't think for one moment it was ever envisaged I would carry out criminal investigations. For one thing, I was not properly trained and it was a task better suited to police, who obviously had the requisite skills and resources.

However, given that sometimes I would be actively involved in attending crime scenes, there would be occasions when certain information would come to light I needed to act on. I certainly had no powers of arrest, other than under s. 458 of the *Crimes Act 1958* (Vic), which stipulated that:

> *1. Any person, whether a police officer or not, may at any time without warrant, apprehend and take before a bail justice or the Magistrates Court to be dealt with according to law… (a) he finds committing any offence(whether an indictable offence or an offence punishable on summary conviction) where he believes on reasonable grounds that the apprehension of the person is necessary…*

I decided to question some students who had remained at the school after being told it had been cancelled for the day, due to the fire damage. A couple of students gave me the name of one boy who had earlier witnessed the fire being extinguished by the MFB. They stated he openly bragged about lighting the fire as he hated the school and the teachers. This information may have been false and possibly a pay back by these two students but on speaking with the principal, it came to light that the named student had been absent for the last two days and previously been disciplined by the school.

Common sense indicated that I should have shared the information with the local CIB detectives so they could make the relevant enquiries but, instead, I made the decision to visit the student's address on my own. On attending his home, I knocked on the front door, received no answer, so I walked around the back to see a young boy sitting in a bungalow. I introduced myself, telling him I was from security with the education department and asked if there was anything he could tell me about the fire. He nervously said 'No', but it was obvious by his demeanour he was lying.

Common sense finally did prevail, so I left his address and notified the CIB, who promptly attended to his house and took him into custody for further questioning. After what seemed hours, the detectives had not been able to obtain any confession from him, so I asked the lead detective if he minded if I had a chat with our suspect. I spoke with the young lad for quite some time, told him a little bit about my life story, explained we all make mistakes and that he would be in a better position if he told me what had happened early that morning. He then confessed to me that he did light the fire and described in detail how he lit it and why. The 14-year-old lad was subsequently charged overnight to appear in the children's court at a later date. At least we had found the culprit, but as I would learn later, s.458 of the Crimes Act would come into play time and time again.

The arson attack on schools continued at an alarming rate and by 19 July, 1975, a total of 14 more schools were set on fire, including a $100,000 fire at Portland Primary School, followed by a $50,000 fire at Malvern Primary School.

In the interim though, school burglaries and vandal attacks were an everyday occurrence, so at this point, I needed to think "outside the square", to appropriate preventative measures, including increasing alarming schools and the detection of offenders. At this stage, Victoria Police had established a Police Dog Squad who were in the process of training suitable dogs.

I would later find out that they would become very effective in catching school crooks.

A Richmond high school fire on 20 July, 1975, causing $100,000 damage was one of those times where I had a bright idea. In my discussions with the school principal following the fire, I was advised there was a rumour circulating throughout the school that the fire had been lit once again by a disgruntled senior student. Despite both investigating police and my further enquiries, we could not establish any possible suspects. Mark Swift, my assistant, was only 20 years of age but looked more like 16. The plan was to place him in the school as a Form Six student who had just arrived from overseas. Our "covert surveillance plan" was done with the full knowledge of the principal.

This brain wave was based on the premise that Mark would attend each class, circulate and befriend other students to see if he could obtain any information which could possibly identify the culprit. It could be argued whether this plan fell under our charter in prevention of school crime, but I thought if we could prevent any further fires, then it was part of our scope.

Mark became a student for three weeks. I would drop him off each morning and then pick him up after school near a local tram stop. Sadly, we wasted these three weeks, as no information was forthcoming, so the idea was abandoned. At least there were no more fires at the school.

Unfortunately, school crime, in particular arson, escalated or perhaps we should say deteriorated. To such an extent that after a spate of five school fires in as many days, Weg, a well-known cartoonist for the *Melbourne Herald*, featured a satirical drawing on the front page of the evening newspaper. It depicted a schoolboy wearing a fireman's uniform and armed with a fire extinguisher. The caption read, 'I'm off to school now, Mum'.

By this stage, we had initiated an extensive preventative program. It involved patrols and surveillance of targeted schools by private security companies and the provision of security rooms, using what was called a multi lock security door to prevent entry to the secured area. The door was invented in Israel and had multiple bolts four different ways with a safety lock.

We also decided to further protect entry into the secured area by placing steel grills over any other entry point. One concern was that the crook, on seeing such a secured area, would consider it to be housing expensive equipment. Each school needed something like a bank type vault if we were to protect their valuable items. We also proceeded with an engraving program for school equipment to enable identification purposes if the items were stolen and later recovered.

It was obvious we still had a major problem trying to control the massive amount of damage being caused to our schools, in particular, damage because of arson. It was apparent the department's concerns were justified and it seemed the only solution was to increase the installation of audible electronic security alarms to be monitored by private security.

All existing school security alarms were subsequently provided with either a land line or telephone connection and were to be monitored by a firm called Rank Security, whose control room was in Burwood, Victoria. Whilst we considered, at this point, to still retain the audible type of alarm, the monitoring could also provide a response by either, a security patrol or police, in the event of an alarm notification.

I was also notified after hours of any alarms considered to

be reasonably close to my place of residence in Bundoora. We had contact details of the relevant school principals who would be contacted if needed, after their school had been checked.

Due to having several break-ins but suffering no major damage, one such school needing a security system was Preston Girls High School. In late July 1975, Mark, the school principal, and I discussed the specifications for the installation of a limited audible security alarm to the school's administration area. As we were discussing the way forward, we were alerted by a very upset teacher that a male, aged in his early 50s, was sitting in his car exposing himself to each student as they walked by.

With our clear charter being the prevention of school crime against building and property, our dilemma was, as security officers for the Department of Education, we were expected to be very interested and would act to resolve the matter. We went outside to see the offender leaving the scene in his banged-up motor vehicle. The decision was made to follow him in my Ford Cortina as he drove down Bell Street to a factory in Preston. It was obvious he was unaware of being followed.

He left the factory 10 minutes later and drove to the Gowerville Hotel on the corner of Bell Street and Plenty Road, Preston. Mark telephoned the police from a local telephone box as I kept watch on him seated at the bar. When the police arrived, we told them what had transpired and he was promptly arrested to later plead guilty to wilful and obscene exposure. Not surprisingly, he had a few priors for similar conduct.

Our initial alarm plan also paid further dividends when, months later, the school was forcibly entered and the offender or offenders were scared off by the local audible alarm. The school council sent us a letter which was addressed to Education Minister Lindsay Thompson, thanking us for, not only alarming the administration area of the school, but also for my prompt attendance some 15 or so minutes after being advised by Rank Security Control room of the alarm. The letter did say though, 'Regrettably, the intruder was not caught.'

Although happy to receive such accolades, I was thankful the letter did not mention our efforts in catching the person charged and convicted with wilful exposure. No doubt, Mr Thompson might have raised his eyebrows wondering what his security officers were doing getting involved in that type of "prevention".

Because the damage to our schools was simply out of control by late December 1975, the state government, courtesy of Mr Thompson, the Director General of Education, Dr Laurie Shears and Assistant Director General, Neville Barwick, made an announcement which was headlined "School Crime Squad Trebled". The Herald Newspaper article, written again by journalist Peter Fitzgerald, followed a meeting consisting of Fitzgerald and the Department Heads, and then subsequently with me. Offences against schools were detailed for the previous five months and included 47 arson offences with damage of nearly $500,000 as at the end of November, 1975. Burglary offences were reported at just over 500 incidents and the total offences in our schools numbered 1,000 separate incidents.

This meant our schools were being targeted, on average, at around 200 separate occasions per month. I made the point that despite our new reporting format, I still felt at least 25 per cent of offences were not being reported to the department and police. I gave clear examples of the type of offending where one school had 201 windows smashed and was closed for two days, while another school had 70 dozen eggs stolen from its home economics wing and then splattered throughout the school.

I also mentioned other types of school crime, some of which included prostitution rings, operated by schoolgirls during lunch times, assaults on teachers and extortion rackets for very young students' tuck shop money by students as young as nine. Fitzgerald backed my comments with his own examples of such crime, including standover rackets, bashings, prostitution and promiscuity. Surprisingly, I did not receive any negative feedback from the department for my comments.

Messrs Thompson and Barwick, however, emphasised that only around 35 schools were deemed a problem out of a total of 2240 Victorians state schools. With no disrespect, the problem we were facing was well in excess of 35 schools and was statewide. There was also the disruption to classes and the education of the students after damage and/or arson had occurred at their school.

This was more than evident in early December 1975 when Preston North-East Primary School was forcibly entered. Vandals scattered classroom materials and student records, poured detergent over the floors, squirted fire extinguishers in nearly every room and scrawled obscenities on walls and blackboards. With the school being closed for a day and 300 pupils sent home, approximately 200 parents attended a working bee to clean up the mess.

Funding for security in our schools had become an issue, despite the planned increase in security staff operatives. Dr Shears had previously announced cuts planned in the school building program, which had been shelved in respect of 69 schools because, as he said, 'Simply, the money isn't there'.

My wishes were granted though, with an allocation of an additional $400,000 for school security, including two government vehicles to be used as part of our duties. The funding was planned for patrols, undercover surveillance and to increase the alarming of vulnerable schools.

By the end of 1975, I was into my second year in charge of school security with a decent security budget. It was obvious to me, though, that not only did I need to keep my focus on the prevention of school crime, but serious consideration needed to be given to more sophisticated methods of detection.

A further press release titled, 'ITS WAR to stop damage to our schools', reiterated there would be a further sustained effort to address a year round problem. As aptly put by Herald reporter, Michael Wilkinson, after my first 12 months in the job, I was a "Vietnam veteran for a close-to-home-war".

In January, 1976, another two officers, Ray Whitehill and Michael O'Mara, were appointed and the title of School Security Control Officer was now upgraded to the Safety and Security Section for the Department of Education, with me as its coordinator. By this stage, Don Woodcock had left the department and while Ray would assist mainly in security operations, Michael would largely be responsible for school safety. He would also assist as required in our efforts to prevent and detect school crime. Our roles were quite distinct in nature and would subsequently be separated, leaving me as officer in charge of the school security section and Michael as safety officer, concentrating on the safety of students and teachers.

Now, with a staff of effectively three officers and, despite a limited funding source, the initial plan was to continue with the installation of audible security alarms in selected schools prone to crime. In addition, we continued equipment engraving, provision of security rooms and engagement of more security firms to complement our limited patrols that we now planned to undertake in the surveillance of school property, which would hopefully result in the detection of offenders.

Unfortunately, the new year was welcomed in with our first major fire at the Maidstone Primary School on 13 January, 1976. The fire, which was started in three places, caused damage estimated to be in the order of $250,000. It prompted a visit to my office in Treasury Buildings from Joan Kirner in her role as President of the Victorian Federation of States Schools Parents Club, which began as an influential education lobby in 1971.

I assured Ms Kirner, in our very cordial meeting, that we were doing everything possible to prevent these sorts of fires, explaining in detail, the preventative measures we had in place and how we were intending to improve our surveillance techniques to detect would-be offenders, in particular, arsonists. Not that we knew it at the time, but Ms Kirner would later become a member of Parliament, occupying the Minister of Education Portfolio in 1988 and subsequently became Premier of Victoria in 1990.

Our field operations increased and not only were we conducting our own patrols in red plate government vehicles but also continuing to utilise the resources of private security. Such surveillance methods included sitting in selected schools waiting for any miscreant to commit an offence. Initially, such surveillance was not overly fruitful and, perhaps my lack of experience or should I say clumsiness, didn't help.

When conducting surveillance on a Saturday afternoon at Preston Girls High School, due to incidents of burglary in unalarmed areas, I observed a youth, about 16-years-old, behaving suspiciously. He was up against a classroom window, holding a large rock in his hand and it was obvious to my "trained eye", he was about to break a window to, no doubt, enter the school.

Forgetting I had a can of coke sitting on the window ledge in front of me, I bent forward for a closer look. Of course, I knocked it over and it fell to the floor. The youth obviously heard the noise, dropped his breaking implement and ran off. I told no one of this event and certainly not the school principal, as I was highly embarrassed. I suppose though, I could have had some satisfaction in preventing an offence being committed.

l continued to be actively involved in liaising with members of Victoria Police, including the arson squad, under Sergeant Howard Cornish followed by John Coffey and local criminal investigation branches. Their daily assistance was critical in addressing the problem of school crime and many visits would take place at police headquarters to discuss the latest school crime, in particular, arson. I would also catch up with my former police colleagues, say hello to Michelle and other members of the Supply Branch, and, of course, Phil and Ken at the BCI.

The Police Association Club was also visited on many occasions after stressful days and, on one occasion, I had the pleasure of meeting and drinking with Jack "Captain Blood" Dyer. Captain Blood played 311 games with Richmond in the VFL and was well known for his football exploits, including the highly publicised photograph of him belting and nearly decapitating Tom Meehan in a game against St Kilda in 1949.

Jack was a former police officer with Victoria Police for nine years from 1935 and, after retiring from football, he became a well-known media commentator. I loved watching Jack and Lou Richards on Channel Seven's World of Sport and League Teams. What surprised me on meeting the football player was that he seemed to be very small, not that I towered over him, even though he played as a ruckman and was reportedly six feet and one inch.

Despite my job being a seven day a week vocation, certainly not a vacation, due to being called out at any time of the day or night, I still found time to play cricket on a Saturday afternoon. I would occasionally take a few catches, keeping and making runs with the East Preston Cricket Club. I could also bowl leg spinners and in one match in a second innings, I "steamrolled" the opposition on the matting wicket, taking 4/1 with my "leggies".

An incident on 4 June, 1976 involved a perpetrator who, unknown to me at the time, would enter my life as head of school security some years later. Three crooks, two named Keith George Faure and his cousin, Norman Leslie Faure, hatched a plan to carry out an armed robbery on the ANZ Bank in Clifton Hill. Constable Michael Pratt, an unarmed, off-duty member of Victoria Police, observed them, masked and armed, entering the bank. After they fired a shot inside the bank, narrowly missing the bank manager and a customer, they ran towards the rear of the building.

Constable Pratt parked his car against the bank's front doors, switched on his lights and car horn and requested a passer-by to contact police. On leaving the bank, the trio told Pratt to move his car but he told them, with words to the effect, to 'bugger off'. He grabbed one robber who he knocked out during the struggle, but Pratt was then shot and seriously wounded by Keith Faure. Constable Pratt was awarded the George Cross for his outstanding courage and bravery but unfortunately, he had to retire from the police force due to his injuries.

It wasn't the first time the Faures had been involved in

serious crime. Keith Faure had priors for armed robbery, the manslaughter of Shane Dennis Rowland in May 1976 and, while on remand for the Clifton Hill bank fiasco, stabbed Alan Sopulak to death in Pentridge prison. For the 1976 hold up, he was sentenced to 10 years imprisonment, and Norman Faure received nearly seven years in jail. Little did I know then that Normie would be committing school crime once he got out. Keith not only distinguished himself in prison but was sentenced to a further 13 years for an armed robbery in 1988.

After his release, Keith and his brother, Noel Faure, carried out the shooting death of Lewis Moran at the Brunswick Hotel in Sydney Road in March 2004. This was then followed by the murder of Leslie Caine two months later in May 2004. It was reported at the time that Faure was allegedly paid A$150,000 by Tony Mokbel for the Moran job.

Before he was sentenced to 24 years imprisonment for the murder of Caine, followed by life with a non–parole period of 19 years for the murder of Moran, Faure fainted in the dock after suffering a suspected stroke during a committal hearing. This was probably from his concern over contemplating turning Crown's evidence to try to get a reduced sentence for both murders.

I doubt that anyone was upset over his health issues, especially after he tried for the reduced sentence, least of all Mokbel and Mark "Chopper" Read, the latter escalating an ongoing feud with Faure while in prison. Their vicious battle was depicted in the AFI Award winning film called 'Chopper', where in the opening scene, a character, obviously modelled on Faure, called Keithy George, was viciously stabbed to death.

In the interim, we continued to experiment with various types of alarms. Being called out on a regular basis became an every day and night occurrence so it was obvious local audible alarms were not the answer. Possibly, all they did was scare the offender from committing any further damage at that particular school.

I am not sure why we didn't just convert all our school alarms to silent, but this was not given any thought and, of course, you can be wise after the event. As the person in charge of school security, I accepted full responsibility as once we converted to silent alarms, we were to go down a very successful path.

Arson in our schools did not, for one moment, dissipate. On Sunday, 25 July, 1976, Harrisfield Primary School in Noble Park, suffered a major fire causing many destroyed classrooms. Ray and I inspected the damage at the school and, after discussing the way forward with members of the arson squad, decided to try something different in an attempt to identify the offender or offenders.

The school held an assembly with their teachers and 350 students where I spoke at length, appealing for any information that would lead to identify those responsible. It paid off when two students came forward to inform Ray and me of their suspicions. They mentioned the bragging by another student who had told them how he had entered the school and lit the fire, all done in retaliation against his teacher and, unbelievably, the classroom piano.

After making further enquiries with the principal, we were confident of a good outcome. The student was subsequently arrested, charged by detectives from the arson squad and ultimately pleaded guilty before the children's court. As a footnote, the school piano was destroyed, along with many other treasured items, including a student's guitar and stamp collection.

Without being disrespectful to the court, his "sentence", for want of a better word, was rather lenient to say the least. In respect of the "slap on the wrist" punishment generally handed down in our judicial system, particularly to school arsonists, I needed to be very careful what I said in respect to this latest fire. I had previously voiced my personal opinion in the Fitzgerald article when I stated, '… too often the children's court only gives a rap over the knuckles on a really bad charge of arson or vandalism'.

I didn't stop there and went onto say, 'If the children's court was a deterrent, perhaps the taxpayer would not be footing the bill for millions of dollars a year for school fires and vandalism.'

It was obvious, at that stage, that most of the offending was being committed by students from the damaged school or from nearby schools but over time, we would determine from the number of arrests we made, that school crime was not just "kiddie crime". These arrests would demonstrate that older and, generally male, offenders were also breaking into our schools, stealing property and leaving behind a trail of destruction and mayhem, usually from fire.

In respect to Harrisfield Primary School, we did receive a letter of thanks from Minister Thompson. He congratulated us on a job well done, not only assisting the school in getting back to normal operation, but also for the 'apprehension of those suspected of starting the fire'.

Mr Thompson went on to say, 'There have been public expressions of gratitude for your efforts and I am pleased and proud of the dedication and commitment which you have displayed.'

We were grateful for the accolades but we still had a job to do. Our patrols were increased and calling cards were left to notify each school that we had been patrolling the area. By displaying a more public presence and leaving evidence of security checks by both us and private security, we thought it may act as a deterrent to would be offenders.

An interesting event in September, 1976 was when an 18-year-old youth, Gregory Ronald Bamford, pleaded guilty in the Geelong County Court to 10 charges of arson, causing an estimated $199,000 damage to two Catholic schools and church halls. In being sentenced to three years in a youth training centre, Bamford was also ordered to pay restitution to the Roman Catholic Trust Corporation.

Despite his father wishing them well in getting the money back, 'if they can get it out of him,' it gave me an idea. In due course, I could attend court and make restitution applications against arsonists on behalf of the Ministry of Education. This view was supported by Mr Thompson who totally agreed with direct repatriation from vandals as an excellent idea.

I also read an article where it was reported in Britain and other countries, courts were ordering vandals to clean up their damage, in addition to any fine or term of imprisonment. It was at this point, we started to consider whether we should make application to the courts for a restitution order against the offender, not that it would be all that easy to enforce.

However, another problem had now reared its ugly head. The installation of local audible alarms in our schools had created a noise pollution issue and led to many complaints from the public to the Environment Protection Authority. Angry residents, living near schools equipped with these types of alarms, were very annoyed. The noise problem was not just as a result of forced entries, but the alarms were prone to be set off on a regular basis, due to either faulty installations, open windows, damaged ultrasonic sensor detectors, heating or air conditioning left on and even from school personnel entering without turning the alarm off.

As a consequence, the installation of local alarms in our Victorian schools was suspended in late 1976 and would not resume until 18 months later. In the interim period, an exhaustive study would be carried out, not only by our security section, but in conjunction with officers from the Public Works Department as to the feasibly of electronic surveillance in our schools. We continued with audible alarms in our schools but in order to reduce and limit the noise pollution, we disconnected all external sirens but left internal sirens active. Hopefully, this would still deter the offender and reduce the noise factor at the same time.

Following the tabling of the Beach Report, it was announced in October, 1976 that over 50 Victorian police officers would be subject to criminal charges for alleged corruption and misconduct, largely brought about via a crusade by Dr Bertram Wainer. Prior to the allegations being made public, a meeting of over 4,000 Police Association members threatened a strike, which did not eventuate, with the Hamer Government agreeing to amendments to police procedures with the involvement of the association, but not based on those of the recommendations by Mr Beach. The charges, subsequently against 32 police officers, failed with findings of not guilty.

The end of 1976 did not get any better though, when one of our well-known rogues, Edwin Eastwood, escaped from Geelong Prison after stealing a car on 16 December, 1976. Police were not only kept busy searching for this escapee but were also faced with, what was described at the time as, "Victoria's most brutal crime". On the night of 10 January, 1977, two unsuspecting young women were stabbed to death. One, a teacher at the Collingwood Education Centre, was stabbed 55 times. It would take Victoria Police 47 years to identify a prime suspect in September 2024, to be extradited back to Australia after his arrest in Rome, Italy.

Just over a month later, on 15 February, 1977, Eastwood kidnapped a teacher and nine pupils from Wooreen Primary School in Gippsland, Victoria. Lindsay Thompson was still Minister for Education at that time. When driving away from the scene, Eastwood also took a further six hostages before demanding a ransom of US$7million, together with drugs, guns and even demanding the release of 17 prisoners from Pentridge Prison. His foray was always bound to fail, just like his previous kidnapping and he was soon shot and captured by police, with the hostages being released unharmed.

Eastwood was sentenced to 21 years imprisonment with the learned judge, Justice Murray, who ordered it to be served concurrently with the remainder of the sentence for the Faraday School kidnapping. For both kidnappings of teachers, students and innocent civilians, he received an effective sentence of nearly 26 years imprisonment, with a non–parole period of just on 23 years. As a footnote, he was later charged with the murder of an inmate when he allegedly strangled convicted rapist, Glenn Davies, but was found not guilty on the grounds of self-defence.

I was given the task of devising a fool proof system to foil school kidnappers and, right from the outset, I told the department there were no easy answers. School kidnappings in the United States of America was also a problem. In 1976, the California Chowchilla kidnapping occurred when a school bus driver and 26 students of varying ages with the youngest being five, were kidnapped and held for a $5 million ransom. Fortunately, they were able to escape unharmed from an underground container in a quarry where the kidnappers had buried them. The perpetrators were ultimately convicted and sentenced to life imprisonment, but with the possibility of parole.

It was apparent that our schools now had an additional problem trying to successfully protect our 759 schools with one and two teachers, from idiots like Eastwood. We approached several security companies, despite our firm view that even with electronic devices in place, a response to any notification through a local telephone network would take some time. The kidnapper could escape with the hostages in any event and the cost would run into millions of dollars.

On being interviewed in March, 1977 by education reporter, Steve Harris, I talked about homing devices attached to teachers' arms or their vehicles, so police could then track down the kidnapper and victims. I also mentioned that one security company we had sought advice from, had also helped protect the United States president, so perhaps they could come up with some fool proof plan. I even suggested local patrols by parents, rostered daily, to check out their designated school. It was obvious there was no real answer as my suggestions were hopeless in trying to come up with any workable solution.

We did have some success at Carlton North Primary School, following a fire at 3.25pm on a Friday afternoon in late April, 1977. It was unusual for a fire to start during school hours and most likely the cause was accidental. On attending at the scene, Ray and I spoke to the Arts Craft teacher who told us that two fires had occurred that day, with the first at 1.45pm and then the second fire in the same area two hours later. Even to our untrained minds, it was not rocket science that two fires in the same area and within two hours of each other, were suspicious.

Lo and behold, two nine-year-old students told us they had seen an old man in the corridor near where the fires had started. When they approached him, he allegedly told them to go away. Interesting though, they also told us they happened to be around the same area at the time of the first fire and even helped put it out. Police had not attended at the scene as it was deemed to be accidental, given the time of day it had occurred and during school hours.

After we considered this information and with some scepticism, we returned to the school five days later to speak with the two students in company with the school principal. In hindsight, we should have requested their parents to be part of the discussions, or should I say, "record of interview", but in those days it was perhaps a little bit different in respect to the rights of a suspect.

We put our suspicions to both boys, who were now in separate rooms and they readily made admissions. Not only did they both give us the same details of lighting the fires at their school, but they also told us about another six deliberately lit fires, including a large factory blaze nearby in Fitzroy, the day after they lit the school fires.

Overall, the damage, as a result of their escapades was in the order of $1 million and they were handed over to Fitzroy detectives. They were never charged because they could not form any criminal intent being only nine years old, too young to be held responsible for their actions. At least we may have nipped any further school fires in the bud and hopefully, the boys received some psychological intervention and assistance.

The fires during 1977 did dissipate to a point but it was

really only a matter of time before schools would once again be the focus of attention by arsonists. We continued our relentless patrols, now under the banner of the Education Department Security Section, again leaving our calling cards in nearly every school door, as did our private security companies, both in the metropolitan area and country Victoria. Our crime reporting system allowed us to develop a dossier on each of our 2,500 schools. Those more prone to break-ins and vandalism were marked with a red asterisk.

With a more effective crime reporting system in our schools, we meticulously planned our patrol areas, selecting several schools for undercover surveillance. This resulted in a number of arrests and over one weekend, in particular, we were able to effect the arrest of two 13-year-old boys, leading to 12 charges of burglary and theft, with these two offenders also being responsible for other school burglaries. Little did these youths know that when they entered the school, usually late at night, they would be surprised with a tap on the shoulder and immediately handcuffed.

Ray and I also had some on-going success and we were lucky enough to arrest one young lad inside Donvale High School late on a Saturday afternoon. On arrival at this school, one of several on our patrol sheet, we observed him walking along a connecting corridor trying each classroom door. We didn't have keys to the school, so we waited at the end of the corridor until he walked out, laden with all his goodies. After introducing ourselves, we took him into custody. Our government vehicles were now equipped with a two-way radio system linked to Metropolitan Security Services, a private security company control room, which enabled us to request police to attend.

It had now become obvious that the role we had originally undertaken was not just about prevention of school crime. Using our effective "hands on" approach, attending every major school fire and noting the enquiries we were making of possible offenders, including the arrest of those caught in the act, Ray and I required proper training. We also needed a greater understanding of our legal system, in particular our powers of arrest and the *Crimes Act 1958* (Vic).

21

Every Contact Leaves a Trace

I was fully aware, on the odd occasion, we had not acted entirely within the boundaries of our legal system when dealing with and arresting offenders. If we continued to act, albeit in good faith, without the proper training, then we could bring the Ministry of Education and ourselves into disrepute.

Mark Swift's main role was collating all the school crime statistics while Ray and I adopted a more hands on approach, as mentioned before. Due to my concerns, we were both enrolled to undertake the five-week Investigators Course No 4 at the Victoria Police Detective Training School in Spring Street, Melbourne, commencing on 30 January, 1978. When Mick Miller was first appointed as Police Commissioner in June 1977 and having been DTS' former head, one of his first initiatives was to restructure the training school. Thanks to him, it now included a dedicated course for other law enforcement operatives, rather than just police.

We both found DTS, colloquially known as "bonehead", to be very informative, particularly in respect to the prevention, detection and investigation of crime, as well as the apprehension of offenders and providing evidence in a court of law. The correct procedures for the collection and preservation of evidence when attending crime scenes, was of valuable assistance as 'every contact leaves a trace.' This would come back to haunt me some months later.

The lecturers were all experienced police officers and included Graham Sinclair and Neil O'Loughlin. Graham later became an Assistant Commissioner of Police, whereas Neil went one higher, being appointed to the role of Deputy Commissioner for Victoria Police. Somehow, both Ray and I passed the final exam with flying colours and graduated on 24 February, 1978.

We obviously were not paying attention in some lectures concerning crime scenes and the collecting of evidence because not long after, we both attended a rather large school fire at Jordanville South Primary School. While on patrol, we were reasonably close to the school when the MSS control room notified us of the fire. On arrival, the MFB had extinguished the blaze, so Ray and I carried out a crime scene check, pending the arrival of local police.

We found six cans of partly consumed beer near where the fire had started and immediately thought they could lead to fingerprints from the offenders. We carefully placed each can in an exhibit bag we now carried with us, since doing our DTS course. Each beer can was picked up with a biro pen so we would not contaminate the prints from the arsonist by leaving our fingerprints.

On the arrival of Mt Waverley CIB detectives who I knew quite well from other jobs, I told them of our find and how thankful we were to the DTS as we now knew how to store possible exhibits in an evidence bag. On opening the bag, our cans were happily floating around in their beer dregs because we had forgotten to empty them before putting them into the bags. One of the sayings from DTS, or should I say, Bonehead, was, 'you want to be a "deetecctive" but you can't even spell it.'

The local CIB sergeant jokingly reminded me of that, as he watched us empty the "vital evidence" into a rubbish bin. Suffice to say, we never caught the crooks and I vividly recall feeling as though Ray and I would have been great as two of The Three Stooges.

Unfortunately, school fires continued to rear their ugly head with major arson attacks at Essendon High School, followed by Maidstone Primary School. The fire at the High School caused damage to the art and crafts wing in the order of $500,000, while the Maidstone fire resulted in the canteen and two classrooms being destroyed, with paint also being splashed around the school. No doubt by the same miscreants.

Major fires at Merrilands High School in Keon Park and Thomaston Primary School in May 1978, caused significant damage, with the high school losing its library, two staff rooms, an audio-visual room and three classrooms. These two schools were in one of our red asterisk areas and had been previously subjected to a number of break-ins in the preceding months.

The fire at the primary school was heart breaking. I literally had the school principal crying on my shoulder because 14 classrooms were destroyed, which meant three quarters of the school was gone. I made the comment to Graham Walker from the media at the time that the remainder of the school buildings 'would most likely have to be bulldozed and a new school built'.

These two schools were less than two kilometres from each other and I had no doubt the same arsonist, or arsonists, were responsible for both fires. With local detectives, we had literally door knocked every house in close proximity to the schools. When we tried our sometimes successful school assembly, looking for information, we were able to apprehend one offender for a number of burglaries at the high school, recovering school property valued at $2,000.

A new "initiative", for want of a better word, was being implemented by the School Security Section because of three major school fires over 10 weeks. We decided to install a special hotline to obtain any information about the school fires which, at this stage, totalled seven over a five-month period. The estimated damage bill was literally in the millions of dollars. There was a press release by young journalist, Tony Wilson, to promote our "brain wave" and the number to call was 651–2627.

It was emphasised that the caller did not have to leave their name and address but hopefully would provide information leading to the offenders. I had read an article at the time where a similar idea had been implemented in Albuquerque, New Mexico. Local detectives had become very frustrated at the progress, or lack of, in a murder investigation. We knew exactly how they felt.

Although an understatement, it was fair to say that our new special hotline was a complete and utter failure. All we received were crank calls, basically telling us to 'get stuffed.'

One caller even suggested that he was the arsonist, 'Catch me if you can'.

Interestingly, Crime Stoppers began in Victoria in 1987 and was largely the brainchild of Geoff Wilkinson, the media director for Victoria Police at the time. On a Churchill Fellowship, Geoff had visited both the United States and Great Britain, witnessing first-hand very successful hot lines in operation, unlike ours. I am not saying that our idea in 1978 was the forerunner to Crime Stoppers, but obviously the latter would go on to have more success than we did.

On shelving our hotline, we had to find another way to reduce the incidence of school crime and the ongoing arson offences. By this stage, the Public Works Department had formed the view, as we did, that a much better standard of school alarm installations was needed. It was also agreed our alarms had to be converted from audible to silent for two reasons. Firstly, it was to stop any further complaints of noise pollution and secondly, to provide us with better chances of not only detecting an offender, but also hopefully placing them under arrest.

The evidence showing us a lot of our school crime was being committed by the same offender, or groups of offenders, moving from school to school, was continuing to mount. If they were scared off by an audible alarm at one school, they would simply move onto their next target, most likely a school nearby.

In the interim and pending a final decision on the conversion of our existing alarms, our patrols continued. At 8.41 pm on 25 May, 1978, when conducting a security check of Brunswick North Primary School, two of our officers detected a fire burning in the school library. One officer, Jeff Stocco, had been seconded from the building branch of the department to assist our three existing full-time school security officers on an as needed basis. They immediately called for assistance and the fire was extinguished without too much damage, despite a second fire also being lit in the principal's office. This was another example when we just happened to be on the scene at the right time but our patrols were certainly not the only answer and we really needed to compliment them with a more sophisticated method of detection.

On 8 June, 1978, I attended a school fire at Tottenham Technical School where the damage was estimated to be around $100,000. The fire, also attended by Senior Detective Robert "Bob" Carr of Sunshine CIB, was suspicious. When being interviewed by a television reporter from Channel Nine, I was asked who was investigating the fire. I proudly said, 'Further enquiries are being carried out by Shunshine SheeIB.'

Unfortunately, I was obviously tired and somewhat tongue tied, but Bob and I would have a good laugh about it in due course.

In 1978, the accolades continued with a glowing letter from the principal of Templestowe Valley Primary School. He asked the department to provide us with additional staff and increased funding for the installation of fire prevention methods in our schools. What stood out in this heartfelt letter, was the principal's mention of the disruption to her school and its students following the earlier fire at Merrilands High School. Templestowe Valley's five modular portable classrooms had been relocated to Merrilands to help them when their classrooms were badly damaged. What this letter emphasised to all and sundry, was that school fires not only disrupted the damaged school and its community, but also had far reaching effects on other schools as well. This was a prime example.

Braybrook High School Council thanked us for scaring away offenders on three separate occasions in July, 1978 due to the installed audible alarm, which was being monitored by Rank Security. The council was extremely grateful the culprits had left the building without stealing property or causing damage, including arson. It really hit home to us that we would have much more success in detecting and, ultimately deterring, other school crimes if we converted to silent alarms to give us an opportunity to arrest the offenders.

On 13 August, 1978, our first arrest following detection by

a silent intruder alarm took place. The penny had dropped and we were progressively converting all school alarms to silent. We commissioned three private security companies to monitor 150 existing separate school alarm systems and we anticipated a dramatic decline in criminal offences being committed against Victorian schools would follow.

Our extensive patrols also alerted us to another existing problem during 1978 when we found 278 schools with either unlocked doors or open windows. Our schools needed to become very diligent in not leaving their school unsecured, particularly over a weekend period. In September, 1978, a fire at Mooroopna Primary School resulted in the loss of three classrooms and a storeroom, again demonstrating that school crime was not just being committed in metropolitan schools but was state-wide.

Urgent silent alarm priority would now also be given to those schools subject to repeated forced entries and vandalism, as determined from our statistical data base collated from criminal offence reports by school principals. Despite having some limited success during 1978, arresting a total of 42 offenders, including 24 detected by our silent intruder detection systems, the total number of major incidents, including 15 major fires, was a serious cause for concern. The damage was in excess of $3 million but, hopefully, I had the answer to this escalating community problem.

22

Silent School Intruder Detection

The upgrade of all school audible alarms consisted of replacing them with SESCOA 2108 control panels. The Sescoa name emanated from and was developed and trademarked by Security Sciences Corporation of America. Each panel had eight channel communicators or diallers, seven to be used for a separate section of the school with the remaining channel used effectively as an on or off, or day and night seal transmission by a telephone line to a control room.

The alarm dialler on activation from a detector would send a signal, via telephone, to the control room using a discrete pulsed tone identifying the school and the section of the school which had generated the alarm. An example was if the school activated its alarm at the end of the school day, being a notification by a section 8, then any alarm from sections 1 -7 transmitted thereafter could be because an area of the school had been unlawfully entered, until proven otherwise.

The detectors initially installed were ultrasonic sensors and they would cover a larger volumetric area using a master and slave arrangement. US detectors operated by transmitting a high frequency, very low power inaudible tone into the protected room via a transducer or speaker. This signal was then monitored by an onboard receiver or microphone. If a sufficiently large change occurred in the transmitted frequency, for instance by a person moving toward or away from the detector at a reasonable speed, it would cause the return frequency to change sufficiently for the master logic circuit to generate an alarm.

The downside with US detectors was they didn't like drafts, canteen fridge motors stopping and starting and, in particular, open windows, because the air movement would disturb the returning signal and cause erroneous alarms. They also required a degree in the electronic "black arts" to tune them to the environment they were working in. US detectors as a rule worked best when walking towards or away from them.

On receipt of the silent alarm notification by our control room, initially Rank Security, the closest available security patrol or officer with keys to each individual school would be advised of the alarm break, either by two-way radio or a telephone call to an afterhours number. As the offender moved throughout the school, the US detectors would continue to activate and report by each section where the offender(s) were in whatever part of the school. This was known as a multi break system but at this point in time, its development was only in the infant stages.

Officers, Peter Haar and Dale Sedgman, from the Public Works Department were in the process of developing an "extent of works" for the installation of the school intruder detection system. The general technical description stated the 'system shall consist of detection equipment, monitored alarm circuits, control panel and communicator,' with the detection units to be 'installed as such that they satisfactorily detected motion in the area specified in the extent of works.'

My main role, amongst others, would be the design layout of each school alarm. I initially would visit a selected school to discuss the installation with the principal, obtain a full set of keys and then return to the school over a weekend period to walk through each building and determine the design layout.

The installation of the alarms, using initially US detectors, were then carried out by selected security firms including Gensec Security under Nigel Buckley, MGA Alarms run by John Humphris and Peter Hickey from Sectight Security. The extent of works following installation also required that 'all detectors must pass a walk test system and alarm following an attempted intrusion into the protected zone.'

Although the alarm would certainly be walk tested by intruders, we also added it to our long list of duties. Walk tests were conducted by our own officers, following the installation of the system, to ensure it was working and that all the US detectors were detecting movement in each specified area and its light emitting diodes were switched off.

It would take time to, not only educate us on the best and most effective type of alarm design, but also Victoria police that when notified of a silent alarm, it would not be a false alarm in all likelihood and may lead to an arrest.

At the time, we didn't consider designing the alarm to allow for separate multiple sections being triggered as the offender moved around the building. In other words, each distinct school building was effectively one section so, for example, the administration part of the school would be section one, the separate Commonwealth library might be section two, the science wing section three, the trade wing as section four and so on. Usually, the remote school canteen would be last as section seven. My design layout was very much in the infant stages but, over time, it would certainly improve to give us a much better chance of detection leading to an arrest.

The newly installed silent alarms had their fair share of false notifications. Most were caused by heaters and air conditioning being left on, students covering up or damaging the detectors, open windows or authorised personnel entering the school after hours and forgetting to switch off the alarm. Although the backup provided by police units was encouraging, I believed they didn't have much confidence in the school alarm network and, to a degree, they treated their response as not urgent and would therefore attend the scene in due course.

Even with 'offenders on', as was now our lingo, it meant we could still find ourselves in a perilous situation, especially if there were several offenders inside the school. Our security section officers were unarmed and all I carried was a pair of handcuffs and an extended, but very effective, heavy black Maglite torch.

In early April, 1979, I received a 3am phone call from Rank Security advising me of a possible unlawful entry at Norris Bank Primary School. One section had been triggered and I was the closest available response to check out the alarm notification. It was my eldest daughter's school and only one minute from where I lived. I attended the scene within minutes, parked my vehicle near the school and advised the control room I was about to check the alarm. On looking down the main corridor, I could see a male offender carrying a bag and entering each classroom.

I decided to quietly enter the school, fully aware I had no back up, as police had not been notified due to the alarm being intermittent. I surprised the offender in one of the classrooms, introduced myself and placed him under arrest. He was in his late 40s, scruffy in appearance and, I suspect, it was not the first time he had burgled a school.

Although he gave up without a struggle, I had many thoughts that perhaps we needed a better form of protection, given that we were not armed. Several staff from the private security companies were licensed to carry firearms but I didn't think the department would have been very supportive of my suggestion of licensing their public servant security personnel to carry firearms.

Approximately two weeks later, I received a similar call late at night to attend Lalor High School where I arrested a young couple having sex in the first aid room. They defended the charge of burglary and being unlawfully on the school premises. The Magistrate dismissed the charge because, in his view, police had not proven the "requisite mens rea", that is they did not have a "guilty mind", as all they wanted to do was enter the school to use the first aid room. I still believed it was only a matter of time before I faced a very serious situation with an offender, or offenders, who were not going to simply put their hands up and let me arrest them.

My concerns paled into insignificance when Victoria Police were faced with a string of bank and TAB hold-ups over two years. The first was committed by twin brothers known as the "After Dark Bandit" or "Australia's last bushrangers", with police initially thinking they were looking for only one bank robber, mainly because they would always wear the same clothes. After shooting Senior Constable Ray Koch during a bank robbery in Heathcote in late April, 1979, their third raid on the same bank in under a year, one of the brothers, Peter

Morgan, was finally arrested and then dobbed in his brother, Doug. They were both sentenced to 17 years at Her Majesty's pleasure, Pentridge prison.

Another series of armed hold-ups in 1978 resulted in two innocent workers being fatally shot by Paul Steven Haigh, who also committed four more murders in 1979. They included a nine-year-old boy and his 31-year-old mother who were innocently sitting together in their car. Haig was sentenced to six terms of life imprisonment without the possibility of parole and even carried out another murder, strangling a fellow prisoner in 1991.

My own concerns of possibly facing armed offenders in our schools was answered when Brian Gray, a security guard with Rank Security, suggested I purchase a three-month-old pedigree German shepherd pup to initially train and then have by my side when attending school alarms. I purchased a young male dog from Edo Karl Kennels and, for the next few months, I relentlessly trained him while also attending private training classes. It resulted in me having this marvellous 9-month-old companion by my side every day.

Although the name originated from his breeding kennel, I named him Edo because the initials stood for "Education Department Officer", an appropriate moniker as he was now part of our team. His training included protecting me but I was to soon find out that he loved the chase and it was all one big game to him. In due course, I would also attend weekly training sessions at the police paddocks in Dandenong with other security staff, including Nigel Buckley and his dog Buddha, under the watchful eye of our trainer, Gunther Krause.

The department also approved the engagement of private security contractors. By this time, Bob Carr had left Victoria

Police and had started his own security business. Given his background, I thought his services would be most beneficial and Bob, with his offsider, Graeme White and several former Rank employees, including Geoff Schofield, supplemented our security operations. It didn't take long for their staff to again become actively involved in arresting offenders, either staying in schools overnight for undercover surveillance or as a result of detection by a silent school alarm.

Graeme enjoyed some early success together with Zac, his trained German shepherd dog, when he arrested a crook at Macleod Technical School who was leaving the building while carrying two television sets. Being a former member of the Queensland Police Force, this offender was very surprised when he was arrested, soiling his pants by the time he had the handcuffs on his wrists. He was unlucky though, as Graeme only happened to be in the area when the alarm notification call came out over the two-way radio network from the Rank Control room for 'any units in the vicinity of.'

By the end of 1979, the success of our new school silent intruder detection system program was bearing fruit, with a total of 226 offenders arrested following alarm detection. The total loss due to burglary, wilful damage and arson was estimated at $1.6 million, an all-time low. Although it could be argued this was still a very high loss, it was certainly down compared to other years. At this point, I was still not satisfied as I believed there had to be a more sophisticated method of detecting offenders in our schools.

A few months earlier in October, 1979, the Police Air Wing purchased its first helicopter, a 14-seater twin engine Dauphin 11, the first of its kind in Australia. Together with the Police Dog Squad, they would both prove to be very effective in providing support in the arrest of school crooks. We also had the support of Police D24 Communications who would stay on the line with our control room so their operators could keep updating responding police units on the location of the offender(s) inside the school building.

The only issue we initially had was educating police units to respond silently without lights and sirens. The department must have also been happy with our efforts, as they announced the Victorian government would allocate a further $500,000 for more silent alarms to be installed in our schools.

In April, 1980, I was fortunate enough to undertake a study tour of school security operations in New York and particularly Los Angeles. The Los Angeles School Police Department was initially formed with a goal to improve relationships between local police and youths with programs like "Officer Friendly", dating back to the early 1960s. By the late 1970s, their role gradually became more focused on crime prevention and law enforcement.

In respect of prevention, they had their own 24-hour, seven days a week manned control room and, like us, they had also installed silent alarms in schools. What stood out to me, though, was the way they designed their alarms on different sections, thereby providing a more definitive alarm signal for detecting offenders breaking into schools.

They first installed reed switches on school windows in one section and when the intruder entered the school, detection would occur by way of an ultra-sonic detector, but on a different section. A reed switch operated by way of an applied magnetic field and had been used in several private security installations. In my view, it was more suited to home intruder systems. I also attended the International Security Conference in London to further enhance my knowledge of the most appropriate methods of detection.

My overseas study tours did not go down too well with Alan Hird, who was in a senior role with the education department and was having considerable debate with schoolteachers over industrial unrest at the time. He referred to me as, 'that cowboy in charge of school security.' A bit rough but then again, my RM Williams style boots and distinct tie I had purchased in the States probably didn't help.

The most important things I learnt from the study tour was that we desperately needed to have our own control room to monitor silent alarms in our schools. Our method of detection had to be upgraded to provide, not just a one section, multi section break type alarm, but one that would function on any forced and unlawful entry by school offenders, notifying the control room of multiple section alarms.

23

Catching School Crooks

My submission to establish our first control room was quickly approved and by early 1980, we began operations from the third floor of the education department at the Treasury Buildings. All existing school intruder detection systems, including ones in country schools, were connected to the control room by way of each school's telephone line and, in some cases, especially for larger schools, we would utilise anything up to three lines, all on different diallers.

Nigel Buckley from Gensec Security installed our control room and we initially provided him with a handheld radio to directly communicate with us for of any technical difficulties. Courtesy of Brian Baker, a technical communications officer with our department, our two-way radio communications network was upgraded, replacing our hand-held units with permanent vehicle installations. Eventually, Nigel would also have a two-way radio system installed in his vehicle and his call sign was "Whisky 42". Other security technicians for call outs, as required, would also have the same and, as it turned out, not just for any technical issues.

The alarm responses to metropolitan schools would mainly be carried out by Mark Swift, myself, and our full-time contract security operatives, headed by Bob Carr and his contracted staff, including former Telecom investigators, Noel Lee and Peter Harrison. In country schools, private security companies would continue to be notified of any alarm and requested to attend.

We had also welcomed Lynn Hutchins to our team in late 1980 but it was not envisaged that she would be one of the responders to silent alarms. A public servant on promotion, she replaced Ray Whitehill who had now joined Bob Carr under contract. Following a nasty incident in the early hours of the morning at Preston Girls High School, Ray, unfortunately, could not continue working as a private security contractor. He attempted to arrest two offenders who threatened him, leaving him very distressed when they departed. Ray subsequently moved to Tasmania to become a prison warder. With a bit of luck, the two crooks who escaped his clutches might have met up with Ray once again in prison in Tasmania.

From August, 1978 we had been reasonably successful in the detection and arrest of offenders in our schools. Once we had converted all Victorian school alarms to our own control room, we expected our arrest rate catching school crooks would dramatically escalate. Our silent alarm system responses were also supported by Victoria Police and, as time went on, the Police Dog Squad and Air Wing played major roles.

An amalgamation of the Breaking and Consorting Squads resulted in the establishment of the Police Major Crime Squad. While its charter was to mainly investigate large burglaries, including safe breakings, kidnappings and prison escapes, they would in time, also assist us in the investigation of several school burglaries, resulting in the arrest of two offenders and recovering large quantities of stolen equipment.

My former office was now our new control room, but it

was extremely small and the control panel could only seat one person. The other problem we faced was that some of us, including our now security contractor employees, Brian Gray and Graeme, had their own trained dogs. Several people thought it was not a good look for animals to be taken into the building, using the lifts and then walking past the Minister of Education, Alan Hunt's office on the third floor. Mr Hunt replaced Lindsay Thompson as minister in 1979, but he certainly never complained about our four-legged friends and, in fact, when he saw Edo, he always gave him a friendly pat.

During our first year of operations in our own control room, we apprehended a total of 360 offenders followed by 497 in 1981, as a result of detection by a silent school alarm. The combination multi break section type alarm had now been introduced, still using the existing school telephone lines and was effective in pinpointing the location of the offender(s).

Our catch cry was, 'Any units in the vicinity of.' If, for example, an offender entered a school canteen, which was always prone to forced entry but was now on two sections, usually six and seven, we knew we had "offenders on" and the call would go out over the radio for any units in the vicinity to attend. We were also now installing passive infra-red detectors (PIRs) initially in canteens as they were generally more reliable in such an environment. As a rule, the PIRs were bullet proof to install and commission but they were more expensive per square metre protected and, as such, used sparingly and generally in school canteens.

As the offender(s) moved around in other parts of the school that were mainly using US detectors, we could track such movements as they went from section to section. When units arrived, on most occasions and with some accuracy, we could guide them to the correct area of detection, within metres of where the school crook was. Because the school administration area was always a target, it was not uncommon for us to design the alarm so we would receive at least two sections on multiple activations to our control room, no matter in what part of this area the crook would move around.

Olympic Village Primary School was experiencing repeated break-ins, so alarm detectors were installed in every room. The school had the identification number of 784 on one telephone dialler and 785 on another telephone dialler, so we were utilising the school's two telephone lines. We placed each detector on different sections and different diallers, so if the school was forcibly entered and multiple sections triggered, we would know we had definite offender(s) in the building.

Now equipped with pagers, every one of our security staff was effectively on call 24 hours a day and would hold keys to any school within reasonable proximity to their private residence. The pager, also known as a beeper, was originally developed in the early 1950s and became widely used from about 1980 onwards. The type we initially used gave off a beep or vibration and we would then return back to the security vehicle two-way radio to answer the call or to the nearest telephone to ascertain why we were being paged.

In the event we had no available patrol vehicle to respond to the alarm, the closest available person with keys would be called out. A special form titled, "Report of Malfunction Intruder Detection System" was also implemented for use by our security staff, including our control room. It would provide, not only the school's details but, the malfunction problem listing the section or area affected and any other relevant information for follow up, usually by the alarm company who installed the system. A copy would also be provided to the Public Works Department, who had the overall responsibility for the proper installation of silent school alarms.

Each alarmed school would have a history card on which the control room staff would log each alarm activation, record the date, day, section and type. The latter would either be a single alarm activation which was a one hit only and would be entered on the history card and no action taken. A multiple break alarm would be treated as "offenders on" when two or more sections were activated.

When I arrived at work at Treasury Place on 12th September, 1980, I read the history card for Harrisfield Primary with much pleasure. At 1.10am, a multi break alarm for sections three and four was reported, resulting in the arrest of one offender. We had missed him two nights earlier in the same area of the school but he wasn't so lucky this time. Both alarms were responded to by Whisky 45, who was Geoff Schofield, a former Rank employee now contracted under Bob Carr. The call out term "Whisky", was given to each security officer and I was Whisky 13. As we were all mainly beer drinkers, I am not sure why we used whisky with a number as a radio call sign to identify each security officer.

Not long after and in the company of Geoff, I attended an alarm from the commonwealth library at Lalor High school. It was a two-section multiple alarm activation, definitely with crooks on. I was called out from home about five minutes away, while Geoff was on patrol covering the northern suburbs schools but mainly in the Lalor and Thomastown areas. We were both on the scene fairly quickly and although we had keys, we decided to wait outside the double storey building with

Geoff on one side, on the ground floor double library doors, and me on the other side.

Armed only with our long-handled maglite torches, the two of us patiently waited until four offenders, carrying VCRs and a television set, opened the double doors. When they realised they were about to be arrested, it's fair to say a scuffle broke out but it was all over quickly. Police arrived, the offenders were placed into their custody and charged with burglary. The offenders were in their late 20s, had just arrived in Victoria from South Australia and obviously needed to fund their trip by carrying out a school burglary.

One of my favourite stories from Geoff, was to do with a traffic incident in Collins Street, Melbourne. He had a distinct broad English Yorkshire brogue and one evening when I was working at our control room at Treasury Place, he radioed us needing assistance. He didn't indicate what the problem was but I drove to his location, only a few minutes away. Unfortunately, Geoff had unbelievably driven his car up a safety barrier next to the tram tracks. With all four wheels still spinning around, it was mounted as though it was a rocket in its launching mode.

Geoff was not on duty and I suspect that he may have had a few too many beers. Police were on the scene when I arrived and had not yet breathalysed him. Random Breath Testing (RBT), which came into force in Victoria around 1976, was still in its early days with RBT statistics at low levels, but testing had increased.

Somehow, I was able to convince the young police constable not to breath test Geoff and, after a tow truck arrived to rescue the offending vehicle, I drove him home. Because I was in a government red plate vehicle with our two-way radio blaring loudly, I suspect the police may have decided it was simply an accident.

Geoff may not have been laughing that night but he was when telling us about how he arrested an offender fleeing from a fire at Preston North-East Primary school. His words were, 'He was easy to recognise and hold because he was running away with no pants on and he was obviously very excited.' One more pyromaniac we didn't need to worry about.

In September, 1980, an arsonist was operating in the Doveton area causing several suspicious fires and not only in schools. Our control room was connected to a number of Doveton schools, but this did not mean we could simply sit back and see what happened. It became readily apparent one weekend when the Doveton Holy Family Catholic School was set on fire, causing more than $200,000 damage. Despite a mystery caller to a radio station, dobbing in the alleged offender responsible for the spate of fires, based on 'no entertainment in the area for young people,' the arsonist remained on the loose.

We saturated the Doveton area with patrols and Edo and I spent many nights driving from school to school. When police were told about a suspicious resident lighting in a fire in his backyard in the early hours of the morning, we were certain it was him but it proved fruitless as all he was doing was cooking some meat over an open fire.

One morning around 3am, I thought I had finally caught our miscreant when I saw a young chap carrying a suspicious-looking bag while walking down the street. After introducing myself from the Education Department Security Section, I asked him to open the bag which contained several household items including a VCR. When I initially saw him, he was merrily walking away from his dirty deed of burgling someone's home. I quickly detained him, placed him in the back seat of my patrol vehicle where, to his horror, he was sat next to a tooth-baring Edo. He was much happier when the police arrived and he was subsequently charged.

The Doveton arsonist was finally caught after setting fire to Doveton Police Station and a patrol vehicle. During the record of interview, he told police that he would often hide in school skip bins to observe any patrols, before hopping out to start a fire. He did mention he was in a skip bin on one occasion at Doveton Technical School when he saw a dog with a plain clothes security officer walking through the grounds. I suspect that may have been me, which shows how close I came to catching him. At least I scored one crook for burglary but not the one we wanted.

As I previously suspected, the job was not without its dangers. One of our contracted security officers, John Ford, was called out from his home at 5am in the morning to Woodville Primary School. The alarm was certainly a multi section break but we all learnt a very salutary lesson. Our control room, still manned by only one officer, took the view that it was most likely not a forced entry at that time of the morning, but possibly the cleaner had forgotten to turn off the alarm. Police were therefore not notified of the callout, so John entered the school, expecting only to see a cleaner at work.

What he saw, unfortunately, was the blade of a large knife which a 15-year-old deranged offender viciously used to stab John five times. Critically wounded, he was immediately ambulanced to the Royal Melbourne Hospital and, thankfully, he survived. John continued to work with us for a number of years but the valuable lesson learnt from this was we treated all our alarms as though they were offenders on.

In 1981, our control room in Treasury Buildings was relocated to leased premises in Gipps Street, Collingwood.

Being a large, empty shoe factory, we could house our control room with four on duty officers for around the clock monitoring and we had vehicle access at all times of the day and night. It also solved the problem of our dogs walking in and out of Treasury Place. This building would meet our needs in the interim but it was not envisaged to be our permanent location.

By late October, 1981, arson was not only a problem in our schools, but now the fastest growing crime being committed in Victoria that year. Over 800 were deliberately lit fires in our state, including a major fire at Glenhuntly Primary School, causing damage estimated at $700,000. One of our newly implemented policies for any school damaged by arson was the installation of an intruder detection system so Glenhuntly Primary was soon alarmed and connected to our control room.

Victoria Police even implemented "Operation Torch", a specially appointed police night squad. When making this announcement, the Head of the CIB, Chief Superintendent Phil Bennett, stated there were several professional arsonists lighting fires for personal criminal profit. This followed two fires causing the deaths of two men and injuring two others at a takeaway food shop.

The personal gain angle was supported by various insurance bodies who said that one in four fires was arson and the cost, including the loss of lives and property, was now estimated at $130 million a year for the Australian community. They also made the comment that school fires had a disastrous impact on thousands of school pupils.

Unfortunately, school burglaries and arson continued in 1982 with 2,626 reports of burglary and 138 incidents of arson, causing damage estimated around $2 million. Our arrest rate still climbed, however, and it was not uncommon for our security staff to attend three to four alarm call outs in one night, with about 50 per cent being genuine entries. By now, we were averaging 70 arrests a month, bringing our total number of arrests to just over 1500 since silent alarm conversion in late 1978. When compared to crime in our community, the school crime rate showed a marked difference. The community crime was at a 12 per cent increase, yet school crime was down by 6 per cent.

By the end of 1982, we had 600 schools connected to our Gipps Street control room, representing approximately a quarter of all Victorian schools and our security budget was now at $1.1 million. The cost to install a multi-section intruder detection system per school was averaging $15,000-$16,000, with total operating costs around $310,000.

We must have been making great advances into the prevention of school crime because we were visited by school security officers from several states, including South Australia and Queensland. An article featured in a New South Wales Education magazine in October 1982 and was written by John Hughes, who spoke very highly of our achievements to date. Schools in New South Wales at this time, were copping a hammering by arsonists where, in a succession of fires, many schools were almost totally burnt to the ground. Trying to find answers to vandalism and arson in their schools, Detective Sergeant Mick O'Brien of the New South Wales Police Arson Squad, contacted me so I offered to visit their state once again, to advise them accordingly.

By this stage, I was totally focused on school security, which was obviously not in my family's best interests, given that I had a wife and two young daughters, Karen and Alison. I was also still playing cricket but now with Glen Waverley Cricket Club.

My brother-in-law, John Fisher, and I had both played with the East Preston Cricket Club for several years but when he and his family moved to Mulgrave, I followed him across, spending two great years with the club and winning a premiership.

I didn't make any runs in the grand final though, as I had a very sore hamstring, a result of making 60 in the semi-final the week before. I told our captain, Mike Jennison, not to call any quick runs when we opened the batting together. Mike obviously wasn't listening as he called me through for a short run about the second over of our innings and I was run out by the proverbial country mile. Good on ya skipper!

My 24 hours a day, seven days a week work obsession wasn't helped by my call out rate at all times of the night and particularly over a weekend. Where possible, I would use Edo as my saviour and protector. By now, we had the Police Dog Squad attending many of our alarms and the policy was, if they were attending, they would be given priority. In other words, we would leave our dog in the vehicle and only arrest the offender, or offenders, if we had no other option. This would also depend on how far off the Police Dog Squad was from the school alarm. If they were only minutes away, they certainly received priority over any of our dogs. A number of our contracted staff also had their own trained dogs and this priority policy usually worked well.

On driving home from cricket late one Saturday evening, the Police Dog Squad priority policy would come into play. A call came out over the two-way radio for possible offenders on at Westbreen Primary School in Pascoe Vale. At this point, the control room had only received intermittent single section activations but it still needed to be checked out. When I was only a few minutes from the school, it went into multi section alarm activations, which confirmed offenders on. After being advised the Police Dog Squad were also attending, I had to leave Edo sitting quietly in the back seat of my car.

As I approached the area in alarm, I observed a male in his late 20s holding a heavy and suspicious-looking bag. He was about to climb down from the roof so I introduced myself in the usual manner, told him to come down slowly and that he would be placed under arrest. He threw the bag off the school roof and climbed down a drainpipe. I expected this would be a simple arrest but, as I approached him, the offender suddenly pulled a small pistol from the back of his pants and pointed it straight at me. I thought my days were numbered, so I immediately put my hands up and asked him not to shoot me. I didn't just ask, I pleaded with him.

I knew at this point that back up was on its way but didn't know how far off they were. I asked him what he was doing in the school and his abrupt reply was, 'You fucking know what I was doing.'

I then said words to the effect, 'I also came here to do a burg, but you obviously beat me to it.'

His response was, 'You said you were a security officer so what are youse on about and I can see you've got handcuffs.'

This true story gets more ridiculous as my response was, 'No, I only said that as I didn't know who you were. I carry handcuffs now because I got caught once before in a school and ended up doing time, so please mate, lower the gun,' which, to my amazement, he did.

It was now or never, so I lunged at him, causing both of us to fall to the ground with me on top of him. The gun was in his right hand, so I grabbed his wrist with my left hand. While trying to push the gun away from my face, I started belting him with the handcuffs in my right hand. Thankfully, police dog Rommel arrived with his handler, Sergeant Russell Moore, who I knew reasonably well. Russell let Rommel off the leash and, as he attacked both of us, I was able to grab the gun and throw it away.

The aftermath was, the offender left a substantial bitemark on my right wrist, resulting in a very prominent scar which is still evident today. Rommel also left his bite marks on me, but these have faded with time. The offender was not so lucky, as he had significant facial injuries from being belted with my handcuffs and Rommel's dog bites were a lot worse on him than the ones he gave me. The offender received a term of imprisonment after being subsequently charged with numerous offences. The gun this offender used on me, turned out to be an imitation firearm, but I was totally unaware of that as it certainly looked authentic and dangerous.

A short period after the Westbreen incident, I received a call at home around 10pm on a Sunday evening, advising me that Bundoora Primary School had offenders on with multiple section activations. I quickly responded with Edo and, as there was no police dog attending, I took him into the school where I saw two offenders who took off looking for a quick exit. I let Edo loose and he chased them out onto the school walkway. The outcome was, he bit both men before they were quickly arrested by attending police waiting at that end of the school.

Unfortunately, Edo also did "a Rommel" and bit a police officer, tearing his pants. This officer, a very young Constable Sol Solomon from Reservoir Police went on to become and still is, the longest serving member of the Homicide Squad and, quite rightly, was awarded an Australian Police Medal. I might add I did pay for the repairs to his uniform after receiving a telephone call from his inspector.

A police dog, and this time it wasn't Rommel, took out a sizeable chunk in the thigh of Nigel Buckley when he attended a silent alarm at Upwey High School late one Saturday afternoon. Police Air 490 was over the top of the school and one of the responding canine units was also in attendance. Nigel didn't have keys to the school and, on seeing two offenders inside the building, he smashed a window so the dog could get inside to effect an arrest.

Unfortunately, in celebration of Nigel breaking the window, our police dog launched himself at Nigel's private parts, luckily missed his vitals but latched onto his thigh and wouldn't let go until Nigel belted him over the head with his torch. The offender hiding under a desk was arrested, while the other one who was known to police, was arrested sometime later.

Due to being one of our main security installers, Nigel attended numerous silent alarms. On one occasion, he was in transit, servicing school alarms in the Western suburbs when there was a call for a response to a silent alarm. Only one section from Footscray's Hyde St Primary School was put over our radio network around 9pm. The sector in the alarm was the administration area and Nigel, being in the area and familiar with the site installation, advised he would attend. Despite only one section in alarm, police were notified at this point.

Quietly parking his vehicle, Nigel approached the main entry doors, which he found open and clearly forced. Unfortunately, he had no dog with him, however, he did have a Maglite long handled torch and a set of cuffs. Both were in the pocket of his father's old green combat jacket that he religiously wore to work. The lights in the building were on, allowing Nigel to see the two young male offenders as they turned away from him.

Given that the silent internal was only running on one section, offenders on was a surprise to Nigel. Hoping the police back up response would not be far off, he took his chances as we all did in those days. Entering behind the offenders and challenging them from about three metres, by introducing himself in the usual way, he asked them to lay down with their arms outstretched. Generally, if you take a gentle but commanding tone to offenders they will comply, but alas, not on this occasion. Suffice to say, while waiting on police units to arrive, Nigel found himself in a predicament trying to subdue two very agitated crooks.

As they quickly moved to either side of him, he managed to get a grab high on their body clothing. A physical struggle resulted, causing Nigel to realise and, in his words, that he 'might be in a lot of fucking trouble here' as they were both extremely strong and wanting to avoid arrest. He was now fully engaged trying to subdue two youths of around 17 years of age who were obviously going to get the better of him, sooner rather than later and no doubt, with unpleasant consequences for Nigel. The ribbing he was going to get from his peers, notably me, if two "kids" escaped his clutches, was possibly of great concern as well.

The struggle continued until he let go of the stronger one on his left side, hoping he would run off, allowing Nigel to subdue the offender on his right side. It was at this point, as he was considering his slim set of options when luckily, they both submitted for a completely unknown reason.

Nigel always loved the navy with their big ships, open seas, smart looking uniforms, see the world, a girl in every port and all that jargon. As he was questioning why his initial untenable position with his two new friends had now improved, a massive hand suddenly came over his left shoulder, grabbed one offender and a voice calmly said, 'I've got him.'

Another very large hand came from the other side and an equally steady voice said, 'He's mine.'

Nigel turned to find himself looking at two of the biggest men you could ever wish to see when needing assistance. Both were dressed in ceremonial Australian navy uniforms. Apparently, on this Anzac Day, the Victoria Dock Australian Navy Shore Patrol were having an unusual quiet night and decided to give Nigel a hand after hearing, 'any units in the vicinity of' transmission over the Victoria Police radio fitted in their vehicle. These strong, tough, fit officers, dressed in full uniform and standing well over six feet, six inches, would have frightened the "bejeezers" out of anyone, despite their impeccable, polite manners. The police response not only included the SPs but also an undercover Drug Squad officer in the area who transported the offenders to Footscray Police Station.

The number of my call outs in the northern suburbs was causing me to think about moving to a quieter area for respite from the job. I made an arrest at Mill Park Primary school at 5am one morning, where I detained two young Aboriginal lads inside the school canteen. After handcuffing them together, Edo and I waited for police to take them into custody. Unfortunately, when police arrived, they determined the boys needed a 'whack over the ears'.

Another arrest I made was at Thornbury Primary School at 6am one Sunday but this time, it was on an older Indigenous male hiding in a cupboard on the first floor. Sadly, it was obvious he was harmless, homeless and looking for somewhere to sleep. By this stage, our silent alarms were clearly pinpointing the offender moving through different areas of a school with some accuracy.

An after hours call out to my old school, Keon Park Technical, resulted in Edo successfully leading me to the offender hiding in a locker in the administration area. A short time later, I made another arrest at this school when detaining a youth in the canteen where he had thrown canteen stock all over the floor. When he was handed over to police, his appearance was filthy. He had 'accidentally' fallen onto the messy floor when I handcuffed him.

My luck finally ran out at 4am one morning when I was called out once again to Keon Park Technical School. A Molotov cocktail, or petrol bomb, had been thrown through the vice principal's window. I was able to extinguish the blaze but having suffered smoke inhalation, I ended up being treated at my favourite local hospital, PANCH.

Related to the incident, a press release by journalist, Tim Pankhurst, stated that I was pulled unconscious from the school, but I thought it was a bit over the top. My efforts went unrewarded because the following night the arsonist was successful in his second attempt, burning down the entire administration block and four classrooms.

Hoping it would give me a well-earned rest from being continually called out after hours, my family and I moved to St Andrews in early 1983. I thought I could pick and choose the number of additional hours I needed to do. Besides, needing some respite, I had another problem. It was becoming extremely embarrassing trying to cover m' ever-increasing baldness, so I needed to do something about my 'comb–over'.

On the recommendation of Lynn from work, I went to a hair regrowth company called Advanced Hair Studio and, after their treatments, I felt like a new man.

Well-credentialed Australian Test cricketer, Greg Matthews, would later become one of their high-profile ambassadors and he made the catchphrase, 'Advanced Hair, yeah yeah,' very popular. Several other test cricketers, notably Shane Warne, Graham Gooch and Martin Crowe followed his lead. My new look was even commented on by Rob Tonkin, one of our contracted security officers, who said that finally I'd had a decent haircut and it was much better now being parted in the middle. 'Yeah, yeah.'

On 16 February, 1983, over 180 fires, with the aid of strong winds, resulted in widespread destruction throughout Victoria. The devastating event became known as the Ash Wednesday bushfires. In excess of 3,700 buildings were destroyed and a total of 47 people died as a result. Damage to property was estimated to be over $400 million for both Victoria and South Australia.

Mount Macedon Primary School and several other schools were either destroyed or severely damaged. Naringal Primary School, one of three schools in the region, was destroyed and I recall attending at this school after the fire. The school sign was the only thing still standing and was situated in front of where the school used to be. Eighty per cent of Upper Beaconsfield, including its school, was destroyed, causing several students to be evacuated and relocated to either Ferntree Gully Technical School or Belgrave South Primary School.

There was nothing we could do except add these schools to our never-ending statistics. As it was determined that most of the Ash Wednesday fires were believed to have been as a result of short-circuiting power lines, with tree branches falling onto the lines, the schools were not classed as arson. At the time though, we believed these fires didn't start on their own or were not a result of accidental causes.

Arson, of course, was still a problem throughout Australia and a press release on 28 April, 1983, suggested that not only had arson increased by 500 per cent in our country in the past 10 years, but it was also the fastest growing crime in the western world. In Australia alone, the damage bill was now estimated to be around $700 million for the previous 12 months. New South Wales had even increased its Police Arson Squad to a total of 19 members. It was a problem everyone needed to urgently address, as we were still losing too many schools from being burnt to the ground or severely damaged by fire.

By this stage, we had a very good working relationship with Victoria Police, particularly with the Air Wing and Dog Squad. Our relationship with the Air Wing resulted in Nigel installing a Phillips UHF Radio Transceiver in their office at Essendon Airport. From our control room, we could then directly communicate our data which was then relayed to the crew of Air 490 as the chopper was call signed. I was also part of the crew with Air 490 on special school security patrols and the chopper had some success very early on.

Regarding the Police Dog Squad, I felt their members were starting to gain confidence in our school silent alarm network and I would liaise regularly with the officer in charge, Senior Sergeant Paul Demos. Unfortunately, Paul passed away and out of respect for this lovely man, I attended his police funeral at Woodend. Paul would be sadly missed as, initially, he was largely responsible for the close relationship we now had with the dog squad and it would continue over many years.

Our contractors had only just finished installing a silent alarm in Southvale Primary School in Springvale and after connecting it to our control room, they left the school late that evening. Approximately 35 minutes later, three offenders entered the building and were promptly arrested with Air 490 over the top of the school. The same thing happened at Clayton North Primary School when, within two hours of the alarm connection to our control room, we arrested two offenders, again with Air 490 hovering above the school. We certainly didn't have to worry about conducting a walk test on these alarms as the offenders successfully tested them for us.

Our close working relationship continued with the Police Air Wing to the point where, after a major school fire, I even went in the police Cessna plane with members of the Arson Squad to Yarram High School. We spent most of the day at Yarram, followed by a few beers at the Sale Air Force Base, before flying back to Melbourne. We had a few more cans on the way back and the empties became very useful as this small aircraft did not have a toilet. We were all very 'relieved' when we landed at the Essendon Terminal.

One of the great features of our Gipps Street headquarters was the amount of space we had in the building. It did not only provide enough area for our security vehicles but we were able to have barbeques where all and sundry were invited, including members of the police force. This became a regular Friday lunch time event which temporarily took us away from dwelling on our stress loads dealing with school crime.

One of our guests was Detective Sergeant William "Dingy" Harris of the Hawthorn CIB. We had the pleasure of meeting Dingy when several burglaries at schools in his area resulted in the arrest of the culprits. I thought it would be a great idea inviting him to enjoy our hospitality at Gipps Street. Being described by some as a 'likeable rogue', I was to soon find out how close he came to that tag. Unknown to us at the time, Dingy was also referred to as the 'Captain'.

During the investigation into the murder of Donald Mackay in 1977, a felon by the name of Gianfranco Tizzone, was charged with conspiracy to murder Mackay. Tizzone, obviously hoping for a reduced sentence, told police of a pending drug importation allegedly involving a Victorian copper only known as the Captain. It seemed that this particular chap had sufficient contacts to short circuit the drugs through customs, without being detected. A task force called Operation Rock was set up and using telephone interception technology, guess who was identified as Captain.

Not long after our barbeque, I received a telephone call from Police Bureau of Criminal Intelligence, telling me, without too much detail, to, 'stop entertaining Dingy Harris'.

I immediately did so as something was obviously amiss. Arrested a few months later in April, 1983, Captain Dingy was subsequently sentenced to 14 years imprisonment with a minimum of 12, thanks also to the diligent prosecutor, Paul Coghlan.

The sentencing judge stated that Harris was a, 'disgrace to the police force and you deserve condemnation'.

Six other police officers were also charged with offences such as theft and perverting the course of justice. Even in my type of job, the lesson to be learnt was to be very careful with who you associated.

Our patrols, including walk testing of alarms, continued and one interesting arrest we made was in the grounds of a Northcote school. Late at night, I found three youths loitering around the buildings and, in my mind, they were up to no good. I had no genuine reason to place them under arrest, so I asked them to leave. They refused, so I called police from my security vehicle who arrived and told them to leave the grounds. They again refused so were arrested under the vague law of trespass.

The *Summary Offences Act 1966* (Vic) under s.9(1)(e), carries a maximum of six months imprisonment if it can be proven that when someone enters a property without permission, they have been asked to leave. If they refuse to leave when requested, they are considered to be trespassing. The difficulty we had was, they technically had not entered a property, as they were only in the grounds. The matter was subsequently defended and heard in the Northcote Magistrates Court where it was thrown out by His Worship. He ruled they were not trespassing as they were on public property.

Graeme White and I had some better success, but this time it was not a school crook. Having finished a patrol in the early hours one morning, we were travelling down the Eastern Freeway returning to Gipps Street when our control room contacted us. They had just received a call from Gensec Security about an alarm activation in a commercial premises in Smith Street, Collingwood.

Only a few minutes off, we attended and, on our arrival, we stepped quietly from our vehicle. After jumping a fence next to a laneway, Graeme and I saw a burglar throwing stolen items out a window. On seeing us, he went straight back inside to hide but it didn't take long for Edo to find him on the ground floor, despite Graeme and I initially belting each other in confusion as we entered from opposite sides. We had just made our first commercial premises arrest, giving us some bragging rights over our other school security officers.

Anzac Day was usually a day for listening to the Last Post and some quiet reflection for me but on Monday, 25 April, 1983, we were faced with two school fires, one causing an estimated $1 million damage at Glenroy High School. Eleven classrooms were destroyed or significantly damaged and it took an hour to bring this fire under control. The thieves stole audio visual equipment before lighting the fire to obviously cover up the crime or maybe as a parting gift. The other burn was at Prahran Technical School but was minor in comparison, with only $80,000 damage.

Graeme's art of catching school crooks was interrupted when there was a strike by prison officers following a breakout at Pentridge Prison. In April, 1983, and prior to the strike, four prisoners, including one of the After Dark Bandits, Peter Kay Morgan, escaped from maximum security Jika Jika Unit, also known as K Division. This unit, opened in 1980 at an estimated cost of $7 million, was termed a 'jail within a jail' and it would house some of our most dangerous and hardened prisoners.

The government had admitted in January that year that security procedures at the prison left a lot to be desired and therefore blamed lax prison officers for this latest escape. The strike went state–wide so the Cain government invoked its *Public Safety Preservation Act 1958* (Vic) and employed, 'anyone it considers necessary to ensure the security and safety of prisoners in Victoria's correctional facilities.'

That anyone, included Graeme as he was contracted under Bob Carr by the government, albeit the education ministry, to provide security to our schools.

Despite Graeme being a well built and tough looking character, he only lasted two nights in Jika Jika. I had to laugh when he pleaded with Bob to, 'Get me the fuck out of this hell hole,' which he likened to an "electronic zoo".

He later said it was the dampness and smell that got to him but I suspect some of its prisoners, including Mark "Chopper" Read, might have had something to do with his jumpiness. Chopper was a well-known crook and leader of the "Overcoat Gang", who would conceal their prison made weapons to rule over other prisoners.

Chopper previously had a reputation for torturing members of the underworld by cutting off their toes with either a blowtorch or bolt cutter. He even arranged for his own ears to be cut off, hence the name "Chopper". His infamous record included priors for armed robbery, assault, firearms offences and also a conviction for arson but, I hasten to add, not one against any schools.

I do have some sympathy for Graeme though as my only sojourn to Pentridge was when I visited Raymond James Saville, our well-credentialed rogue school arsonist. I arrived one sunny afternoon to serve him with some papers, putting him on notice that the Ministry of Education would be seeking restitution against him by court order and if that failed, they would sue him civilly if he was ultimately convicted of his latest school fire.

Pentridge was certainly an unforgiving cold place and that is the exact welcome I received from Saville. He tore up the paperwork, threw it back and told me to piss off. I was very tempted to reply with some smart remark but thought better of it and got the hell out of there. I also tried serving a crook in Eltham, who had been charged with a school fire, only to be told by his parents in no uncertain terms to 'get the fuck off' their property.

Applying for a restitution order became part of our overall

effort in deterring school crime. Following a major school fire with offender(s) charged, we would seek an ancillary order from a court for restitution. Often the person charged and, subsequently, convicted would not have sufficient means to pay an order for compensation, causing us a problem. When making application for an order, I recall giving evidence in the county court at Melbourne and as far away as Wodonga but without much success. Some years later in 1991, the *Sentencing Act 1991* (Vic), specifically made provision for a restitution order.

By observing a senior detective from the arson squad giving evidence in a county court trial, I noticed a particular strategy. When being cross examined by the defendant's counsel, his answers were either 'yes', 'no', or 'I don't agree'. Taking his time, he would also gaze around the court room before he answered. The lawyer would often get very frustrated and repeat the question two or three times before he received an answer. I tucked this idea away for my personal use.

We continued to think "outside the square" to increase our arrest rate and one new idea was to place a temporary alarm in any school that had been subjected to repeated forced entries. The installation of a complete alarm system usually took many weeks, so a portable type seemed to be the answer. Using a passive infra-red detector (PIR) coupled with an Astrol microwave, Nigel put one together where both detectors needed to be in alarm to send an activation to our control room. After placing one in a long corridor, we were successful in achieving a good result.

With the detection of offenders in our schools being so successful, we were provided with a direct line to Police D24 now relocated to the first floor at Russell Street Police

Headquarters in May 1982. I arranged this with the officer in charge at the time, Superintendent David Triplow, who would give us immediate priority on contacting D24. The radio call would go out, 'EdSec alarm-any units in the vicinity of…,' with our control room providing updates as they stayed on the line providing continuous feedback to police units responding.

My view, deducted from the overwhelming evidence, was that we needed to respond within six minutes of the alarm activations if we were going to be successful in making an arrest. I believed anything longer than six minutes would drastically reduce our chances. It would also be a matter of time before we would add the Police Dog Squad to our radio network. At this point, though, we all needed some stress relief and several offenders were to give us a bit of a laugh and put smiles on our faces.

24

Comedy 'Arrest' Capers

While the pressures and stress of the job were never ending, there were moments that can only be described as hilarious. Up until this point, I have painted a rather bleak picture, certainly with several incidents that could have and did result in serious consequences for our school security officers.

Some arrests or memorable incidents could be seen to be something out of comedy capers or even Keystone Cops, however, they were not fictional. They were also not based on incompetent police officers or, in our case, "school cops" for want of a better term, but at times would have been excellent material for a film based on slapstick comedies.

One of my much-loved movies was, in fact, *Abbott and Costello Meet the Keystone Cops*. The latter even became a catch cry in some sporting events when things went horribly wrong. In our case, it would be things going bad for the crooks we arrested or in some situations missed, albeit in comical circumstances.

Apart from what I said to the imitation gun-toting crook at Westbreen Primary, one of my favourite comedy arrests would have to be the one I made at a technical school in Preston. The silent school alarm went off around 1.30am and, as I was now residing in a small house in Preston, I was only a few minutes away. With Edo sitting in the back seat and about a minute from the school, I was advised by our Gipps Street control room that there had been no further alarm activations.

I was in my red plate government vehicle with an aerial on the roof and, for all intents and purposes, it probably looked like a taxi. Just before turning into the street where the school was situated, I was waved down by a male in his late 20s carrying a heavy looking bag. At this time of the morning and given that the school alarm activation had ceased, the chances were, he could possibly be the offender. As I stopped my vehicle, he opened the back door, threw his bag next to Edo and climbed into the front passenger's seat. He then said to me, 'Didn't think I would see a taxi at this time of the morning. Can you take me to Lalor?'

He saw the two-way radio, which was, thankfully, quiet at the time with no voice transmissions, so there was no doubt he believed he was in a taxi. Before leaving to take him, supposedly, to Lalor, I asked him what he was doing at this time of the morning.

His reply was, 'Mate, you don't want to know.' Without a doubt, he was our crook. I grabbed his wrists and handcuffed him. When he tried to struggle, Edo fired up, which resulted in the guy being too frightened to move. I told him who I was and that he was under arrest. Upon checking his bag, I found it to be full of computers and other items, obviously stolen from the school.

Suffice to say, he readily made admissions. After advising the control room that I had one in custody, I drove him to Preston Police Station. The young constable on the front desk was in fits of laughter upon hearing the story. The unlucky crook was subsequently placed in the cells after being charged with burglary and other related offences. The lesson to be learnt is, looks can certainly be deceiving so be careful who you wave down after committing a crime, as you never know who they could be.

If you are going to commit a crime, especially arson, it is also advisable not to hang around and marvel at your work, because you never know when someone might tap you on the shoulder. This happened to Nigel Buckley when he attended a fire at Burwood High School. Living close by, he was the first unit on the scene. On arrival, he noticed a young chap in his early 20s, wearing jeans and a flannel shirt and looking very pleased with himself, while watching the school burn. Nigel tapped him on the shoulder and commented, 'What a great fire!' As the chap replied that it was superb, Nigel noted he was very "excited".

The crook, looking at Nigel dressed in his usual scruffy dirty casual attire, obviously thought he was just someone passing by, so Nigel asked him how he lit the fire. He replied that he broke into the school, gaining entry through a window and then splashed the accelerant around, before setting a match to it. Nigel asked where the accelerant was and he said, 'I'll show you' then led Nigel under the Burwood overpass where a five-litre plastic bottle was located. He was taken back to the fire scene and Nigel handed him over to police. Believe it or not, some crooks are just plain dumb.

Nigel's unkempt appearance was probably the main reason he had a police service pistol stuck in his ear by a "jovial" member of Police Traffic Operations Group (TOG) who assumed him to be the offender. It occurred at 2am one morning when he entered one end of the corridor at Donvale High School, while the TOG members entered from the other end.

Nigel thought he was about to meet his maker but thankfully the other police TOG member yelled, 'No, he's not the crook.' Suffice to say the "real" crook escaped while this was all going on.

Some offenders do like to dress up and one was arrested by Graeme White at Richmond Girls High School. Attending the school following a multiple section break alarm in the main administration block, he detained a male dressed in women's clothing. On handcuffing him and patting him down, Graeme found that the crook was also wearing a lace bra and knickers. During a further examination of the first aid room, Graeme saw a female student's dress laying on the bed and upon picking it up, his hands were soiled. Our friend had masturbated into the clothing much to Graeme's disgust, but it gave his workmates a good laugh.

Graeme insisted he had arrested Raymond Edmunds, also known as "Mr Stinky" and the "Donvale Rapist". Edmunds had previously been arrested in Albury in March 1985 for indecent exposure and was fined $400, which then saw his prints being matched a few months later with a 1966 crime murder scene prints. When his photo appeared in press releases, after Edmunds had been arrested and charged with the 1966 murder of Garry Heywood and the rape and murder of Abina Madill in Shepparton, Graeme was adamant that Edmunds was who he arrested at Richmond, but I am not so sure about that!

Edmunds also had a previous conviction for a series of rapes in the Donvale area in the 1970s, hence the title, Donvale Rapist. He was also a suspect in the case of Eloise Worledge, who went missing from her home in Beaumaris in 1976. Edmunds also allegedly bragged to fellow sex offenders that he had murdered dozens of women but was eventually eliminated as a suspect in the unsolved early 1980s Frankston and Tynong North murders, where a total of six female victims were murdered and their skeletal remains left in scrublands near main roads. A total of $6 million remains as a reward leading to the conviction of the person(s) responsible for these unsolved murders.

Edmunds is now serving two life sentences with no minimum term for the Shepparton murders and police still believe he committed at least 32 rapes and a number of murders over nearly 20 years. Hopefully, he will never be released.

Another offender who liked to, shall we say, "expose himself", was one I failed to arrest on two separate occasions. After entering Mt Eliza Primary School, he would go straight to the administration area's photocopier and take a picture of his exposed and excited genitals. On the first occasion, he made several copies which he placed on the students' desks before leaving the school. Because he was only in the school for a few minutes to carry out his dirty work, our response was not quick enough. On his second time at the school, I must have disturbed him before he could finish, as I found his photo still in the photocopier tray but no signature messages on the kids' desks. The one positive was the children didn't have to witness his handy work at school the following day.

Sometimes you need to think outside the square and one example was when I attended an alarm at Lalor North Primary School on a Saturday afternoon. I disturbed two young lads who took off down a street. I gave chase but they were too quick and were making an easy escape. An elderly gentleman was riding his bike with his shopping bag on the handlebars, so I stopped him, showed my identification, grabbed his bike and took off after the fleeing miscreants.

Taking only a few moments to catch up with them, I lunged out causing the three of us to crash to the ground. After escorting them back to the school in handcuffs, I found the poor old cyclist sitting in a driveway with his shopping strewn all around him. Obviously assuming I had stolen his bike, he was very relieved when he saw me. I took his name and address and we sent him a thank you letter the following week.

A bicycle wasn't needed at a Whittlesea school when offenders carrying stolen goods were seen running from the school. I just yelled, 'Stop or we'll shoot,' and would you believe it, they stopped in their tracks and walked back to a police officer and me, holding their hands in the air. It didn't work at a school in Prahran about 1am when police were pursuing two crooks who ran even faster when the warning was yelled out.

I am not sure whether this arrest qualifies for comedy capers but I found it laughable, and stupid into the bargain. On driving down Tooronga Road in Hawthorn early one morning, I came across two males stopped by the side of the road. They were busily engaged in loading portable traffic signs into the boot and back seat of their vehicle. The signs were placed along the extremely busy road while road works were being carried out. Asking what they were doing, I was informed they were just having a bit of fun and thought the signs would look very impressive at home in the garden and their bedrooms. Placing them under arrest for theft, we waited for the responding police who included a very young constable. Having just graduated from the Police Academy, this was to be his first arrest on duty and he could not get the smile off his face.

We were running a competition at work where the security officer with the most arrests at the end of each year would be awarded a trophy for his efforts. Small things amuse small minds but it gave us a laugh in what was a stressful occupation. Geoff Schofield was leading at the time so I tried to add this arrest to my work tally but the consensus vote was, it could not be included.

After Bob Carr unsuccessfully let a few rounds go at Maidstone Primary School, a Police Dog Squad member fired two warning shots at offenders running down the connecting corridor from the administration block at Lyndale High School. We arrested the offenders as they quickly lay on the floor in obvious fear of being shot. Following an arrest of any offenders or, even when we attend a school after hours for any reason, we would always leave a report on the principal's desk at what had transpired.

For good reason, I made no mention about the shots being fired but simply wrote in the report that there was an alarm activated at 1.45am and two offenders were detained. The principal contacted me that morning to advise his air conditioning wouldn't work. It also appeared to have two bullet holes in it. I did a "Sergeant Schultz", but I have no doubt he knew what had transpired.

Talking of gunshots, one memorable moment, although it wasn't an arrest, was when a few shots were fired by a well-known Detective Senior Constable from a crime squad. Being a good friend to Nigel and me, we caught up with him one morning after working a night shift but he was very down in the dumps. While stopping at a set of traffic lights in St Kilda Road with three other detectives in their unmarked police vehicle, hoons pulled up alongside them. They obviously knew they were coppers so yelled abuse and poked their tongues out while giving them the finger.

Our friend was taking none of this nonsense, so he wound

down the passenger side window and shot out two tyres before calmly driving off. The idiots with flat car tyres then filed a complaint to Police Internal Affairs (IID), so he was rightly concerned. On reflection, perhaps he should have just given them a "bunch of roses" (in reference to a former officer, which should give a few ex-police reading this a laugh) and wished them well. However, nothing ever came of it and he went on to hold a very senior and successful position with Victoria Police.

One morning around 4am, offenders on at Thornbury High School with multi section breaks had units coming from all directions, including members from Northcote CIB. We detained one crook as he was leaving the building but his mate was missed and had disappeared into the cold dark night. After talking to the offender in custody, he agreed to take us to their vehicle which was two streets away from the school.

After a plan was hatched, one plain clothes member hid under a tarp in the back of the ute, while another drove the vehicle around the streets beeping the horn, hoping the other crook would think it was his mate. We all left the area with the guise underway and about five minutes later, the missing offender hopped into the passenger's side seat and said to his mate, 'I didn't think you got away, let's get the hell out of here.'

With the pointy end of a pistol stuck in his ear, he was told, 'Sorry mate, but you're busted.' Another crook bites the dust.

One Saturday afternoon, being in the throes of boredom, we decided to have a "hoon fest". A few of us planned to meet at the Bundoora Hotel and sink a few beers while waiting to be paged by the control room. One security officer would not drink as he was the designated driver. The publican wasn't happy though on seeing Edo sitting near me close to the bar.

It wasn't long before we were paged and advised of offenders on, once again at Lalor High School. After our arrival at the school, three of our hoon team waited at various areas outside the school, while I quietly entered with keys through the east end double doors of the main administration block.

While I was walking down one part of the corridor, unaware the offender was walking in the same direction towards me from a connecting corridor, Nigel was unsuccessfully trying to warn me from outside the building. As the offender and I came around the separate corridors, we walked into one another. It was unexpected and I lashed out with a right hook, causing him to heavily hit the floor. He was only 14 years old and stated that after finding an open door, he was just walking to his locker to retrieve schoolbooks so he could go home and study. He had priors, so why would he be believed?

Nigel had success at Fairhills Primary School attending a silent alarm with his well-trained wonder dog, Buddha. He arrested one young offender in the early hours of the morning while the other one took off. Buddha was so well trained he chased after the escaping felon, ran past him then sat about 10 metres in front of him where he did nothing else but bark. The best part about this arrest is that the subdued offender was escorted back to Nigel by Buddha and the only one with a grin on his face was our wonder dog.

Drinking on the job was indeed a welcome pastime but at times it could have landed us, well me, in a spot of bother. I was traveling further these days as I had moved to Mount Martha on the Mornington Peninsula, where I pictured myself spending more time snorkelling and surfing. On one occasion, I consumed a few too many beers at work and, on leaving the control room, I drove straight into a breathalyser manned near Monash High School in Blackburn Road.

While waiting in a line of cars to be tested, I advised the control room of my problem. The plan was, when the police officer conducting the breath test approached my window, on my notification the control room would say over the two-way radio, 'Chief (me), that alarm is still going with further multiple breaks'.

After showing the senior constable my identification and telling him of offenders on at Monash High just around the corner, he eagerly stopped all other vehicles on hearing confirmation from the two-way radio transmission. He then waved me around while, at the same time, yelling out, 'I hope you get the bastards'. A very successful plan but obviously not one of my better moments despite it being worthy of being a comedy caper.

There were times when you wanted to "hang a school burglar out to dry", meaning you wanted to allow someone to be punished or made to suffer in some way. This is what literally happened at St Kilda's Ardoch High School, a school for disadvantaged and homeless youth. At about 1am, following a multi section alarm activation, we attended in company with the Prahran Police uniform night shift. After entering the building and proceeding up to the first floor, we saw four well-dressed offenders in their 20s, all running in different directions, however, we did manage to detain two.

On having a "chat", we found them to have strong Russian accents but, no matter how hard we tried, they would not tell us their mates' names or where they had parked their getaway vehicle. After opening a window on the first floor, one police member grabbed one of the crooks and hung him upside down out the window by his ankles. He screamed his head off, while his mate, also threatened with the same fate, quicky gave up the location of their vehicle and the names of the other two offenders. Another four crooks were to be added to our scorecard following detection by a silent school alarm.

Talking of getaway vehicles, it always pays to make sure you have the right car. We missed two crooks at a Mt Waverly school and, like Nigel, I also had a police service pistol stuck in my ear when one of the members, on entering the school, thought I was one of the miscreants. I decided to get a haircut after this as possibly my "yeah, yeah" hair was too long.

We searched the area, however, to find a vehicle parked at a very odd angle near a back lane adjacent the school grounds. A member of the Police Dog Squad had also arrived with his dog who followed a scent right to this car and would go no further. On a balance of probabilities, it had to be the crook's vehicle, so with a jemmy in hand, we decided to force open the boot as no doubt we would find evidence of stolen goods.

The boot was jemmied open and we hit the jackpot as it contained all sorts of items, including a television set. This had to be the offender's vehicle but, unfortunately, it wasn't. A very angry household owner came out into the street wanting to know why we had forced open and damaged his car boot. The goods did belong to him as he was moving house the following morning. The department subsequently paid for the damage but I had a lot of explaining to do before they would even consider paying.

On attending an alarm at a Balwyn school with police back up, the four offenders were leaving the building when I arrived. I chased after them, but they took off at a fast rate of knots and as I was not the fastest on two legs, they made their escape quite easily. I started to search the streets in my vehicle when a police officer waved me down to say they had just run past him and, unfortunately, he couldn't prevent them getting away. Obviously, not thinking clearly, I just thanked him and took off down the street in hot pursuit. In hindsight, I should have opened the passenger door so he could come with me, but no, I just left the stunned officer standing there.

Upon seeing their vehicle, I drove up to the driver's side thinking I now had them in my clutches but they took off before I could do anything. You would wonder why I never had the policeman with me but also, why did I just drive up alongside their vehicle, when I could have rammed the front thereby preventing them from taking off? Obviously, one of my three stooges attempts at an arrest.

Despite our great success rate in catching school crooks, we had several problem schools where we continued to miss the arrest of the offender(s) when responding to the silent alarm activation.

Deciding to think outside the square once again, we installed listening devices in a school in Brunswick as it had been prone to repeated burglary. The idea was, following an alarm activation, we could turn on the device and listen to the crooks while they burgled the school. I had no idea what listening to their chatter would prove, let alone assist in their arrest but at the time it sounded like a good idea.

On receiving the multi section alarm activations, we turned on the devices and listened to them chatting, laughing and obviously enjoying their foray. Police Air 490 was quickly over the top, but the problem was, the chopper, being too close to the school, was drowning out their chatter. Our control room asked the Police Air Wing at Essendon to get the chopper to go higher so we could continue to listen to the conversation.

There was method in our madness and I am pleased to report we arrested the two talkative felons.

Comedy capers always put a smile on our faces and they were desperately needed as there was certainly no letup in catching school crooks as the incidents of school arson remained an ongoing problem. We again needed to up the ante as there would be no letup in our efforts to bring school crime under control.

25

A New Direction

My initial broad charter, following my appointment in late 1974, was the overall responsibility for the prevention and detection of crime against school buildings and property. We initially commenced operations with three security officers and a limited funding source where we engaged several private security firms. We undertook numerous patrols and surveillance of school property, together with the installation of security rooms and the engraving of school equipment.

The installation of silent alarms in our schools, which was an Australian first as a means of detecting offenders and placing them under arrest, was further complimented by our own central control room, originally at Treasury Buildings and then Gipps Street, Collingwood. Up to June 1984, our surveillance system in terms of personnel was to, not only man our control room, but to undertake field operations which, under my direction, was carried out by respective contract security companies.

We now had 900 schools state-wide connected to our central control room, which was manned 24 hours a day, 365 days a year. Since the inception of silent school alarms in August 1978, we had arrested a total of 3,200 offenders on school property, being charged with a multiple range of offences including burglary, wilful damage and arson. The value of our alarm system was further demonstrated by the on-going support provided by the Victoria Police, in particular, the direct access we had to D24 Communications under the call sign 'Edsec,' Air 490 and the dog squad.

In early 1984, I spent a week in Western Australia, assisting John Marrapodi, who was my equivalent in that state for the education department's security division. Following my visit, John then converted all their school alarms to silent in the hope they would also have the same success we were experiencing. John would ultimately visit Victoria in late 1988 to obtain a further update on the preventative measures, including detection, we had put in place. In the meantime, both Lynn and Mark had successfully completed the Investigators Course at the Victoria Police Detective Training School.

On 1 July, 1984, school security in Victorian schools was to take a new direction. It was announced that our public servant team of three would be substantially increased to carry out our security operations and we would only use private security companies for the installation of our silent alarms, with alarm attendances for country schools by local security. In addition, our control room was to be relocated to permanent premises at the State Schools Nursery in Mount Waverley. It was envisaged that our new direction would be fully operational by March 1985.

Unfortunately, my personal life had also taken a new direction. Following a lengthy separation, my marriage to Marjorie ended and certainly not through any fault of hers. I had initially moved to temporary accommodation at Gipps Street, then to a small house in Preston and by early 1985, in anticipation of our new control room location, I was renting a house in Mount Waverley with Edo. It was only a few minutes from the State School Nursery.

Continuing to play cricket, I captained East Preston Cricket Club to a premiership for the 1984/85 season, winning the competition batting with an average of 88. I must admit, my average was helped by a lot of not outs and I think my highest score for the season was only in the mid-70s, but not out, of course.

Our new "state of the art" control room would be equipped with the latest technology including Ademco 685 receivers supported by multi plexers, IBM compatible computers, Tecom Communicators and Dindema computerised surveillance systems. The school alarm system would still consist of both ultrasonic and now additional passive infra-red detectors, all communicated to our enhanced control room by Ademco 678 Digital Communicator units. This meant we could receive concurrently, as many as eight school alarm notifications, a copious amount of school alarm activations.

In our early days, when we were using the Sescoa type dialler transmitters, we found it could take anything up to a minute to receive the alarm activation, as the Sescoa dialler initially had to seize the telephone line, get a dial tone and then put a momentary short circuit across the line to dial each digit of the number in sequence.

All up, this process could take anything up to 20 seconds and, if the telephone line was a bad connection, often the case in our country schools, the receiver would not accept the first transmission of data. In fact, it would request a second round of notifications and, even then, repeat itself. This meant, by the time we received the first alarm notification, we could already be up to a minute or more behind the crook.

With the advent of tone dialling, the alarm dial up time dropped dramatically from upwards of 20 seconds down to around 5 seconds, so connection times to our control room were much faster and the actual alarm notification time was one third less than our Sescoa diallers. As we gradually upgraded all the Sescoa diallers with Ademco 678 units, now fitted with DVM operating modules, our alarm receipt notification was sub 15 seconds, which meant we were now not far behind the school crook, following entry into the alarmed building.

The completion of our new headquarters was not without its problems. When we transferred over all our school alarms to Mt Waverley, we found that the telephone network was not supporting the alarm notifications. Telecom initially were unsuccessful in diverting the telephone link lines from the Public Switched Telephone Network, being the Collingwood prefix, to the Mt Waverley prefix.

This meant that on changeover from our Collingwood control room to our new base at Mt Waverley, alarms state-wide were not being received. Thankfully, our technicians and, in particular Nigel Buckley, were able to solve the problem, but for about four hours on the Saturday afternoon changeover, all silent school alarms throughout the state were inactive.

We also engaged the services of Drake Personnel to undertake an exhaustive interview process for our new staff. Our multi-disciplinary team was to consist of a deputy manager, two coordinators for Control Room and Patrol Operations, 10 security officers, one technical officer and a word process operator. My team totalled 17 officers in varying classifications from my ADM 6 classification to CO 6 levels for our coordinators. Several security officer positions would be classified as exempt and employed, pursuant to the Victorian State Award for security employees.

Our security staff would be equipped with a Motorola Maxtrac Trunked Radio System, together with a handheld portable and the call sign was now changed from "whisky" to "security" with each officer given a designated call sign number. My identification for example, was now "security 13", and our control room would be identified as simply "Mt Waverley".

The manning of our control room would remain at one officer per eight-hour day shift, but the afternoon shift, commencing at 3pm and night shift from 11pm, would be manned by a total of three officers with one as supervisor. Our patrol staff would come on duty at 6pm and generally work though to 2am, seven days a week. We would allocate at least one security patrol for the north, west, south, and eastern regions, which were supported by the Police Dog Squad units and the Air Wing, as available.

The main tasks of our school patrol officers were to respond to any silent alarms and patrol nominated schools subject to crime, in particular, burglary and arson, as compiled from our criminal offence reports collated and assessed by Mark. Each officer would also hold keys to alarmed schools within reasonable responding distance from their place of residence. In addition, because our officers would continue to walk test alarm installations, they were also provided with an electronic intruder detection walk tester.

One frustrating problem we still had was school staff were failing to turn on their alarm when departing for the day. Our afternoon control room shift would compile a list ready for the night shift of schools where no turn on code had been logged. The shift coordinator would check the list before a designated patrol officer would attend at the school to determine why we had not received any on signal. In most cases, it simply had not been switched on, leaving the school exposed overnight.

The same procedure would apply in country regions and contracted private security would also be notified to attend and check the school. At one point, the lack of attention by several schools in not turning on their alarm became so annoying, I tried to implement a policy for one school in Syndal. They were warned if they continued to be negligent, we would power down their school alarm for the next 24 hours.

When the principal lodged a complaint with the Southern Region Director, Dr Jean Russell, we received a telephone call of admonishment. I never intended following through with the threat as all hell would break loose if the school was set on fire due to its alarm being powered down from my direction. However, my threat worked because from then on, the school religiously made sure their alarm was switched on when vacating the building.

My efforts with Edo were very rewarding because he loved the work he was doing, as did all the dogs who worked with their handlers but I did fall foul of Dr Russell once again and it was partly to do with having Edo in my vehicle. While working at our Mt Waverley headquarters one Saturday afternoon, a multi break alarm was activated at a school just off Waverley Road. After speeding to the school, I arrested two young offenders with their pockets full of pencils.

Some days later I received a "please explain" from Dr Russell, following a complaint from a conscientious member of the public. Apparently, this do-gooder noted my vehicle's red plate registration number and reported me to Dr Russell for speeding. She was also informed of a German shepherd in the back of the vehicle. How this person knew that I was with the Ministry of Education, no longer known as the Education Department, I had no idea. My response to Dr Russell was quite short and very blunt when I told her in a written reply with words to the effect, 'Yes, I was speeding and Edo wasn't wearing a seat belt.'

As Manager of the Ministry of Education Security Services Group, I was reporting to Neville Rohan, the Senior Facilities Officer under Dr Russell as part of the Southern Region for the ministry. Our overnight operations, together with recommendations for the ongoing installation of security systems in high-risk schools, were part of my daily reports. Other duties included the continuance of preparing design specifications and cost estimates for the installation of intruder detection systems to our school network. Neville was also provided with a two-way radio in his government vehicle and his call sign was "security 12".

As we were not entirely relying on silent alarms, my role included, not only overseeing daily rosters, certifying log sheets and mobile duty returns and approving annual leave applications, but also the implementation of special covert operations and continuing to liaise with Victoria Police, Metropolitan Fire Brigade and the County Fire Authority. I was required to also liaise with regional directors, school councils, principals and various state and federal government representatives.

I continued to prepare court briefs of evidence in relation to seeking restitution following acts of major criminal damage, in addition to answering ministerial and parliamentary questions, particularly following a spate of school fires.

Our new Mt Waverley headquarters, including our control room, was now fully operational and we had also added dog pens to the rear of our building. The Police Dog Squad, now connected to our two-way radio network, would also kennel their dogs at Mt Waverley and use our base as a patrol point, before commencing their shift.

Dog squad officer, Sergeant Gary Morrell, was one of six police officers shot by Pavel Marinof, with four being shot in one night of mayhem in June 1985. Gary, luckily, wore a bullet proof vest but was hit by a bullet piercing his wrist. One officer, Sergeant Brian Stooke was not so fortunate and was paralysed as a result of his injuries. To his credit, Brian returned to the force working in administration until his retirement in 2007.

Unfortunately, shootings involving police and private security were becoming common place. In November, 1984, a gunman by the name of Kai "Matty" Korhonen, shot at two police in Beaumaris, wounding one with flying glass from their van's now shattered window. Hours earlier, the officers had responded to the fatal shooting of security guard, Peter Poole, who was seated in his vehicle when shot dead by Korhonen. Following his escape at Beaumaris, Korhonen then fired at an unmarked police vehicle, seriously wounding Senior Constables Paul Gilbert and Ron Fenton from Caulfield Police Station. He was subsequently arrested and convicted of the murder of Poole but, despite being sentenced to a total of 88 years imprisonment for his mayhem, he only served 15 years.

Following the shooting death of Poole and, considering my experience at Westbreen Primary School, the near fatal stabbing of school security officer, John Ford and numerous other incidents involving our unarmed security officers, I did consider applying for all our officers to be armed. I prepared a submission for consideration by Robert Fordham, Minister of Education and State Deputy Premier at the time.

The ministry also had a legal office comprised of three lawyers who were tasked with reporting on all legal matters to the Director General of Education. To say my submission fell on deaf ears is an understatement and I don't think it even got as far as our legal office.

Even though we only wanted to provide our officers with better protection in an afterhours situation, clearly the ministry didn't want to go down the path of the United States of America with a school security policy of having armed security officers effectively patrolling schools. I also think the arrest rate by our staff, suggested it would only be a matter of time before an offender was shot, bringing unheralded and unwelcome publicity on the ministry.

We had maintained a very close working relationship with the Police Air Wing, now under the direction of Inspector Kieran Walshe as Officer in Charge. I always held him in high esteem as he was a pleasure to work with and, not surprisingly, Kieran went on to become Deputy Commissioner of Police in charge of public order, counter terrorism and emergency management. He was appropriately awarded the Australia Police Medal and a National Medal, together with a Victoria Police Service Medal in recognition of his 44 years of exemplary service. Following his retirement from Victoria Police in 2012, Kieran joined the Adult Parole Board and was then appointed to head an investigation into a riot at the Melbourne Remand Centre. What a stellar career from the time he joined Victoria Police as a 16-year-old in 1968!

My second in charge was Bill Herman, ably assisted by Kevin Batchelor, who had replaced Mark Swift, following his promotion to a country region headquarters. Lynn Hutchins had now left the public service to pursue a career as a dermal clinician, while our control room coordinator was Rob Tonkin, together with Graeme White, in charge of our patrol group and Chris Shoebridge, formerly of the Public Works Department, as our technical officer.

Most staff continued to be available for call out and also held keys to schools in their close vicinity in order to attend active alarms at any time of the day and night.

In respect to our school alarm installation, we now adopted a process where, following our design of the multi section breaks system, the specification would be sent to the selected school to obtain three quotations from nominated installers. After my perusal of the quotations, the school council would proceed with the installation on my recommendation. Following the introduction of the *Education (School Councils) Act 1975* (Vic), there was an expansion of the school contract system and this included silent intruder detection systems.

I would usually design the alarm specification over a weekend period as I needed to walk through all the school buildings, to ensure the layout would have the most effect in detecting offenders. On average, I needed three to four hours to work out what was required but in some large schools, anything up to three alarm diallers with 21 separate alarm detection sections was the norm and I could spend all weekend drafting the design.

In most instances, the approved contractor would supply all the equipment as part of the installation and, if an existing audible alarm system was to be replaced or an upgrade of the existing silent alarm was needed, the selected contractor would remove the equipment and return it to us. On average, a primary school alarm would cost $8,000 to $9,000, while some large secondary schools costs were as high as $15,000. It was a small price to pay to be successful in protecting school buildings and equipment. On completion of the installation, we would carry out an inspection and walk test and, if in satisfactory working order, the installing security contractor would forward an invoice for payment from our security budget which was now in the vicinity of $1 million annually.

Although the school council was obtaining the quotes, it was to our specification and it required that I have a better technical knowledge of alarm systems than what I had. I was not the most technically minded person, unlike my father. I therefore attended an Intruder Detection System Installation and Maintenance Course at Preston TAFE and, unbelievably, graduated on 18 December, 1985 with flying colours. The procedure of the school council obtaining three quotations and then submitting them for my approval, generally worked very well.

Overall, our security contractors were excellent to deal with but one contractor didn't last very long after he attempted to bribe me to ensure he would be given favouritism over other alarm contractors. Another contractor, despite knowing the installation would be walk tested, had a habit of not connecting up all the detectors, which we soon uncovered during the walk tests. That installer also didn't last very long as one of our seven preferred contractors.

As manager in a day-to-day operational sense, I had to ensure I utilised and directed our staff and resources appropriately. This required a degree of discretion, initiative, creativity and overall, I had to make decisions that were appropriate in meeting the security needs of our Victorian schools.

Our criminal office report forms indicated a total of 4,591 offences were committed against our schools during 1985 with loss of equipment and property now exceeding $4 million. Our silent alarms were again proving to be very effective with 682 offenders arrested from a total of 704 "offenders on" alarm activations.

It was fair to say that working in school security operations was a highly active but stressful occupation and the next few years would prove to be very eventful for, not only myself, but also our officers and Victoria Police.

26

An Eventful Year

The first six months of 1986 were not without its problems and while we continued to have reasonable success with our school intruder detection systems, arson raised its ugly head at six schools. The largest fire was at Knox Technical School on 8 April, 1986, with damage estimated to be approximately $500,000.

Compared to some of our previous school fires, I suppose we could consider that overall, the fires were not the usual destructive school arson. School burglaries were on average around 120 per month, with a total of 763 offences of burglary reported with an estimated loss of $430,000. Wilful damage totalled 1178 offences with a damage bill in the order of $325,000.

During this six-month period, we responded to a total of 401 silent school alarms with a total of 416 offenders arrested. For the financial year ending June, 1986, we had arrested a total of 802 offenders, 152 more than for the previous financial year. This brought the total number of offenders arrested, on silent alarm intruder detection systems since inception in August 1978, to a total of 4,140.

When compared to offenders who escaped our clutches, a

further analysis determined our arrest rate was hovering around the 40 per cent mark. More than half were still being missed but certainly not from a lack of endeavour by us and Victoria Police. We still needed to improve our arrest rate following detection by a silent school alarm and, at least, apprehend more than 50 per cent of offenders.

The excellent alarm response also provided by Victoria Police continued unabated, notwithstanding crime in our state during this six-month period was not just focused on our schools. On Tuesday, 25 February, 1986, Pavel Marinof, better known as Max Clark or "Mad Max", met his maker in his last shoot out with members of Victoria Police.

He added two more to his scorecard, bringing his total to six wounded police officers before he was fatally shot by detectives John Kapetanovski and Rod MacDonald from the Major Crime Squad. Both these officers were seriously wounded but would eventually recover from their injuries and ultimately be awarded with Victoria Police Star Awards.

Unfortunately, Victoria Police could not rest on their laurels, as on Thursday 27 March, 1986, a car bomb exploded outside the Russell Street Police Headquarters complex causing injuries to 22 people. Sadly, Constable Angela Taylor became the first Australian policewoman killed in the line of duty, passing away 24 days after suffering horrific injuries. This was despite the heroic efforts of Bernie Balmer, a clerk working in the city court opposite Russell Street, who carried the mortally wounded constable well away from the smouldering wreckage of the car that had detonated. His heroism was subsequently acknowledged by Victoria Police when he received their citizen commendation, the highest civilian honour that can be awarded by Victoria Police.

Bernie, who was quite handy in the ring as a heavyweight boxer, was also in the vicinity in November, 1979 when Raymond "Chuck" Bennett was shot dead inside the court building. It is with credit to Bernie that he later became a well credentialled lawyer and is nicknamed "Bernie the Attorney".

Bennett was believed to be the key mastermind in the Great Bookie Robbery carried out on 21 April, 1976, when around $14 million was stolen from selected bookmakers. The murder of Bennett was believed to have been carried out by one of his bookie robbery cohorts, Brian Kane, but there was also an unproven allegation the murder was because of his feud with members of Victoria Police, notably Brian "Skull" Murphy.

Constable Carl Donadio, who was only 19 years old and having served just five months with Victoria Police was also severely injured by bomb shrapnel, as was Magistrate Ian West. Fortunately, they would both recover and Constable Donadio returned to light duties five weeks later.

The car bomb caused extensive damage, in the order of $1 million, to not only the Russell Street complex but surrounding buildings. Michelle, my former colleague from Supply Branch, was now second-in-charge of Police Stores in Wellington Street, Collingwood and she worked closely with Police Uniform Issue Section who were situated on the ground floor basement at Russell Street. She later told me of staff being thrown around, luckily without suffering serious injuries, as a result of the impact from the blast.

There was damage to several computers and furniture but, of more concern to Michelle and everyone else at Police Stores, their truck driver Paul Bellinger, was missing for hours. One of his deliveries that day was to the ground floor at Russell Street

HQ and his truck had been sighted entering the courtyard but was not seen leaving. Thankfully, hearing of the bomb blast on the radio but, unaware that people were searching for him, Paul contacted the office when he had a free moment. He had left Russell Street HQ only moments before the blast and had continued making deliveries to various police stations.

Because 60 sticks of gelignite did not detonate, it was felt at the time that if the bombers had more experience, there would have been worse consequences with mass casualties. In addition, the car was initially going to be placed in the quadrangle of the Russell Street complex, which would have brought the whole building crashing down.

The Russell Street bombers were soon arrested but not without two more police members being seriously wounded when they raided the home of a crook by the name of Peter Michael Reed. Reed's house uncovered drill marks, like those found on the two vehicles linked to the bombing, together with fingerprints identifying the four suspects.

Following a six-month trial in 1988 in the Supreme Court of Victoria, well known rogues, Stanley Taylor and Craig Minogue were sentenced to life imprisonment, with Reed being acquitted of any involvement in the Russell Street bombing. In respect of Rodney Minogue, the jury found him guilty of being an accessory after the fact.

Reed, however, was sentenced to 12 years imprisonment for his involvement in the shooting of the two police at the time of his arrest. Taylor, prior to the bombing, had served a total of 17 years in prison for several bank robberies and was ultimately to die in custody in 2016, supposedly of natural causes.

One of the police officers involved in the investigation was Bernie Rankin from the Major Crime Squad and I would have the pleasure of working with some of their officers in due course. The Major Crime Squad and their investigators were very well credentialed and experienced detectives who were also well known for dealing with some of our state's more hardened criminals.

Attacks on police were certainly heightened by the death of Constable Angela Taylor and it was now considered that any police officer on duty may be subjected to violence, resulting in death. Those fears were confirmed six months after the Russell Street bombing, when Senior Constable Maurice Moore was shot dead in Maryborough by his own police-issued service pistol, when arresting a one-legged offender by the name of Robert Nowell, for stealing a motor vehicle. After a struggle, Nowell had grabbed the pistol off Moore and shot him a number of times.

Nowell was sentenced to a life term of imprisonment but was released on parole some 15 years later. One of his parole conditions included a restriction that he could not go within 50 kilometres of Maryborough. I have no doubt that gave no solace to the family of Senior Constable Moore.

Our genuine entries into schools continued with more arrests, including one crook at Ararat Technical school. Kerry Andrew Dristoll forced entry into the school at 0201 hours on the morning of Thursday, 3 July, 1986. He entered through a skylight and activated two alarm sections in the administration area. The response by police and security was nine minutes and they arrested him leaving the school after putting the skylight back in place.

Dristoll gets a mention as he was already on bail for 12 counts of burglary and he told investigating police he entered the school to find some cash to pay his lawyers for his court case the following Tuesday. You must give him some credit for thinking that far ahead!

On Tuesday, 8 July, 1986, a two section multi alarm break at 2119 hours resulted in the arrest of two 15-year-old youths at Eltham East Primary School, followed two hours later with the Police Dog Squad arresting a 21-year-old offender at Wembley Primary School in Footscray at 2345 hours, following a three section multi break. Our arrest rate was still hovering around the 40 per cent mark and I noted our response time for the Eltham East job was seven minutes, with Wembley Primary taking nine minutes, the same as Ararat.

No matter how hard we tried, it felt like our response times to school alarms would be slightly over the six-minute mark, which I had previously considered we needed to achieve if we were to be certain of making an arrest. While we had direct access to Police D24, two-way radio communication with our control room to, not only our officers, but also the Police Air Wing and dog squad, I think we all believed success was dependent on being lucky enough to have units in reasonably close response proximity to the school.

On the other hand, luck went both ways. When telephoned at home by our control room in the early hours one morning and told of an intermittent one section break alarm at a Glenroy school, I first declined to respond, suggesting we just monitor the alarm and see what transpired. In one way, I was placing faith in my design of the alarm giving, at least, a two section multi break, which at this time was not being received.

After a second telephone call 35 minutes later, again to be told of an intermittent one section break alarm, I reluctantly headed to the school. As I got closer, it finally went into multi section break and I arrested two male offenders leaving the school by a classroom window. They would have been in the school for at least 40 minutes and, lucky for me, they didn't cause any damage or set fire to the building in that amount of time.

While waiting for police, they confessed that all they were doing after forcing entry was sitting in a classroom having a chat and occasionally would walk into the corridor to make sure they hadn't been seen. It was after having a few cigarettes they decided to steal some equipment and hopefully also find some cash in the administration area of the school. This was why our alarms in the first instance were spasmodic but only until they went on to carry out the burglary.

After nearly 12 years as head of school security, the breakdown of my marriage and another relationship disaster, I decided to have a well-earned holiday in late July, 1986. Nigel Buckley was traveling to Israel as a representative of MAGAL Security Systems, who were designing and managing many of the most complex world security projects. He also needed to inspect their taut wire indicative fence along the Israel/Lebanon border.

The fence known as YAEL, was a physical security barrier combined with performance sensors, to keep control and provide a buffer zone following the 1982 Lebanon War, which was also known as Operation Peace for Galilee or the South Lebanon conflict, with the Palestine Liberation Organisation (PLO).

Following the withdrawal of most PLO operatives, an accord was finally reached in 1983 and, by January 1985, Israel commenced withdrawing most of its military but still maintained the necessary security buffer along the border due to other warring factions, such as the South Lebanon Army and Hezbollah, who refused to disarm. Nigel and I were to find out that cross border attacks were an intermittent problem on the border. Following our visit to Israel, we would visit the New York School Police and the Los Angeles Police Air Wing after a short stopover in Greece, London and France.

Despite this three week "holiday" not being a rest from school security, I was looking forward to it. As Officer in Charge of our Police Air Wing, Inspector Kieran Walshe, was kind enough to provide me with a letter of introduction to his counterpart of the Los Angeles Police Astro Division. They had been operational from around the 1960s with a fleet of Bell 47 helicopters, followed by a Bell 206 Jet Ranger.

Following two days in Athens, our passenger jet began its descent into Ben Gurion Airport and looking out the window, I noticed we were being accompanied by an Israeli jet fighter. It seemed that the never-ending fracas with its border neighbour, Lebanon, was still a cause for concern. This was readily apparent when, arriving at the airport, we were subjected to a strict security regimen and by armed guards holding Uzi open bolt submachine guns. It was the main international airport in Israel and situated approximately 20 kilometres from our hotel in Tel Aviv.

We stayed in excellent accommodation and I was lucky enough to visit Jerusalem and Bethlehem. It was apparent that school children on excursions were always accompanied by Uzi carrying security guards. The Western Wall in Jerusalem, also known as the Wailing Wall, is one of the most religious sites for Jewish people, who would place paper slips with written prayers into its cracks. What I found fascinating was the practice of the worshippers, regularly moving back and forth as they prayed, which looked like they were weeping or wailing, hence the name. Believed to be the birthplace of Jesus and situated about 10 kilometres south of Jerusalem, Bethlehem was where Christians make pilgrimage to the Church of Nativity, particularly during the Christmas season.

I learnt very quickly that you should carry your passport everywhere you go in Israel. Prior to inspecting the security buffer along the Israel/Lebanon border, Nigel and I decided to spend a day in the busy and popular resort town of Eilat which was approximately 352 kilometres from Tel Aviv, situated near the northern tip of the Red Sea. The city was a major tourist destination and we had to fly, leaving from Ben Gurion Airport to Ramon Airport in Eilat.

Unbelievably, I passed through security at Ben Gurion without my passport but wasn't as lucky when arriving at Ramon. An Uzi armed security officer demanded to see my passport which I had left in my hotel room and, being unable to produce it, I was escorted into a dark room for a strip search. And I mean a strip search. He even ran his fingers through my "yeah yeah" hair and was not happy, despite being intrigued with my hair style. Nigel was able to explain what had transpired with my passport, told him where we were from and, thankfully, due to having my school security identification card in my wallet, he allowed us through the armed check point.

I have been to several extremely hot places in my travels but Eilat was in a world of its own with temperatures getting up to 45 Celsius. It is worth visiting though, as you can see Saudi Arabia, a distance of only 20 kilometres from the resort beach, and the Ramon Crater in Israel's Negev Desert, the latter being the world's largest erosion crater.

Our inspection of the taut wire fences along the border, separating Israel and Lebanon, took a whole day and not without incident. The barrier technology provided a very cost-effective solution, as it also had 24-hour monitoring of sensors which provided aggregate signals and was mainly in place to prevent and deter Palestine terrorists from crossing the border into Israel undetected.

It was still prone to mortar attacks and, as we were enjoying a coffee and a chat with a lovely Israeli family, I heard a very distinct sound which caused me to hit the floor from their couch in full panic mode. A rocket attack landed just over the border from the Lebanese side and, as we would see later, it left a gaping hole in the road on which we had been travelling.

Everyone, including Nigel, enjoyed a good laugh at my expense but I had a good excuse after serving in Vietnam. The rocket launcher used was most likely a Russian made Katyusha type, also used in the Vietnam War and usually mounted on trucks which allowed mobility as needed. The sound of it incoming was very distinctive and, unfortunately, happened to be a regular occurrence for the Israeli people.

Conscription under the *Israeli Défense Service Law* (IDSL) also applied to all Israel citizens. Unlike our conscription, from the time of turning 18 unless they qualify for limited exemptions, including on religious grounds, women were required to serve for two years, with men serving for two years and eight months. The IDSL replaced the *Security Service Act 1949* which only required military draftees for national security emergencies.

I left Israeli feeling very uneducated. Compared to my school leaving certificate pass, Israel had one of the most well-credentialled, educated populations worldwide. The country generally offered free and compulsory education to its people from kindergarten through to year 12, with many graduating in due course with university degrees. In addition, their population, both linguistically and culturally, had no limits, with its people speaking at least two languages, including English and Hebrew, with the latter being the country's official language.

Our visit to New York was eye opening, especially for me. Under the Board of Education, New York's Board of School Safety had a security division which consisted of 1700 unarmed uniformed officers in 1982 with a $24 million allocation. Their 1986 security budget now included $5 million for a new security guard at each of the 95 elementary schools and two security guards at each of the 32 school districts. One of their main problems was serious violence during school hours, including attacks with weapons and students requiring medical treatment. Most schools were alarmed back to a central control room.

Schools in the United States had already been subjected to shootings, particularly in the mid to late 1970s, one of the most violent periods in their history. There were numerous school shootings, with one involving a 6-year-old girl at Grover Cleveland Elementary School where she fatally killed two students with a gun gifted to her from her father.

Two months prior to our visit, a hostage situation occurred at Cokeville Elementary School where a married couple held 150 students and teachers under a ransom demand of $300 million. It came to a very abrupt end when the wife set off a bomb, then was shot dead by her husband before he committed suicide. All hostages survived, although 79 were sent to hospital.

The New York Board of School Safety was in the process of reconsidering the introduction of metal detectors into each school. They were introduced into Thomas Jefferson High School in 1982 as an experiment but were discontinued following a protest by students. It was obvious our school security problems back home, thankfully, were not on the same violent scale as New York. Following our fleeting visit to Los Angeles Police Aero Division and, after spending a few days enjoying the sun in Hawaii, it was business as usual back home catching school crooks.

I was reasonably happy with our statistics for the year ending 1986 as the number of burglaries, when compared to 1982, was down from 2,626 to 1,553, as were our incidents of arson, dropping from 138 reports to 72 during 1986, with a total damage bill around the $2 million mark. I didn't place much weight on this figure because a couple of large fires in our light timber construction design schools would considerably raise the damage estimate.

Our silent intruder systems were a godsend, with 898 offenders arrested for the year, 68 per cent being juveniles under the age of 17 years. This brought our total number of offenders arrested by our alarm network to just over 4,600, many being repeat offenders and known to police. At this point, we determined that most of the juvenile offenders were attending the schools they burgled or other schools nearby.

We looked forward to 1987 and were increasing our security staff from 17 to 25 officers. Our message was hopefully getting through; that you ran the risk of being detected and arrested if you broke into a Victorian school. However, there were to be two defining arrests I made which would ultimately determine, once again, what direction in life I would take.

27

Two Defining Arrests

On the way to visit my two daughters in St Andrews late one evening, a call came over the two-way radio system for, 'any units in the vicinity of Diamond Creek Technical School.'

A Police Dog Squad unit and I both radioed our control room advising that we would respond but we were both about 10 minutes off. Edo was sitting in the back seat excitedly, listening to the chatter coming from the radio.

Unfortunately, he had to remain in my vehicle as the Police Dog Squad unit had priority, or as we would often say, 'had first bite of the cherry.' The multi break alarm activations were coming from the trade wing area located at the southern end of the school. I was the first unit to arrive, so I quietly proceeded to the outside of the building in alarm where I observed a 25 to 30-year-old male methodically searching several areas. I waited for him, knowing the dog unit would not be far off. He then opened a set of double doors, threw some items out and was about to depart with his goodies or so he thought.

I really had no choice but to place him under arrest before the dog squad unit arrived. To say he was a smart arse was an understatement, but I handcuffed him and waited for police. The senior constable from the dog squad was rather annoyed because I made the arrest despite knowing the police dog unit was attending. I tried to explain I had no choice, to no avail and he left the area very pissed off.

A few months after I made a statement to Eltham Police. Our burglar was pleading not guilty as he stated he had been walking through the school grounds, minding his own business when, without cause, I placed him under arrest.

The matter was listed at the Eltham Magistrates Court where, after giving compelling evidence of what I observed on responding to a silent alarm and why I arrested the offender, I was subjected to vigorous cross examination by his barrister.

He said words to the effect, 'Mr O'Neill, I put it to you the defendant was simply walking through the school grounds and you placed him under arrest without reason, that's correct, isn't it?"

Luckily, I recalled learning from our experienced member of the Police Arson Squad to keep your answers short and where possible, limit them to one word. After looking around the court room, I replied, 'No.' He then responded, 'So you say Mr O'Neill, you had good reason to arrest him?' My reply was, 'Yes.'

The barrister put the same question again, about walking through the school grounds and his client being detained without cause. By this stage, I was getting rather annoyed and said words to the effect, 'You have already asked me that question.' Learned counsel tried it again, so I just looked at him and then slowly said, 'I have already responded to that question.'

He kept at me, causing me to say, 'Sorry, but I don't understand your line of questioning.' His blunt reply was, 'Don't you understand the Queen's English?'

By this stage, I was more than aware of conducting myself

in a professional and appropriate manner, but my reply was very unprofessional and inappropriate because of my annoyance and frustration with his repeated line of questioning, 'Yes, she lives in England!'

The magistrate was very unimpressed, as was the police prosecutor, who both gave me a dressing down and I left the court with my tail between my legs. The defendant also left but at least I got to go home that night, whereas he didn't, due to being found guilty. He had priors for burglary and was sentenced to a term of imprisonment.

In my position as Manager, Security Services Group, this defining moment was the first time where I believed I could do a better job than some of these lawyers. So, maybe I should give some serious thought to a career in law.

I had already determined I needed to achieve a higher standard of education, even if it was only the Victorian Certificate of Education (VCE), which was replacing the Higher School Certificate (HSC). After returning from Israel, I felt I needed to hold more qualifications than just my leaving certificate and passing the Investigators Course at the Victoria Police Detective Training School. Compared to a lot of other people, I was not highly educated.

My second defining moment involved an arrest I made at Coomoora High School, once again bringing me a step closer to our legal system. This time, though, it involved me as the alleged perpetrator, albeit a civil cause of action citing battery or assault. Defending the claim against me involved, not only the Ministry's Legal Office, but a well-known top silk who would be appointed later as Victoria's Director of Public Prosecutions and then become a well-respected Supreme Court trial judge.

The moment came about due to our concern with school

crooks becoming more sophisticated when addressing our silent alarm approach. This became readily evident in late 1986. We were experiencing several break-ins at schools in the Springvale South area, where the telephone line providing the mode three connection to the school would be cut at the Telecom pit, before the school premises were forcibly entered and selected equipment, especially computers, would be stolen.

By cutting the selected school's telephone line, there would be no activation of the alarm by our control room. This meant we would not be aware of any issue until we were advised of the burglary by the school principal or on determining we had not received any day or night switch off or on activation. One of our technicians would then attend the problem school to determine if there was a technical fault but would find that the alarm mode three, being the line connection, had been cut.

It was obvious we had to think of a way to defeat this new determined approach by a particular group of offenders. On consultation with our security contractors, Nigel Buckley came up with the idea of transferring one mode three connection to the other adjacent school, so the two school alarm lines were connected to each other. In other words, if there were two schools within close proximity, we could simply wire up one separate school's mode three connection to an adjacent school.

The two schools close together in the targeted radius were Coomoora High School and Coomoora Primary School, both practically adjacent to each other. This meant if Coomoora High School was targeted by our perpetrators cutting the mode three connection for this school, there would actually be no disconnection because the mode three was connected to the adjacent primary school phone line.

The other alternative was to swap over the mode three

connections so the high school alarm and primary school alarms were reversed. If one selected line was cut, we would still receive an alarm notification from the targeted school. The problem with this alternative approach was one school was still exposed with its line being cut, so the preferred approach was to connect two schools together. Coomoora High had already been targeted with its mode three connection being cut and we believed the miscreants would try again, having succeeded the first time.

I was staying at a friend's place in Mount Waverley when I was paged around 4am one morning by our control room who stated Coomoora High School was in alarm with multi section breaks coming from a portable classroom. Being the closest unit, I immediately responded and D24 Communications were also advised to assist with a responding unit.

On my arrival at the school, the alarm notifications had just stopped, so it was possible we had missed the offenders or, at best, they would still be in the vicinity of the school building. As no Police Dog Squad unit was attending, I took Edo with me to the alarmed portable and saw two adult males about to leave with computers.

One offender was still on the roof of the building but he was about to climb down. The other offender was placing a number of items into a bag, when he looked up and saw us approaching. He immediately dropped everything and took off, so I let Edo loose as he loved the chase. However, the other offender, now on the ground, distracted Edo so he made a beeline for him, only to be hit over the head with a jemmy bar, which momentary stunned him. It was obviously painful, as poor Edo yelped.

To say I was very miffed with my dog being belted over

the head is an understatement. I managed to detain our friend after a rather vigorous scuffle and it's fair to say, we both got a few good punches in before Edo left the offender with some decent dog bites on his thigh, which was bleeding profusely, as was his nose.

When one of our school security officers, Phil Brown, arrived on the scene, his first words were, 'Geez Chief, you've given him a good smack around.'

I explained to Phil that it went both ways and he totally agreed when he saw the cuts and abrasions around my head.

We placed the offender into the back of the security vehicle and I "politely" asked him where he and his mate had parked their getaway vehicle. At this stage, police had still not responded so we drove around the back streets of Springvale South looking for their vehicle. Our handcuffed friend, sitting beside a very angry Edo, was more than happy to direct us to their parked vehicle in a nearby street.

The plan was for Phil to hand over our arrest to police, who had now arrived at the school, while Edo and I would hide behind a bush in a local residence's front yard, hopefully to arrest the other offender on returning to the vehicle to make his getaway.

I waited impatiently for about 30 minutes but the only activity was the houseowners enquiring why I was sitting in their front yard. After explaining what I was doing and showing my identification, they retreated inside. No luck in catching the other crook so I made a statement at Springvale police station on what had transpired, noting our arrested felon was not at all happy. That morning, I decided to see a doctor due to a rather large cut above my eyebrow and a thumping headache, plus I thought a medical certificate regarding my injuries might be useful.

We subsequently determined that the offenders had cut the telephone connection, thinking there would be no alarm activation from their targeted high school. It explained why they were still at the school 15 minutes later after forcibly entering the building through the roof. Their sophisticated attempt had been outsmarted and all the arrested offender copped, apart from me belting him in self-defence, was several charges, including assaulting me under s.31 of the *Crimes Act 1958* (Vic). Despite police making several enquiries without assistance from the one in custody, they were unable to determine the identity of his co- accused.

Months later, I received a telephone call from a process server who needed to personally serve me with a writ, alleging assault causing serious injury and loss, in respect of my arrest at Coomoora High school. Deciding to accept service, as I didn't have any choice, I arranged to meet the process server at the local Mt Waverley 7 Eleven, where he handed me the documents. It was now obvious I needed to obtain urgent advice, so our legal office arranged for me to meet with Paul Coghlan, an eminent barrister.

My previous exposure to the legal system was with making any necessary statements to police in respect of an arrest and then, as required, giving evidence in court and being subject to cross examination. My only introduction to a lawyer was in court so this was a first for me. Paul could only be described as a very affable person who always got straight to the point. I think his counsel was not only because he specialised in criminal matters but also because the lawyer from our legal office personally knew him.

Paul was normally involved in prosecuting for the state, notably as lead prosecutor of our former friend, "Captain

Dingy" Harris and "Mr Stinky". I was not going to tell him about my innocent involvement with Harris at our first and only conference when he asked me to tell him what transpired.

I had only said a few words when he stopped me, saying, 'Don't beat around the bush, tell me exactly what happened.' I did that and then produced my medical certificate, which set out in detail the injuries inflicted by the now plaintiff with me as defendant.

It was explained to me, if the matter proceeded and I defended it, it would be before a jury and the plaintiff only had to prove, on a balance of probabilities, meaning more likely than not, I had committed a battery on him, causing injury and loss. In other words, I made intentional contact with his body which was either harmful or offensive. Of course, the problem our plaintiff had was that he was committing a burglary, resisted arrest and I used as much force as necessary to not only defend myself but to place him into custody.

If it did proceed before a jury, they would consider the reality of what had taken place, that the force I used was proportionate when under pressure and handcuffing him was warranted to prevent him escaping. Paul felt it wasn't worth the effort providing a defence, unless agreement couldn't be reached. It was highly likely the plaintiff was only going down this path in order to negotiate the withdrawal of some of the charges laid by police, possibly for assaulting me.

His learned counsel was most welcome and our legal office was able to reach an agreement with, not only police prosecutors withdrawing some of the charges including those relating to him assaulting me, but with the defendant's lawyers on the basis the writ was discontinued. This was finally agreed to and he appeared before a magistrate at the city court in Russell

Street. I also attended to see him being sentenced, hopefully to a term of imprisonment but that didn't happen. The miscreant was sentenced with conviction to a corrections order and to undertake unpaid community work.

Despite this whole saga being quite stressful, I again considered whether my future career should be in law as I found the legal system fascinating. It was obvious with the stresses of my current job, I would most likely burn out but if I went down the path of qualifying for the legal profession, it would be a much less stressful occupation.

Time would tell if that was the direction I would take, whereas Paul Coghlan, subsequently appointed as a Supreme Court Judge in 2007, would eventually preside over many highly publicised criminal trials, with his usual no frills but fair approach.

As to our offender, sorry, former plaintiff, I am not sure whether he went on to bigger and better things, but I did come across him some months later and this time not by way of an arrest. While on patrol one Saturday afternoon, who should I see but my "boxing mate" carrying out his community work in the school grounds and obviously under supervision. I enjoyed the fact that he recognised me by the huge grin on my face.

28

Crime has no Boundaries

In June 1987, I was one of many guest speakers at a three-day Crime At School Seminar in Canberra. It was to look at all aspects of crime in schools, including burglary and arson, offending during school hours, assaults, sex offences, offensive behaviour and the illicit use of drugs and alcohol. A number of papers were presented by various speakers, including one on preventative policing in Queensland schools, arson and vandalism in schools in New South Wales and even a paper on an actual school community-based police officer in the Northern Territory.

It was interesting to note that our security orientated initiatives, providing silent alarms in our Victorian schools, was a first in any Australian school system. Although, we were now gradually being closely followed by New South Wales and Western Australia.

I listened attentively to Queensland's approach, particularly the adoption of a preventative program, which included the reciprocal approach between school principals and their State Police Juvenile Aid Bureau. This community relations policy also included a Police School Liaison Unit tasked with providing lecturers to schools to discuss topics such as crime and its consequences, while at the same time, explaining the legal system to its participants. They even had a special booklet titled, "A Guide to Professional Workers".

One program I found very interesting was called "Adopt a Cop". It was about schools and their students forming a close liaison with a police officer, who would regularly visit selected schools and gradually become more widely known in each respective school community. It was so successful that by the end of 1985, 167 Queensland schools had become involved.

In respect to New South Wales, I had previously spent a week in early 1976 with their school security officer, where it was again confirmed this state was also experiencing numerous incidents of school crime, especially arson. The speaker from the Education Department's Community Liaison Unit, Frank Meaney, largely focused on what he termed "guerrilla warfare", which was costing the taxpayer a massive repair bill of around $16 million per year due to school fires.

To combat this ever-increasing burden, the department had installed security rooms, steel bars on doors and over windows, security lighting, live-in caretakers and back to base silent security alarms. Frank was very complimentary when he referred to our very successful electronic surveillance system, which was now being followed in their schools. By this stage, they had only 50 schools connected to a control room by way of a silent alarm, with 77 arrests, but like us, there was still over 50 per cent of detected offenders escaping arrest.

While Frank was concerned about the cost of repairing and, in some cases, rebuilding schools, following a criminal act, he was also worried about the high costs involved in initially acting on notification of a school silent alarm activation, then costs for apprehending offenders, including the cost to the police department.

Mention was also made of the United States model, where armed guards were patrolling schools 24 hours per day, seven days a week. One comment he made was that our highly sophisticated silent alarm approach was in some way self-defeating. This was on the basis that, the more sophisticated our means of protection developed, our offenders would also become more sophisticated in evading protection. I was to subsequently find this very evident regarding the two schools in the Springvale area.

The Northern Territory approach was to introduce School Community Police Officers. They had 14 officers covering 13 schools and the scope of duties undertaken by each officer was not just in respect of a physical presence. Each officer would effectively become a member of the school staff and attend all related activities, including school council meetings and be seen as a valued member of the school community.

Their approach of having a uniformed police officer on site, generally on a day-to-day basis, might deter crime being committed after hours, especially against the school. Staff and students' acceptance of having police at their school would not happen overnight and, at the time of the presentation of this paper, the jury was still out as there had been no discernible reduction in school-based crime.

Evidence was also presented by three distinguished academics whose research found that juvenile offenders who attacked schools did so as a means of aggression and pay back, not just against their own school, but the education system in general. They also found that several young offenders in youth training centres told why they committed offences against schools. One reason was because of dissatisfaction with their school and its teaching staff.

In the last paper presented, teachers didn't escape without a mention. It was obvious that not only were students in the education system committing offences but teachers were also being subsequently charged and convicted. The paper also discussed how best to deal with their offending.

Another paper referred to the abolition of corporal punishment in Victorian schools. With the double hands strap punishment, I could personally relate to being given six of the best. In the Year of the Child in 1979, our Minister for Education, Lindsay Thompson, received a recommendation for the abolition of corporal punishment, which he rejected at the time but preferred and published a set of guidelines to retain such punishment only as a last resort.

However, in 1983, it was effectively banned. A set of guidelines titled "School Discipline Procedures" followed, setting out the adoption of detention and suspension of disruptive students. Regardless of this and, without the rigours of corporal punishment, I believed students would continue to attack their schools after hours as a form of pay back.

Before returning from the seminar, I was fortunate enough to spend an evening with Chief Inspector Phil Walliss, who was now seconded to the Australian Bureau of Criminal Intelligence (ABCI). The ABCI was established in 1981 to provide a means for the collection, collation and analysis of criminal intelligence for dissemination to other Australian-wide law enforcement bodies. This was in order to combat the ever-increasing threats of organised crime and, more specifically, in relation to the trafficking of illicit drugs. It was headed by Fred "The Cat" Silvester, a well-known and respected Victorian police officer, who would also achieve the rank of Assistant Commissioner. Fred was a former London "bobby" and also served in World War II. His exemplary service with Victoria Police also included being a detective in the Fraud Squad and with Licensing, Gaming and Vice.

We spent an enjoyable dinner consuming too many fine wines and, on returning to their unit headquarters located at a suburban police station, Phil jokingly breath tested me. At the time, the legal driving limit in Canberra was 0.08% and I recorded a reading of 0.11%, not much over it but it didn't cause a problem as, thankfully, I wasn't driving.

In April, 1987, the new Victoria Police Forensic Science Laboratory (FSL), which was initially located in Spring Street, Melbourne was opened at Macleod. By August, 1987, the actual strength of Victoria Police was 8,876 but its authorised strength was 9,100 sworn officers. Our arrest rate continued with an average of around 90-100 offenders per month, thanks to the excellent support provided by, not only our security officers, but also Victoria Police, in particular uniform units supported by the dog squad and Air Wing. However, before the end of 1987, two mass shootings, attracting extensive media attention, would occur and would have a profound impact on our state.

After being discharged from the Royal Military College at Duntroon due to his unsatisfactory conduct, Julian Knight, an unknown perpetrator at the time, carried out a mass shooting in Clifton Hill, Victoria. It became known as the Hoddle Street Massacre. Days earlier, upon returning from Canberra to Melbourne on his not so honourable discharge, Knight discovered that his girlfriend had moved on and his mother had converted his former bedroom into a living room. With no money and no ability to earn any, he took his frustrations out around 9.30pm on Sunday, 9 August, 1987. Over a 30-minute period, he had shot dead seven innocent civilians and wounded 19 others, some seriously, as he fired at passing cars.

I recall being on patrol that evening when our control room issued a warning to our officers to stay away from Hoddle Street due to the mayhem that was unfolding. A Police Dog Squad unit and the Air Wing headquarters at Essendon had advised our control room what was transpiring and said that many police units were responding, including Air 495.

Knight was subsequently arrested 45 minutes later but not before he fired three shots at Air 495 piercing the main fuel tank and causing the chopper to do a forced emergency landing on a sports field nearby. Knight, represented by defence barrister, Robert Richter QC, received seven concurrent sentences of life imprisonment with a non-parole period of 27 years. I personally don't think he will ever be released while he remains a risk to the public. Still, to this day, Richter appears pro-bono for Knight in respect of his unsuccessful applications for parole.

Unfortunately, on 19th August, 10 days after Knight's massacre, Michael Ryan went on a similar shooting rampage in Hungerford, England, where he shot dead 16 people, including his own mother and an unarmed member of the police force. Fifteen others were wounded but survived and Ryan subsequently committed suicide before he could be arrested. The excessive media publicity given to Knight's despicable crime was mentioned as a possible motive for the Hungerford massacre, despite no firm evidence.

Our continuing efforts paled into insignificance compared to these two massacres when a member of the Police Dog Squad and I attended a Coburg school alarm to find a fire burning in a classroom, following a forced entry. Fortunately, we were able to bring the fire under control by using portable fire extinguishers located in the school corridor.

This was followed by an arrest at a special school in Dandenong when I responded to a silent alarm from my then girlfriend, Edith's place. Despite Edith's home being only a few minutes away, I missed the crook by 10 minutes but I did find items left behind in the roof walkway between two classrooms and near overhead louvre windows. Two of the louvres had been removed to gain entry. Thinking the offender might return, Edo and I waited patiently in the classroom below. About an hour later, the offender arrived to collect the remainder of his stash, only to be arrested. He was about 12 years of age, which made me wonder why he was out doing a burglary in such early hours of the morning. Attending police were very concerned with his demeanour as he wouldn't stop crying.

As school crime has no boundaries, Catholic schools were also subject to burglary and fires and the Board of Education for Catholic Schools soon became aware of our successful school alarm program. I spent several days designing alarms for them, based on our specifications and even considered connecting their schools to our control room. It wasn't long before I realised, we had enough problems in our own schools and didn't need any more, so private monitoring was recommended.

The Victorian Public Service Association (VPSA), of which I was still a member, also represented prison officers and therefore welcomed the closure of K Division, also known as Jika Jika, following a fire which killed five prisoners on Thursday 29 October, 1987. It initially appeared to be the fault of the deceased, as they had barricaded themselves in their separate cells then set a fire causing them to die from the fumes. A subsequent coronial inquest, however, was to determine that the automatic cell door controllers had failed.

One deceased prisoner, Jimmy Loughnan, was a former close associate of Mark "Chopper" Read, who was serving a lengthy term of imprisonment after attacking and trying to abduct a county court judge in a vain attempt to get Loughnan released from incarceration. Loughnan then paid Read back by stabbing him repeatedly in a premeditated attack in jail. I don't think police would have been happy when it was announced that Craig Minogue, the convicted Russell Street Police HQ bomber, was one of the four other prisoners who survived by stacking a tennis net against their cells' section doors.

The year didn't end well for the police, our community and us, with our ever-present plague of school arson. In our case, a major fire at the Swan Hill High School on Sunday, 22 November, 1987 destroyed most of the school buildings. Graeme White attended the blaze and, as part of our normal practice, he made enquiries with local shopkeepers for any information. A milk bar owner provided some information about a young Aboriginal lad who came into his shop the day before boasting about his exploits with matches.

Graeme passed this information onto Detective Sergeant Neville Taylor of the arson squad who moved swiftly, arresting two boys, aged nine and 10, for burglary and criminal damage by fire. In the interim, the school's 800 pupils needed to be rehoused in temporary alternative accommodation. One of those arrested, subsequently moved to the Heidelberg area where he set fire to Olympic Village Primary School in Heidelberg West, causing extensive damage. The school, renamed Charles La Trobe Junior School, was set on fire for a second time, destroying several classrooms in March 2012.

Our community was rocked once again when another mass shooting took place on 8 December, 1987 at the Australian Post Offices in Queen Street, Melbourne. Frank Vitkovic, a university law degree dropout, shot and killed eight office workers and injured five others. Three office workers, including two wounded, tackled and disarmed him before he jumped from the fifth floor of the building, dying on impact.

A coronial enquiry, headed by Coroner, Hal Hallenstein, initially heard some criticism of attending police, but counsel assisting the court, Joe Dickson, immediately put that to rest when he submitted that the police response was satisfactory and no one died because of any perceived delay by responding officers.

Evidence was also given of the killer's mental state, that he hated a former school acquaintance who worked at the Queen Street building. Ultimately, it was open to determine that he could have been declared criminally insane under the *Mental Health Act 1959* (Vic), as it was clear he was a paranoid schizophrenic and could be likened to Julian Knight, the Hoddle Street gunman. Mr Hallenstein, as I was to later find out at a major school fire in Blackburn South, was a no-nonsense magistrate, who refused to allow suppression of images taken of Vitkovic from a fifth-floor security video. They were subsequently published after the inquest.

My personal life certainly changed for the better with my engagement to Michelle, my former colleague at Victoria Police, on Christmas Day, 1987. We had kept in touch over several years and her youngest brother, Tony, who also worked with my father, had played cricket against me a few times. Not knowing I was in a faltering relationship with Edith, Michelle sent me a 40th birthday card on 21 March, 1987, with the caption, 'You can't have your cake and ~~eat~~ 'Edith' it too'. Uncanny when you think about it and it certainly caused me to ponder on my chances, or perhaps lack of, with Michelle.

I got lucky, so to speak, and we were married in Box Hill on 12 March, 1988. The reception was at the State Schools Nursery and we honeymooned in Fiji. Nigel Buckley was my best man but my other best mate, Graeme White and I very nearly didn't make it to my own wedding. The night before, I was speeding along Waverley Road with Graeme in the passenger seat, when I accidentally ran into the back of a vehicle and wrote off the government car. As a result of the collision, we were both very sore from our aches and pains and I suffered a knee injury, causing me to struggle when kneeling at the appropriate times in the church. Neville Rohan was our Master of Ceremonies and, despite my injuries, it was a memorable wedding day. After renting out my Mt Martha home, I moved into Michelle's rental place in Toorak Road, East Hawthorn and back into suburban life with more call outs to alarmed schools nearby.

Our close liaison with Victoria Police also included arranging for schools and vacant ministry premises to be used for special investigations, particularly the importation of drugs into Victoria. One covert surveillance in 1983 was organised with police undercover operatives sitting in after hours at the Aspendale Primary School. It was not for me to enquire who was under surveillance, but I was told in confidence they were looking at a crook by the name of Christopher Dale Flannery, also known as "Mr Rent-a- Kill". Flannery had an extensive criminal record including terms of imprisonment for armed robbery, assaults, firearms offences and rape.

According to police, after his release from prison around 1980, Flannery became disenchanted working as a bouncer at Mickey's Disco in St Kilda, so he ventured into contract killings, hence his nick name. One of his first contracts was the murder of Melbourne solicitor, Roger Anthony Wilson, evidently over a failed business venture, for which he was subsequently acquitted in October, 1981. He became a suspect in up to a dozen murders, including the attempted murder of Sydney police officer, Michael Dury. Flannery's luck finally ran out on 9 May, 1985 when he disappeared and was believed to be murdered. He has never been seen again.

We also assisted Chief Inspector Graham McDonald, officer in charge of a covert group of police who used one of our vacant buildings in Ferntree Gully Road as a base. We arranged for them to conduct covert surveillance from Templestowe High School which overlooked a suspected drug importer's place of residence. At the time, police had just been provided with phone tapping powers following amendments to the *Telecommunications (Interception) Act 1979* (Cth) in September, 1988.

Graham was eventually appointed as an Assistant Commissioner of Police in charge of its Ethical Standards Department. We held him in high esteem as, of course, did Victoria Police and he even attended Graeme White's wedding. Sadly, this well respected and very likeable police officer was to pass away from illness and is still sadly missed.

I already had the pleasure of previously discussing school security with the Principal of Templestowe High, Ken Fraser, and, without hesitation, he gave us permission for Graham's undercover police to utilise part of the school for overnight covert surveillance. Ken, a former Essendon player with 198 VFL games to his credit, including two premierships in 1962 and as captain in 1965, was also later inducted as a member of the Australian Football League Hall of Fame. I telephoned Ken one day to explain how we missed arresting two offenders in the process of a burglary at his school the night before, so that of course gave me the opportunity to tell him of my days when barracking for Essendon. I didn't dare mention Essendon's three-point loss in the 1968 Grand Final against Carlton.

Regarding the two that got away, I admit that was my fault. On responding to a silent alarm, I went to enter the school from a set of double doors at the end of a corridor, only to find they were locked from the inside. This gave the offenders a warning they had been detected and they took off before I could get anywhere near them. Ken was fine and had no problems with me because they escaped without taking the stash of stolen school property left behind in their haste to get away.

Drugs in schools had previously been discussed very minimally at the Canberra Crime at School Seminar and so I wrongfully assumed it was not a problem for us. It is fair to say that our schools do play a significant role in not only educating our children but also in preventing the illicit use of both drugs and alcohol. Around this time, the possible trafficking of drugs, in particular, marijuana, was occurring at certain schools and was brought to our attention. Arguably, it fell outside our charter of the prevention and detection of school crime but, nonetheless, I was more than happy to assist investigating police.

As a result and with the permission of each school principal, we attended at two secondary schools in Dandenong and another one in Croydon with Police Drug Squad officers and tracker dogs. After hours, a student locker search was carried out at each school but nothing was uncovered. Given I had concerns as to whether my role as Head of School Security included such a preventative measure, I still considered we needed to liaise and cooperate with Victoria Police in any event.

On 12 October, 1988, sadly two more police officers would be shot dead and, as a possible consequence, we began to assist Victoria Police in alarming their non 24-hour police stations with monitoring carried out by D24 Communications. The Walsh Street, Prahran shootings occurred when Constables Tynan and Eyre, who were responding to a possible stolen vehicle, were fatally gunned down in what would be known as the Walsh Street murders. The day before, Police Armed Robbery Squad officers had shot dead a crook, Graeme Jensen, in Narre Warren when he allegedly produced a firearm to prevent being arrested. Eight armed robbery officers were subsequently charged with murder with only Detective Robert Hill subsequently proceeding to trial.

Hill was acquitted by the Supreme Court in August 1995, noting the jury took less than 20 minutes to reach its unanimous not guilty verdict. Sadly, respected homicide squad investigator, Detective Senior Sergeant John Hill, after being charged as an accessory after the fact to murder for allegedly concealing evidence, committed suicide two months after being charged. He always maintained the charge had no merit.

The Walsh Street murders, allegedly carried out by a group known as the "Flemington Crew", including the notorious Victor Pierce, a member of the infamous Pettingill family clan, were considered by some to be a payback in respect of Jenson's death and two other deaths of armed robbery suspects by police in 1987. Four suspects, including Pierce, were ultimately charged but later acquitted by a jury in the supreme court, while two other suspects, Jedd Houghton and Gary Abdallah, an associate of Jenson's, were shot and killed by investigating Police before they could be charged.

As a footnote, Pierce was to cop his right whack in May, 2002 when shot dead by Andrew "Benji" Veniamin who claimed, 'If I don't get Victor, he'll get me first.' Benji didn't last long as he was later killed by Mick Gatto, who successfully pleaded self-defence and was acquitted by a jury.

In respect of Abdallah, police officers, Cliff Lockwood, who had emptied seven shots into Abdallah, and Dermot Avon, who never fired a shot, were both subsequently acquitted of the murder in 1994. Coroner, Hal Hallenstein, effectively found the deceased had brought it upon himself and said, 'Abdallah has contributed to a sequence of events leading him to being fatally shot by picking up and pointing at Lockwood an imitation revolver reasonably believed to be real.'

In due course, I would be lucky enough to witness firsthand, the brilliant defence of Lockwood by Robert Richter, QC.

29

Not a Good Year

We were still being well supported with funding by the Victorian government and the never-ending involvement and support of Victoria Police. There was immense satisfaction in arresting offenders in the act of burglary, especially before they could carry out anything more sinister. We still needed to think outside the square though and, by this stage, our expanded covert surveillance team was to be used mainly as a stop gap measure on an as-needed basis.

The installation of our silent alarms continued at a very effective detection rate and we put in temporary measures, such as portable silent alarms as required. Our undercover operatives, known in the media as the "school sleep patrol", would also move from school to school.

In addition, our patrol group continued to conduct regular patrols of schools which were being subjected to repeated acts of vandalism. Graffiti was now starting to rear its ugly head. Our operational role also extended to assisting investigating police in particular the arson squad and local CIBs, following major school fires. I also needed to continue to broaden my knowledge of state-of-the-art security measures to stay ahead of offenders who were hell bent on entering our schools to steal and cause damage.

With that aim in mind, in April, 1989, I attended an International Security Conference and Expo in London, England, which focused on the use of security technology in crime prevention and other countermeasures in protecting public buildings and property. With some satisfaction, I found we were still ahead of most other government organisations in our prevention and detection of school crime, but it was certainly very evident that crime in schools was an ever-increasing worldwide problem.

When in England with Michelle, we were both saddened by the fatalities at a football match at Hillsborough Stadium in South Yorkshire. The "Hillsborough disaster" occurred during a FA Cup semi–final soccer match and because of overcrowding, 97 supporters died and 766 suffered injuries. According to local police, it initially appeared that drunkenness and hooliganism was the main factor, but a later investigation initially determined it was due to a lack of crowd control. The aftermath subsequently resulted in several safety improvements at English football grounds but following a coronial inquest, there was also a finding of a lack of a duty of care by both police and ambulance responders.

After a few weeks touring Europe by train, the final leg of our holiday was a week in Hong Kong. Unfortunately, our flight home to Australia was delayed due to a massacre in Beijing, China. The student-led Tiananmen Square protests, demanding greater political freedoms, were at first ignored by the communist government, but on 3 June, 1989, Chinese troops took control, firing bullets at random, crushing and arresting the protesters. On 5 June, 1989, a civilian stared down a line of tanks and the photo taken would ultimately become the protest's defining worldwide image.

In support of the Tiananmen Square protesters and, showing their disdain for the Chinese Communist Government, large protests also took place outside our hotel in Nathan Road, Kowloon. Out walking that night, Michelle and I came across thousands of protestors running down the road, also known as the Golden Mile. Many were carrying placards written in Chinese. We couldn't understand them and had no idea what was happening. It was certainly not a peaceful protest with many police in riot gear charging at the protestors. Michelle and I were ordered off the streets and told to go back to our hotel. It was not until the following morning when we were informed by the hotel staff what had occurred, both outside the hotel and in Beijing.

The Chinese government announced that only about 200 civilians, including several dozen security personnel, perished in the Beijing Massacre but the toll was believed to be in the thousands. Over the coming days, numerous aircraft were diverted from Hong Kong and other countries to Beijing to pick up passengers trying to leave the city, thereby also causing our flight home to be delayed.

It was with some relief that we arrived home safely, but family news, both happy and sad, awaited us. We were overjoyed to hear that Michelle's sister, Bernadine, had given birth to her first child, a precious daughter, and they were there to welcome us home. Our sad news was, despite being given an all clear from cancer before we left Australia in March, Michelle's father, Mick, had passed away in our absence. His cancer was to return with a vengeance and the Beijing Massacre had put a stop to us being home in time for his funeral, which had only been a few days earlier.

Another sad passing was soon to follow. Nigel had been

looking after Edo during our absence and on our arrival home, Edo enthusiastically greeted us. He had been well looked after and loved by Nigel's family, but he couldn't wait to get back on the job.

Waiting on my desk on my first day back was a briefing note raising concerns over the exposure of our schools and students following an incident in a local kindergarten in May, 1989. Staff and students had already been subjected to two previous kidnappings, courtesy of Edwin Eastwood, but the kindergarten incident was on another level.

On Tuesday, 9 May, 1989, an angry and disgruntled armed man, separated from his wife and children, poured petrol over four children and held them hostage for seven hours at a kindergarten in Hawthorn. We certainly had no jurisdiction over kindergartens but this was an incident which again highlighted how our education facilities and its occupants could be targeted. After surrendering to police, the offender, Serafettin Huseyin, was to ultimately serve 14 years in jail for the kidnapping and serious injury to four children, who suffered extensive chemical burns.

There was no easy answer to whatever preventative measures we could put in place, other than having security officers at all our schools, which was ultimately the New York school security approach. Earlier on 17 January, 1989, another shooting at a Cleveland school in Stockton, California saw five students killed with 29 wounded, when a lone gunmen fired over 100 rounds into the schoolyard using an AK47.

A survey, conducted by the American School Health Association, found around three per cent of school students had carried a handgun to school on at least one occasion, during a school year. In Victorian schools, the only thing in our favour was the limited access to weapons. Hopefully, the Hawthorn incident and our two previous kidnappings would not lead to more incidents and follow the path of the United States.

Despite Edo being quite well and happy in himself, it was obvious he was having issues with his back legs. He was nearly 10 years old, so retirement time was fast approaching where he would have to forget about chasing crooks. This became readily apparent early one morning when I was called out to attend a school alarm just off Princes Highway, near St Kilda. I let him off the lead to chase after an offender who was making a getaway down the middle of the street.

Unfortunately and being very unusual, the crook outran Edo and made a clean escape, albeit leaving items stolen from the school behind on the roadway. Edo limped back and, at that point, I had no choice but to place him into retirement where he could live a life of comfort and eat his favourite food, roast chicken.

This now left me, not only without a four-legged companion, but effectively, without any personal protection in what was becoming an increasingly dangerous occupation. This was so apparent when an offender escaped from my clutches at John Gardiner High School, which was only one minute from where Michelle and I were living in Toorak Road. I failed to make the arrest when he quickly realised he had been detected.

Some weeks later, though, I arrested two young offenders at Auburn South Primary school, adjacent to John Gardiner High, when they forcibly entered the canteen and were detained within minutes of the silent alarm activation. However, given I was being called out on a regular basis to attend silent alarm activations, I needed a trained dog to, not only protect me, but, of course, assist in the arrest of school offenders. Hopefully, I could find one who loved the chase.

I made enquiries with Sergeant Russell Moore from the Police Dog Squad, hoping they had another Rommel. They did have another German shepherd, Rajah, who was quite well trained, or so Russell told me, but not in the same class as Rommel. The only problem they had with Rajah was, he would run off on every discharge of weapons at pistol practice. Despite this quirk and Edo's annoyance at having to contend with another dog in the house, Rajah was soon to become my faithful companion and, at times, not so faithful.

To say Rajah was determined, had his own ways and a very stubborn streak was an understatement. On one occasion, when he was sitting in the back seat of my security vehicle, he would not allow me to get in. He was snapping away and banging his head against the rear side window. On another job, when seeing a police divvy van with lights and sirens pull up at a school, he literally jumped from the back seat headfirst into the front windscreen, leaving a rather large crack and also stunning himself. On other occasions, when he would see police, Rajah would become very excited and try to jump into their cars, so I think his problem on a pistol range was one of many.

Despite his faults, he made a number of arrests, one occurring in the early hours of the morning at Ashwood High School, when he chased down an offender fleeing the school after being detected by its silent alarm. There were two offenders, both working as Telecom technicians but one, unfortunately, got away. Apparently, they would commit burglaries while out working on faulty telephone lines. He eagerly took Graeme White and myself back to his work vehicle, but I think he was very cooperative only because of Rajah baring his teeth before leaving a decent bite mark.

Regarding all types of school crooks and their diverse occupations, there was another interesting arrest we made at Prahran High School in company with the Police Dog Squad. I left Rajah in my vehicle as the canine unit was already in attendance and we searched the school building in alarm but it first appeared we may have missed out on making an arrest. The police dog, however, had other ideas and he kept going back to one office in the administration area and barking, wanting to get in. The call took place after hours and I was with my brother-in-law, Trevor, so he attended the school with me. As we had already searched this admin office, we were not all that interested when the police dog would not leave it.

However, the dog had other ideas, so we decided to have another look. Lo and behold, there was our felon, hiding under a desk. Like our Telecom worker, he was also out on the job, but this time it was with a well-known clinical and pathology agency. He just "happened" to drive past the school and, seeing an open window, decided to have a look inside. Good luck in telling that one to the court. Trevor was so impressed with our arrest, he started to think about leaving his government employment working in fraud investigation, to join our security staff but eventually decided against such a career move.

As we approached the end of 1989, one of our busiest nights on the job was "Muck Up Day", being the last day the Year 12s would supposedly spend at their school, prior to end of year annual examinations. Unfortunately, many students went out on the grog before returning to their school at night to carry out a number of practical jokes. They would often enter school buildings in whatever way they could, to leave behind a message in respect of their attendance and school experiences. If they didn't enter a building, they would, nonetheless, leave a parting message known as "dicktation" on the school oval.

End of year pranks became a regular occurrence across Victoria and we would always put as many security vehicles as possible on the road to patrol schools. It was not uncommon for responding units, including police, to make as many as 100 arrests every muck up day and I recall our best effort was 126 offenders arrested, either in school buildings, tripping alarms or committing offences in the grounds. Our radio network was constantly abuzz with never ending calls for units "in the vicinity of" and it was not uncommon to finish responding to calls until around 6am the next morning.

Many schools would have their own staff in attendance overnight to try to prevent damage from happening but, unfortunately, Mt Waverley High School did not take any precautions and were targeted. I knew the school well from having previously arrested a crook after Edo had chased him down. Luckily for the school on this particular night, it was the last one on our patrol sheet before eating a well-earned breakfast at Dennys, our favourite 24-hour restaurant in Burwood.

In company with Graeme at about 5am, we were checking a portable building at the rear of the school when we came across a fire lit in the doorway and about to take hold. As we had fire extinguishers in our security vehicle, we were able to extinguish the blaze without too much damage but little did we know at the time, what was awaiting us over the next 18 months regarding school fires.

We thoroughly enjoyed our breakfast at Dennys after a long night patrolling schools but, on a funny note, I went to the toilet after we ordered. Being absolutely exhausted, I inadvertently entered the ladies. Sitting in the cubicle, I happened to notice a pair of red heels clunk past, followed by another pair but of a different colour. It was obvious I had made a mistake, so I sat there for at least 10 minutes until the coast was clear before quietly tiptoeing out of the toilets and back to our table. For a fleeting moment, I could see media headlines that evening, 'Head of School Security arrested in women's toilet'.

'No intent, Your Worship,' and I could honestly plead it was entirely due to fatigue.

It was not a good end to the year with the passing of Edo on Christmas Eve morning after his back legs finally gave out. With much sadness, he was put to sleep after eating a whole roast chicken fed to him by my good mate, Graeme White, Michelle and me. My very faithful four-legged friend was sadly buried just outside our control room in a grassy tree area at Mount Waverley, so he could be close to his other home that he loved so much.

30

School Arson Out of Control

The number of school fires was to escalate during the period 1990-1992, to a degree where I finally came to the conclusion that, despite our hard-earned efforts, it was simply out of control. Since 1985, fires, burglary and vandalism were averaging around $5 million a year in costs to the Ministry of Education, of which half could be attributed to arson.

By the end of the financial year in 1992, we would unfortunately experience 136 school fires over a two-year period at an estimated cost of around $5 million alone and this was despite arson only accounting for one in every 50 offences involving school property crime.

The ministry, however, was not the only education body being subjected to school fires, noting a fire at Wesley College in Prahran in the early morning hours on Sunday, 19 November, 1989. Damage was estimated to be, at the very least, around $3 million. Being one of Australia's most famous and private schools, it had past students of some note, including former prime ministers, Sir Robert Menzies and Harold Holt. The fire not only destroyed the school library, but a collection of rare Greek and Roman antiques and a valuable collection of Australian books.

It was also noted at the time that school fires in the United Kingdom had increased from $18 million in 1987 to $55 million in 1990. In due course, they would introduce an amendment to their *Criminal Justice Act 1967* (UK), which would hold parents liable to pay compensation for their child's acts of vandalism. This was certainly a new approach but, despite us making inroads in seeking compensation restitution against the actual offender, suing parents was another level and I was not convinced of the success they would have with this approach.

At common law, the general principle is that a juvenile cannot be held liable in the absence of any statutory provisions, which then extends to parents and the question of vicarious liability. There clearly would have to be a distinct set of circumstances to make a parent liable. It would also raise the issue whether the parent had, in fact, been negligent and therefore directly liable for the actions of their child.

On Monday, 2 July, 1990 at 2141 hours, Frankston High School was set on fire with damage in the order of $1 million to its north wing. Unfortunately, fires lit by the same two offenders on another five occasions took place at this school over the next 12 months. Following the first fire at Frankston High, a further eleven schools were subject to arson attacks before the end of 1990. They included a major blaze at Upwey South Primary School on Monday, 9 December, 1990 at 0238 hours and 14 minutes later at 0252 hours, a fire at Ringwood High School, where the trade wing was effectively destroyed with damage estimated to be in the order of $300,000.

These two fires, although in reasonable proximity to each other, could not be considered connected and caused by the same arsonist as the travel distance between the schools was about 14 kilometres. But then again, the first fire, once lit, may not have taken hold for some time, giving the offender(s) time to travel to the high school to light the second fire. In any event, both fires were never solved.

On Sunday, 17 March, 1991, at 2157 hours, the trade block at Darebin Parklands High School in Thornbury went up in flames, causing $750,000 damage. It was followed by a massive fire at Lilydale Primary School, where the complete light timber construction (LTC) building was gutted and damage was estimated around the $1million mark. This school had already been subjected to a fire in 1980 when its annex was destroyed and the LTC wing was replaced, only to be burnt to the ground once again.

In addition to the five Frankston High School fires, 1991 didn't end well with a major fire at the Forest Hill Secondary College's Blackburn campus. On this occasion, two LTC wings, being the northwest and southwest wings, were set on fire and completely destroyed. I was working a night shift in the early hours of Monday, 7 October, 1991, when the call, for any units in the vicinity of, came over our radio network at 0223 hours.

Being only 10 minutes from the campus, I was flashed speeding through a red light but arrived to witness both wings burning furiously. Leaving Rajah in the vehicle because the flames would be intense, I could hear the Metropolitan Fire Brigade in the distance. I checked the school grounds hoping to find our arsonist watching intently but all to no avail. The MFB extinguished the fire after a solid one-hour battle but all that was left was a smouldering ruin.

The intense fire and the publicity given to, not only this fire, but our previous 17 fires for the year, resulted in our State Coroner, Hal Hallenstein, attending the next morning. Mr

Hallenstein had previously attended at the Wesley College fire, but this was the first occasion he would attend any of our fires.

Whilst the state coroner, under the *Coroners Act 1958* (Vic) (as amended), generally had the function to oversee and coordinate coronial services in our state, they also had the power to investigate deaths and could conduct an independent investigation into any fire in the public interest, how it happened and make recommendations to prevent similar fires.

I subsequently spent most of the morning with Mr Hallenstein going over the fire scene and found him to be very easy to talk with, not that he smiled much. Then again, given the nature of his charter, which would not be an enviable task, I could understand why. Many years later, I would appear before "His Honour", certainly not in similar circumstances, but this time, he would be very happy to smile back at me.

Our usual practice, following a school fire, was to either alarm the school if it was without that type of protection and, in the event the school was alarmed but still suffered an arson attack, we would carry out covert surveillance for at least a week with one of our officers sitting in the school after hours. A good example of this was on Saturday, 19 October, 1991, when there was a major fire at Deepdene Primary School with damage estimated around $500,000. Given our recent success in arresting two offenders in the process of lighting a fire at another school, we sat in Deepdene Primary for many nights after the fire. Unfortunately, one of our covert operatives possibly disturbed the same offenders at the school in the early hours of the morning only a few days after the first fire, so they avoided arrest.

The problem was, many of our school fires were not as a consequence of a forced entry, but a combination of either

Molotov cocktails thrown through a classroom window or simply papers and whatever else would burn, being stacked against a doorway. Because many of our schools were made of a light timber construction, they were quite combustible. It was around this time we again considered whether schools should have smoke detectors fitted and sprinkler systems installed.

Smoke detectors were widely used in large commercial and industrial buildings and generally connected to a central fire alarm monitored system. The United States had developed a standard for smoke alarms in 1967 but this was with residential home settings. In 1989, the National Fire Protection Association required that all US homes be protected by smoke alarms.

There was no such legalisation in Australia at the time and it was not until August, 1997, that smoke alarms became compulsory in all Victorian residential homes. As far as schools were concerned, smoke detectors would really only serve as a warning during school hours and, after hours, would be of little value. With arson attacks in Victoria, we were finding our schools very quickly became engulfed in flames.

Fire sprinkler systems were only ever used historically in factories and commercial buildings and history suggested that 99 per cent of buildings protected by fire sprinklers were completely protected and controlled any fire. The *Hotel and Motel Fire Safety Act 1990* in the United States required all hotels and conference centres to be equipped with sprinkler systems. In the early 1990s, many new American educational facilities were equipped with automatic fire detection systems monitored by local fire departments, which saw a dramatic improvement in reducing losses due to fire.

Fire sprinklers were first used in Australia as far back as 1886 and since then, they have become more prevalent in hotels, aged care homes and hospitals. Installation in our schools would certainly be a first but the problem was the cost of each installation, not to mention they would have to be student tamper proof. We did give some thought to at least equipping our new schools with fire sprinklers systems as part of their design specifications.

Portable relocatable classrooms, often situated away from the main school building, were also prone to attack and a number of relocatables were destroyed in a large fire at Pascoe Vale Girls High School in the early hours of Thursday, 21 November, 1991. The science block at Forest Hill Secondary College, was once again subjected to a fire just prior to midnight seven days later. This time though, it was not at the Blackburn campus.

Our view was the majority of school fires were arson, unless determined otherwise. It was also a matter of record that a vast majority of our school fires were late at night, with many occurring in the early hours of the morning. On that basis, you could only reach the conclusion they were not started by spontaneous combustion but the handiwork of some misguided miscreants in our community.

Our cooperation with Victoria Police reached a new level in 1992 when the number of flying hours for its Air Wing were doubled in an effort to, not only provide a rapid response to silent school alarms, but to reduce the troubling and repeated arson attacks. We still had direct radio communication with the Air Wing operations room at Essendon Airport. Effectively, the sky police or flying divvy van, as the Air Wing was later termed in a press article by journalist, Greg Thom, increased its airborne time by one hour per shift, meaning an extra 10 hours a week flying time solely concentrating on selected schools.

This also meant the chopper could respond and be above,

or land at, a designated school within minutes, whereas it would normally take our ground units much longer to arrive. A number of our officers, including me, would also be part of the "astro patrol crew" with Air 490 coordinating what schools we would patrol from the air.

The scourge of school fires continued with one of our largest fires in the first half of 1992 being the gym at Kealba High School which was extensively damaged. The school canteen at Glen Waverley High was set alight on Thursday, 16 April, 1992, causing damage around $50,000. This was followed by a major fire at 2328 hours on Monday, 25 May, 1992 at Box Hill North Primary and once again a light timber construction building suffered extensive damage in excess of $350,000. Unfortunately, Montmorency Primary School also suffered at the hands of an arsonist at 0203 hours on Saturday, 20 June, 1992, again a light timber construction building, causing damage estimated at $100,000.

The year ending 1992 was not to finish well with three major fires causing untold damage affecting, not only the schools in question, but their teaching staff, pupils and the community. On Sunday, 8 November, 1992, the Ringwood High School once again suffered a major fire which destroyed a number of classrooms, important school records, musical instruments and sports displays.

It didn't take long for another heartbreaking fire, this time at Patterson River Secondary College around 2345 hours on Tuesday, 1 December, 1992. I also attended this fire and, it's fair to say, the new principal, Bruce Devlin, was in a state of shock. An entire wing, including six classrooms, a staff room, typewriters, science equipment, school records and about 100 computers, were destroyed in the fire.

This school was effectively in its inaugural year as a new college, following the amalgamation of Bonbeach and Seaford Carrum High Schools. Much of the equipment lost had been donated by the local community and the computer centre that was destroyed was named after Mr Victor Mallett, a Bonbeach resident, who had donated $30,000 in equipment to the school. He also visited the scene and it was very obvious he was absolutely devastated by what had happened. The only shining light for the school was that students had minimal disruption as they were able to be relocated to a number of recent on-site portable classrooms.

One week later, Mitcham Primary School went up in flames destroying seven classrooms in the early hours of the morning on Wednesday, 9 December, 1992. Just prior to this fire, arsonists had tried again to burn down Blackburn Secondary College which was only one kilometre from the now destroyed primary school. The smouldering rags they left behind in a desk drawer failed to ignite, so most likely, they had another attempt at the primary school.

The fire at the primary school was dangerous enough to threaten neighbouring houses and the billowing smoke could be seen for many kilometres. Interestingly, the officer in charge of the fire investigations unit from the MFB made a comment to the media that, 'too few schools had sprinklers or smoke detection systems.'

Once again, I was faced with another shocked principal, Alan Cole, but he was resilient in that the school and its community would battle on with classes continuing as normal.

It was not all doom and gloom though and it's time to reflect on our most successful investigation including undercover surveillance, in trying to arrest school crooks. Our close liaison with Victoria police certainly came to the forefront when a concerted effort was put in place to finally arrest the Frankston High School arsonists on 12 August, 1991 and see them sentenced in June, 1992 to terms of imprisonment.

I was to form a close liaison with Detective Inspector Laurie Ratz, Crime Coordinator for Delta District and Frankston CIB who, like me, also said when he first started in the job, that he didn't know what he was in for. The small sign above his desk in his office stated, 'When I grow up I want to be a detective'.

At least he spelt it right and he would get a laugh when I told him about the floating cans saga at my first crime scene effort after completing DTS.

The Frankston High School arrests were indeed going to be a major victory for both of us. However, before detailing Operation Firebug, Laurie deserves his own chapter for his outstanding police service.

31

Laurie Ratz

Laurie was certainly going to experience some highs and lows in his distinguished career of 28 years with Victoria Police, joining the job in 1980 and reaching the rank of chief inspector. He was a well-respected Frankston copper, albeit Inspector in Charge of Crime Coordination on the peninsula, prior to being promoted to the rank of chief inspector and in charge of research, planning and budget control in the Victoria Police's Crime Department.

It's fair to say Laurie attracted publicity and in his words, he was a "media moth". His job saw some sad and horrendous crimes with investigations carried out under his watchful eye. These included the disappearance of Sarah MacDiarmid and the abduction and murder of Sheree Beasley.

Sarah was a 23-year-old woman who emigrated to Australia with her family from Scotland in 1987. On Wednesday, 11 July, 1990 she boarded a train at Caulfield station and after her friends disembarked at Bonbeach, Sarah alighted at Kananook railway station, never to be seen again.

Investigating police quickly formed the view she had been assaulted as they found Sarah's cigarette lighter, blood stains near her 1978 motor vehicle and drag marks leading into nearby bushes. Despite an extensive 21-day search by police members, including the Air Wing and Motor Boating Squad, Sarah was never found and was believed to have been murdered. Laurie was the police officer in charge of the investigation and was liaising with the homicide squad as well as Sarah's parents. He noted that the first day of the investigation was Friday 13th and, as it was to turn out, nothing would go well from an investigation point from that day on.

Despite the state government offering a $1million reward, no arrests were made, much to Laurie's frustration and annoyance and sadly for her parents who could not have any closure, let alone know what happened to their much-loved daughter. Police did have one strong lead when an informant told them she had been murdered by a group of drug addicts and they should have a close look at Jodie Jones, a known prostitute who had boasted to others that she had murdered Sarah. Before dying in 1991 from a drug overdose, Jones had numerous priors, including manslaughter and, although she remained a person of interest for some time, she vehemently denied she was involved and was never charged.

Upon his promotion to chief inspector, Laurie said if there was one thing he could change, it would be to bring some closure for Sarah's parents. To his credit, he still had hope and at a memorial service to mark the 20th anniversary of Sarah's disappearance, her parents also remarked they had never given up that one day there would be an answer to what happened or that their daughter would still come home. Although Laurie remained very frustrated the case was never solved, he still holds the firm view that you never know what is around the corner.

Another sad moment in Laurie's distinguished career was the kidnapping, rape and murder of 6-year-old schoolgirl,

Sheree Beasley. This innocent little girl disappeared on Saturday, 29 June, 1991 and her badly decomposed body was not found until three months later in Red Hill on Tuesday, 24 September, 1991. Laurie was on leave when Sheree's remains were found and her death and subsequent investigation, understandably, had an untold impact on him and other investigating police.

Following the abduction, witnesses told police they saw a middle-aged male driving a vehicle containing a very distressed child. Some months later, a psychotherapist with a client by the name of Robert Arthur Selby Lowe, became suspicious with some of his comments and notified police of her concerns. Due to a number of convictions for indecent exposure involving young girls, Lowe was well-known to police.

After further investigation, including police covertly taping his psychotherapy sessions, Lowe was subsequently charged and, during his trial, he finally made admitted to strangling Sheree and disposing of her body. He was sentenced to life without parole and died in prison in November, 2021. I don't think any of us, including Laurie, would have felt any remorse for the passing of this former Sunday school teacher and church elder.

Laurie was to gain immense satisfaction with the charging and imprisonment of two offenders for the Frankston High School fires in what he described as a "major victory", for not only him and Frankston CIB, but our Security Services Group. When interviewed by journalist, Matt Deighton, and prior to his promotion, Laurie stated, 'It was not only due to police, but the state school security who put in hours and hours.'

I think it is fair to say we both became very frustrated not being able to identify those responsible until after the sixth fire but in our numerous meetings, Laurie always tried to keep us positive. He often said, 'They will make a mistake, just wait and see.'

How right he was because it all came to fruition around 2330 hours on the night of Monday, 12 August, 1991.

Highly respected, Laurie was a pleasure to work with and, after leaving Victoria Police in 1998, Laurie took up a position with the Qantas Group Security. He became Special Risks Manager with the Insurance Council of Australia about 10 years later and was involved in the coordination of the industry's response to national disasters such as the Victorian bushfires in 2009. A very distinguished career to say the least and in his own words, Laurie was, 'certainly a bloke who tried his best.'

32

Operation Firebug
Frankston High School Fires

Frankston High School was a large multi campus co–educational facility situated in Foot Street, Frankston. Occupying two interacting sites and built in 1924, it offered education for years 7-10 and senior years 11 and 12. It was considered to be a very proud school, not only in providing academic excellence but with strong parental support had formed close links with the local community.

The school's principal, Ken Rowe, was ably supported by a diverse range of excellent teachers but they were soon to have their spirits lowered by a spate of deliberately lit fires.

Following the first fire on Monday, 2 July, 1990, effectively destroying the school's north wing, our firm policy was to place any school that had suffered a fire, under patrol for a number of weeks. The school was already alarmed and the first notifications to our control room was the fire itself as it had been started from outside the building. The close surveillance given to the school seemed to be successful as nothing more happened until January, 1991 when two fires were lit: the first at 0015 hours on Wednesday, 2 January, 1991, followed by another only seven days later at 2302 hours on 9 January, 1991.

Like the fire in July, 1990, we only received alarm notifications at 0015 hours when the actual fire was burning and certainly not as a result of any forced entry. The second fire was clearly due to a forced entry and it appeared the arsonist(s), using an accelerant, had set the fire in a stack of papers. The fire on 2 January, 1991 had occurred in the junior block of the school with damage estimated at $175,000. The fire on 9 January, 1991 was in the senior administration block causing damage in the order of $100,000.

Following a meeting with Inspector Laurie Ratz, we decided the school needed to be placed under better surveillance by the use of close circuit television cameras, as well as our patrols. This type of video surveillance would allow video cameras to transmit a signal to our control room by the school telephone line. In view of two of the fires being lit without any forced entry into the building, the thinking at the time was we could then observe any activity that was taking place after hours.

Such surveillance methods were not uncommon as in 1968, New York became the first city in the United States to install video cameras as a means of fighting crime, particularly street crime. Similar initiatives had been tried in the United Kingdom and a number of businesses prone to burglary had also implemented this form of surveillance. It was also hoped by installing CCTV cameras around the school it would serve as a form of deterrence to any would-be offenders.

A problem we had was achieving real time pictures back in our control room. We were receiving the images but there was a time delay of 45 to 60 minutes. The technology we were effectively experimenting with meant that, while the CCTV was recording around 25 frames a second, once it was being fed into a telephone line, it was in a time lapse. This meant one to three frames every second were being fed to a telephone line as in the example of a fax machine.

Another issue we faced was too much data was being transmitted, resulting in it banking up while waiting to gain access before being received by our control room. We tried this form of surveillance but technically, it had its issues and therefore the idea was soon shelved. Back to square one.

At around 2336 hours on Wednesday, 20 March, 1991, a Molotov cocktail was thrown through a window setting fire, once again, to the senior block but this time the staffroom was affected. The damage was only minor but it was obvious that after the 4th fire at the same school, it had to be placed under covert surveillance until such time we were able to effect an arrest.

Following a further meeting with Laurie and members of the Frankston C.I.B, Peter Shrubsole and Alan Poole, led by Aubrey Findlay from our under-cover surveillance team, were given the task to coordinate after hours covert surveillance inside the senior and junior blocks of the school buildings. It was determined this would provide a good view of the main areas being targeted and hopefully at some point in time, the offender, or offenders, would attempt further mayhem.

As part of our planning, we had to determine what hours we would sit inside the school. Given the four fires, apart from the first one on 2 July, 1990, had been set late at night with one occurring after midnight, we decided the covert surveillance would commence around 2200 hrs until 0300 hours, seven days a week. Part of our thinking was that a five-hour shift would not be as tiring on our operatives but in the event it became too tedious, we could replace them with other security officers.

In addition, the school was equipped with a silent intruder detection system so if the offender(s) gained entry to any of the buildings prior to the covert surveillance, at least we would be notified. Although, this type of surveillance had not worked very well to date.

We clearly made an error in determining the hours of the covert surveillance as on Sunday, 5 May, 1991 at 2142 hours, a multi section break alarm activation was received by our control room from the school's administration building. Aub was only a few minutes away from the school as his covert surveillance was to commence at 2200 hours. Unfortunately, not only did we once again fail to arrest the offender(s), but the fire had quickly gained control. On arrival a few minutes after receiving the alarm notifications, he radioed in that the school was once again on fire.

This was now the fifth fire in the space of 10 months and the impact this was having on the school community, in particular staff and students, was totally devastating. Although our security staff was also very disappointed and frustrated at our lack of success, we were not going to let the offender(s) continue with such acts of arson. We believed it was only a matter of time before an arrest would be made.

Unfortunately, our positive thinking received another setback as around 2051 hours on Thursday, 8 August, 1991, a fire causing around $100,000 damage, was set inside a portable classroom after being started with an accelerant. This now meant a total of six fires, with damage in excess of $1.5 million and, despite our undercover surveillance now in its fifth month, we were still no closer in identifying any suspects.

Laurie and his team of investigators, now working in close liaison with the Police Arson Squad, led by Detective Sergeant

Neville Taylor, were also at their wits end trying to determine who was responsible. They had convened a task force named Operation Firebug after the fifth fire, to try to bring this mayhem to an end. Finally, at around 2315 hours on the night of Monday, 12 August, 1991, the nightmare was to come to its final conclusion.

A very urgent radio transmission from Aub was received by our control room, notifying us of offenders on and requesting immediate back up. Hiding under a table in the senior school administration wing, he very quietly whispered that two offenders were actually right above him on the school roof. He could hear them talking while at the same time, they appeared to be drilling a hole in the building's roof, obviously to place an accelerant before setting the fire.

After being notified and driving to the school, which was 45 minutes from home, I directed that all units switch over to channel B on our radio network as Aub needed to have direct radio communication without any interference from other users on channel A. Our control room had notified Police D24 Communications of "offenders on" and, it's fair to say, the dog squad and police units from all directions were on their way to the school.

The offenders continued drilling directly above Aub, placing him in serious danger, so a decision was made to try and effect an arrest before they could place their accelerant and light a fire. By this stage we had a number of police officers virtually surrounding the school, so Aub was able to safely leave the building. When finally seeing the police and Aub, the offenders took off but were quickly arrested, handcuffed and placed separately into police divisional vans.

An examination of the building's roof left us in no doubt

we had finally arrested the offenders for the Frankston High School fires. We found an incendiary-type bomb device with more than 30 rifle cartridges, a bag of tools and a portable drill. No doubt we would have the pleasure of seeing the offenders in the dock in due course.

I had the pleasure of unbolting the police divisional van rear doors to introduce myself to each offender, wishing them well and trusting they would enjoy prison. I also had a vivid memory of when drunken spectators are escorted from the cricket ground with the crowd cheering and singing the Painters and Dockers song, "You're going home in the back of a divvy van".

In the county court dock before Judge John Nixon in June, 1992, were Evan Rees Williams, 19 years of age and Jonathan Cleveland Loftes, 17 years, both now formers students at Frankston High School. They were sentenced for arson for the four fires they lit between 9 January, 1990 and 8 August, 1991 and also the attempted arson on 12 August, 1991. They were not charged with the major blaze on 2 July, 1990 nor for the fire on 2 January, 1991. I have no doubt these two miscreants were most likely responsible for those two fires as well.

Regarding the fire on 9 January, 1991, they were equipped with a green army type carrier bag which contained, not only tools, but two containers of a mixture of kerosene, turpentine and petrol. They cut a hole in the school roof, climbed down into the administration area and set fire to a stack of papers. Their modus operandi on 20 March, 1991 was courtesy of a Molotov cocktail and while Loftes held the bottle, it was lit by Williams and then thrown through a smashed window.

On 5 May, 1991, a similar accelerant was used which Loftes poured around inside before setting it alight and leaving to walk home with Williams to Cecil Street, Frankston. As we suspected, the portable classroom fire on 8 August, 1991 was started by pouring petrol down a drilled hole into the classroom after Williams had passed up the necessary tools and equipment.

Prosecutor, James Bowen, submitted to the court that the raids were somewhat sophisticated. He gave examples of the type of arson committed on public buildings, in particular, schools. He also noted these offenders also placed responding fire units in grave danger if the incendiary devices left behind had detonated while the fires were being extinguished.

Loftes was represented by barrister, Peter Cash, who provided the court with a variety of reasons why his client set the fires, including wanting days off from school and not wanting to sit exams or complete assignments. Counsel further submitted his client had not considered the amount of damage that would be inflicted on the buildings but also saw himself as some modern day Batman by scaling school walls and climbing onto the roof of various buildings. Mr Cash also blamed the other offender's parents, who appeared to have no control over their son, Williams. He said that Loftes also carried out this type of offending because of his loyalty to Williams.

In the case of Williams, barrister Ron Clark noted the fires were an aberration for his client as he was a dedicated member of the Church of Jesus Christ of Latter-Day Saints in Frankston, in addition to his work in the community. Overall, it was admitted he was equally involved in the offending with Loftes. His excuse was he had a grudge against teachers and in some way, 'wanted to get back at those who crossed his path.'

His Honour was not impressed and, on remanding both in custody pending pre-sentence reports, noted it would be practically impossible for either counsel to submit they should be freed. Williams was subsequently sentenced to two and a half years in a Youth Training Centre and, noting Loftes had previously been "inadequately" sentenced by a learned magistrate in an earlier children's court sentence for only six months, the young offender was given 18 months. Williams was also ordered to make restitution to the Ministry of Education for the sum of $527,427, with Loftes receiving a lesser amount of $156,736 for reasons unknown to me.

Overall, we were extremely disappointed with the meagre sentences of only two and half years for Williams and a lesser sentence of only 18 months for Loftes. I say this on the basis there were two arsonists who caused absolute mayhem, setting fire to Frankston High School on four separate occasions but were not charged for two other fires, noting one of the fires was only seven days prior to the fire on 9 January, 1991. They were also ordered to pay a piddling restitution amount of only $680,000, yet the total fire damage bill was well over $1 million. Of course, such compensation would never have been recovered in any event.

Also not taken into account was the effect these fires had on the school community and, in the words of principal, Ken Rowe, who gave a victim impact statement before the court, 'The impact on the morale of pupils and staff was devastating, it caused untold concern and anxiety.'

The school lost, not only buildings, but furniture and equipment, including computers, irreplaceable school records and memorabilia. In addition, after two of the fires, over 700 students were sent home for two days before they and the staff could be subsequently relocated.

To quote Lord Chief Justice Gordon Hewart, in the matter

of *R v Sussex Justices, ex parte McCarthy* [1924] 1KB56 [1923] All ER Rep 233, when he set down the often quoted maxim, 'Justice should not only be done but should manifestly and undoubtedly be seen to be done.'

In the case of the Frankston High School arsonists, on this occasion those principles were in no way given such relevance.

With their subsequent arrest and conviction, it was a highlight for Laurie Ratz and me, as it had been a lengthy and frustrating period of 13 months, particularly the last five months of continuous covert night surveillance. The dedication and effort put in by Aub Findlay was rewarded and I had much pleasure at our yearly awards night, in presenting him with the "Security Officer of the Year" medal.

33

Rogues Gallery

Williams and Loftes would top our list of rogues, but a number of others are worthy of our gallery line-up. Bringing the Security Services Group into disrepute, three in-house rogues would be subsequently charged and convicted of criminal offences. We were absolutely shattered and disgusted with their conduct.

Regarding my decision to ultimately leave as Head of School Security after 19 years, not only did the Frankston School fires wear me down, but the conduct of three of our own officers was probably the final straw that broke the camel's back. Firstly, though, a tale of a lovable rogue who sadly fell on hard times.

On Wednesday, 13 April, 1983, a silent alarm was received from the music block at Oak Park High School late in the evening. It was definitely "offenders on" with multi section breaks. The first responding unit was a crime car from Broadmeadows. A rather tall, imposing police sergeant observed a short indigenous male inside the music block, stealthily stacking up musical instruments to take with him when he left the building. Our police officer immediately recognised the crook and arrested him when he left the building.

On placing him under arrest, the sergeant said, 'Now Lionel, you are not going to give me any trouble, are you?'

Lionel responded rather sheepishly with, 'No Sir, I won't.'

Lionel Rose won the World Bantamweight boxing title when he defeated Japan's Masahiko "Fighting" Harada in Tokyo in February 1968. The first Indigenous Australian to achieve such success, he was later to also win the first Indigenous "Australian of the Year" award. In 2003, he would be inducted into the Australian National Boxing Hall of Fame and subsequently elevated to legendary status. He also had reasonable success with a modest singing career but, it is fair to say, after his exemplary boxing achievements, he spiralled down the path of alcoholism.

It was at this low point in his life that Lionel was arrested and appeared in Broadmeadows Magistrates Court, where he was fined $750 for the school burglary. His former manager and trainer, Jack Rennie, gave character evidence before the court and to Lionel's credit, he still remained an Australian hero. He was honoured with an Australian stamp showing a replica of his boxing gloves, followed by a full-length movie of his life in 1995. Sadly, Lionel passed away in May, 2011 following a stroke.

Another rogue who was lots of fun in Edo's eyes as he certainly "enjoyed" his company, was Jimmy Ristevski. I would prefer to call him just a plain, dumb rogue who lived in the Thomastown area and had a penchant for breaking into schools. I first came across our friend at a school in Lalor when, late one evening, he triggered a silent alarm only to be arrested by me in Edo's company. Some months later, Ristevski was at it again but this time it was at the Thomastown East Primary school.

As I approached the building in alarm, in the early hours

of the morning, Ristevski, carrying his loot, was departing via a window. When I politely suggested he should stop and lay down with his arms outstretched, Ristevski took off, only for Edo to quickly bring him to the ground where I was able to handcuff him.

Now you would think Ristevski would learn a salutary lesson, but no. He had to try one more time. On this occasion, it was the Diamond Creek East Primary School and, unfortunately for him, I was called out to again to attend the school's silent alarm. With the same old outcome, I arrested him after Edo gave him another bite and on enquiring why he hadn't learnt his lesson, Ristevski responded that he thought by breaking into a school away from his normal habitat, he would be successful in stealing school property. Sorry Jimmy, but you were my only ever hat trick and just a "plain, dumb crook".

Raymond James Saville had 20 previous arson convictions, including his foray in trying to burn down Shepparton Technical School in January, 1975. His 20 previous arson convictions stemmed from four court appearances as far back as 1973, with two substantial terms of four years in 1976 and five years from 1983. Saville had a penchant for lighting fires in stormy weather and in October, 1989, he was at it again, setting fire to a church, followed by a school in Eltham causing damage in the order of $250,000. Needing to witness his handiwork, he actually returned to the scene of his crimes where he could watch the buildings burn. Once again, he was arrested.

In August, 1990, Saville appeared before His Honour, Judge Cash and the learned judge commented that Saville had chosen the crime of arson as his criminal speciality. He went on to say Saville was a menace to society with an appalling history of lighting fires, particularly in schools. His modus operandi was to search a building looking for money and, in the case of the Eltham Christian Church and School, where he only found three dollars, he became so annoyed he set the fires which almost gutted each building.

The judge noted Saville had poor social skills and, on release, he would need to get help for his pyromania. At the same time, he could not be seen as someone who did not know what he was doing. On that basis and, given his prior convictions, he was jailed for 10 years and six months. Another rogue out of action for some time.

In-house rogues have to get a special mention as their conduct was appalling. At no stage did I ever think that our own trusted security officers would bring our operation into disrepute by entering schools and stealing property. Heading the list was former security officer, John Didik, and his partner in crime was Phil Brown another of our trusted security officers, who up until Didik joined our staff, had also been a close friend of Graeme White. On being selected to join our staff, Didik was on the recommendation of Brown and, as he met all our selection criteria, we welcomed him into our team.

Graeme and I initially suspected Didik when we observed patterns emerging, where he and sometimes Brown, always seemed to be a few minutes behind any crook on activation of a school silent alarm. When the call went out for "any units in the vicinity of", we noted Didik or Brown would come up on the two-way radio, advising the control room they were only minutes off and would attend. A few minutes later, either one would then notify the control room that the school in alarm had been forcibly entered and it appeared that equipment had been stolen.

This happened on a number of occasions, particularly at

Aspendale Technical School. We realised something was amiss and, despite placing both of them under surveillance, we still did not have enough evidence to confirm our suspicions. The fact they always seemed to be "in the vicinity of", happened too often and Didik and Brown's luck on always being close by was becoming very questionable.

Our suspicions were further confirmed when I received a telephone call from Didik's previous employer, the manager of a Board of Works Depot in Springvale. They were also being subjected to burglaries and, on one occasion, a master key was used. They eventually concluded Didik was the culprit as he had never returned a master key when he left their employ in questionable circumstances. I was never made aware of this when he applied to join our team.

The type of equipment being stolen was also similar to that taken from our schools, mainly trade equipment, including saws, hammers and cutting tools. At this particular time, Didik had made an application to the Ministry of Education for WorkCare, as he was alleging, he suffered a back injury from lifting boxes of school keys. Pending approval, he was now unable to work.

Our relationship with the Police Major Crime Squad was very close and early one morning on Friday, 2 December, 1988, Didik's house was raided and he was placed into custody. What was found in his garage was mind-boggling. Of course, it was mainly trade type equipment and it took three large truck loads to remove it all. Didik readily made admissions and also dobbed in Brown as his accomplice.

Their modus operandi stealing school equipment was for Didik to break into the school while Brown waited outside. They would then load the goods and quickly leave, advising the control room they were close by and would respond to the alarm activations which were caused by Didik inside the school building.

Brown was next on our list and, as he was not aware Didik was in custody, I requested he call into our Mt Waverley headquarters at the start of his shift as I needed to speak with him. What he didn't know was a Major Crime Squad detective was waiting for him. My staff always called me "Chief", so in his usual jovial fashion, Brown walked into my office, greeting me with, 'Hi Chief, what can I do for you?'

My answer was, 'No Phil, it is what I can do for you,' as the handcuffs were placed on his wrists and he left the building, certainly not as jovial as when he arrived.

Suffice to say, both Didik and Brown were summarily terminated from their employment with the Security Services Group.

On 20 March, 1989, Didik and Brown pleaded guilty to 10 charges of burglary and 50 counts of theft valued in excess of $100,000, including, not only thefts from schools but the Board of Works. Unfortunately, they only received a 12-month suspended sentence. Suffice to say, I wasn't happy with the sentencing as they both should have been sentenced to a term of imprisonment. Their deplorable conduct left their co-workers and me totally gobsmacked and very angry.

After he was arrested and convicted, Didik seemed to have luck on his side because his alleged bad back claim for Workcare came before the Accident Compensation Tribunal for further adjudication. The Ministry and the State Insurance Office (SIO) had applied to get Didik taken off weekly compensation payments because of his criminal conduct. His alleged bad back clearly was not caused by lifting school key boxes but from the heavy industrial type of equipment he and Brown had been stealing from schools and the Board of Works.

As Didik had not fully recovered from his bad back, the tribunal arbitrator, Bernie Collett, somehow determined he was to remain on weekly payments. This was despite clear evidence of his criminal conduct but Collett was unmoved saying that, while he was somewhat unhappy with his decision, he had no choice. Didik denied he aggravated his back lifting heavy equipment and even said it was Brown who did all the heavy lifting during their criminal foray.

His solicitor, Simon Garnett, submitted that his client's criminal convictions were totally irrelevant to his Workcare application and, noting he was only on a suspended sentence, he should only lose such benefits if he was jailed. Didik kept saying his 'back was crook', he 'would dearly love to return to work' and that his actions were 'foolish'. He even told the court he was 'like a bellbird, I just liked material things.'

To say this ruling caused some outage is an understatement. Journalist, Phil Skeggs, gave it media coverage with the headline, "Anger over compo for law-breaker". Even the managing director for the Accident Compensation Commission, Michael Roux, stated, 'I do not believe the community would accept the results of this case as being natural justice.'

He went on to say that the Commission's agent and the SIO would appeal the decision and require Mr Collett provide a detailed written explanation how Didik could possibly be allowed to remain on WorkCare.

I was also incredulous, so I made a statement to the press saying, 'Under the laws of this state, a person on Workcare benefits can steal from his employer yet that employer must still pay the person his Workcare benefits.'

Unfortunately, this statement wasn't well received by Dr Jean Russell, our regional director, who called me to her office once again. I was raked over the coals for speaking to the media in matters other than school security. With respect to Dr Russell, I felt I had every right to voice my concerns about Mr Collett's appalling decision.

What followed was a recommendation by the state government to make urgent changes to the Workcare system, including replacing arbitrators such as Mr Collett with an Appeals Board. WorkSafe Victoria, under the name of the Victorian Workcover Authority, was subsequently established in December 1992 and the various Occupational Health and Safety Acts governing Workcover were further amended under the *Accident Compensation (Workcover Insurance) Act 1993* (Vic). Regarding Didik, his Workcover benefits were ultimately cancelled and Brown died of an undisclosed illness some years later.

Those two were followed by another one of our school security officers, Graham Mahoney, who had only been in our employ for a short period of time. Just like Didik and Brown, the same pattern emerged with Mahoney always being in close vicinity of school alarms, responding and then advising the control room that a burglary had occurred but with no sign of the offenders. He was placed under surveillance and both Graeme and I determined we had enough evidence to call him into my office to put our suspicions to him.

This decision was made following a burglary at Warrandyte High School's trade wing where, once again, Mahoney just happened to be close by, attending within a matter of minutes with the offenders already decamped. Our view was, he would carry out his burglaries, steal what he wanted before quickly leaving the school, possibly to park around the corner while waiting for the alarm call received by our control room.

Mahoney made no admissions but was extremely nervous, so we decided to hand him over to Lilydale CIB. After they subsequently took out a warrant, searched his house to discover numerous items of school equipment, Mahoney realised he was in a spot of bother.

His career as a security officer with the Ministry of Education came to an abrupt end. A few weeks later, on a Saturday afternoon, he was observed in the back of a limousine heading past the Mt Waverley control room towards the State School Nursery's function room, which he had previously booked for his wedding reception. As they drove past, Mahoney, sporting a huge grin on his face, waved to all and sundry, including me, in the control room.

Postscript is, that smirk came back to bite him because I received a telephone call from his new wife, Mrs Mahoney, a few days after their wedding. She berated me for her husband having to resign, because apparently, I wouldn't give him leave from the job to get married. Is that right, Mrs Mahoney? I told her, in no uncertain terms, that he had been sacked from the job and filled her in on what he had been up to, all without her knowledge, of course.

To the best of my recollection, the marriage came to an abrupt end and Mahoney, with his tail between his legs, returned home to his parent's house in Maryborough to complete his community service, as ordered by the court.

An unidentified rogue is also included in my gallery but to this day, he has never been brought to justice. "Mr Cruel" was the moniker given to this person described by police as a serial "super cool and super cruel" invasion rapist, when in November,

1987, he wore a balaclava and forcibly entered a home in Lower Plenty, tied up both parents and then raped their 11-year-old daughter.

This was followed by an abduction in Ringwood in December, 1988 where, once again, he bound and gagged the girl's parents, before abducting and then releasing her 18 hours later in the grounds of Bayswater High School. The same *modus operandi* then followed in July 1990, when a girl, taken from her Canterbury home, was molested for over two days before being released in Kew.

At first, police investigators, during Operation Spectrum, mistakenly adopted a school holiday abduction angle, when they looked at a number of suspects, including teachers and other males linked to both state schools and private schools. Because we had ready access with keys to most metropolitan schools, we assisted detectives in checking school staffing records after hours.

Following the disappearance of Karmein Chan in April, 1991, who also attended the same Presbyterian Ladies College (PLC) as the young Canterbury victim, males, including teachers at PLC, received a knock on their door from detectives looking for any evidence to link them to the crimes. Sadly, Karmein's decomposed body was found twelve months later and, to this day, Mr Cruel remains at large, despite a $1 million reward.

I have left this particular rogue for last as he tops my list. Late one evening in 1983, after working at our Gipps Street headquarters, I was returning home to my rental property in Preston when a silent alarm with multi section breaks was activated at Heidelberg High School. I had Edo with me so, despite not holding keys to the school, I advised our control room that I would attend, although I was 10 minutes off.

The alarm activations were coming from within the administration area and as I had designed the alarm, I had a fair idea of the school layout. Approaching the school, I could see an open window and, as the alarm activations were still being received, I thought I would sit off it with the view the offender would leave the school from that exit.

A few minutes after positioning myself 20 metres from the window, a bag was suddenly thrown out, followed by a short male offender. When he landed on the ground, I told him he was under arrest and to lay down with his arms where I could see them. After telling me to, 'Get fucked', he took off.

Within seconds, Edo had the screaming offender down on the ground with a nasty bite on his leg. I handcuffed him, told him he was under arrest and asked his name.

'Normie Faure, you prick,' was his reply.

Being a northern suburbs boy, I knew the background of the Faures, in particular the Clifton Hill bank robbery in 1976 and the shooting of police officer, Michael Pratt. I very quickly placed Faure into the rear of my vehicle with Edo and, hoping there were no other Faures watching, I made a quick dash for Heidelberg Police station. I could always return to the school later to secure it, so I told our control room to inform responding police who I had in custody.

I did have a fleeting brain wave to see if I could find his motor vehicle but quickly changed my mind. On the way to placing him in a police cell, my good mate Normie left me in no doubt that he would get me back and it wouldn't be pleasant. I must admit I didn't sleep well that night after the adrenaline wore off.

Our friend was actually on parole for the Clifton Hill bank job and was now back in prison to see out his eight years that he first received in 1977. Knowing his history, I always thought he would most likely come after me and the outcome would not be to my liking.

In June 1984, Faure asked his prison mate, Vincenzo Delouise, who was about to be released from custody, to look after his de facto, a very attractive heroin addict by the name of Darlene. Normie was to be released some weeks after Vince and thought nothing of asking his cell mate to make sure he took care of her until his release.

The old adage, 'Never introduce your donah (girlfriend) to a pal', particularly another crook, was overlooked by Normie. Vince, being the lad he was, certainly looked after the highly sexed Darlene and Normie, on his release, was to subsequently find out she was sleeping not only with him, but Vince on alternative nights. It was always going to finish badly and better Vince and Normie, rather than me. When Faure discovered what was going on, they had a knife fight and stabbed each other to death.

The following morning, I was greeted with the news on the radio about two well-known Melbourne rogues who had met their maker. No loss to mankind and good riddance to Norman Leslie "Normie" Faure. I think Constable Michael Pratt may have received some satisfaction from that outcome as well.

Another school demolished by arson.

Only two portables were left standing.

EDO, an amazing security dog and my loyal protector.

IT'S WAR... to stop damage to our schools

SCHOOL'S out this week. But there'll be no let-up in the Victorian Education Department's war on vandals.

In fact, the battle's being intensified.

There'll be more secret lookouts, more undercover patrols, more hidden alarms.

by MICHAEL WILKINSON

Education Department security officer Colin O'Neill was asked: Isn't Christmas-New Year normally a quiet time — how can there be vandalism at empty schools?

He has detailed files to prove that — as in Britain — violent wrecking of classrooms and playgrounds has become a big, year-round problem here.

In the past six months equipment worth more than $1 million has been vandalised at Victorian schools in 153 offences, 67 of them arson cases.

One school was so badly damaged that it had to turn away its pupils for two days.

The files show that offenders have been as young as 8.

The extent of the problem has spurred the State Government to earmark nearly $500,000 for improving school security in the next year.

The improvement will begin during the Christmas-New Year holidays with the Education Department's hiring of more security officers to bring the total to seven.

Also during the holidays the department will buy two patrol cars so that schools can be patrolled on a circuit system.

And there will be an extended use of private-enterprise patrol firms, some of the men will be hired to live in a school all weekend to stake it out.

Throughout the 12 months there'll be a continuing program of installing sophisticated alarms. These will be set so they're sensitive to movement in the building at nights or weekends.

It is hoped to have an alarm in every school of any size by the end of the year.

The Education Department's school security section is just a year old.

Colin O'Neill, 27, a Vietnam veteran, was hired last December to head it.

Since then he compiled a file on each of our 2300 schools, detailing its security risk, marking with a red asterisk schools incurring the most vandalism.

Said Mr O'Neill at his office fronting Treasury Place: "Our effort can't be reduced at all during the Christmas-New Year break.

"That's the time when kids can get really bored and into mischief at deserted schools."

Mr O'Neill said: "Generally vandalism is more of a problem in the northern and western suburbs, although it's not only confined to those areas — we can get it anywhere."

And the typical vandal?

"That would have to be a boy 11 to 15 years old. He's most likely been in trouble at school — not what you would call a perfect student.

"But I stress that the problem is not confined to this type. In the past year we've caught a boy who went to a well-known grammar school, and even a girl."

Mr O'Neill's policy on offenders is to hand them over to police with the recommendation that charges be laid.

The maximum penalty for such offences for an under-16-year-old is detention in a State Government youth institution.

But such a sentence is rare. The Children's Court normally puts school vandals on a bond or probation.

Mr O'Neill favors more realistic penalties.

He would like guilty students to be made to help repair their damage at weekends or holidays.

And he favors the British move of making parents pay for at least some of the damage.

Blackboard jungleground ... $2 million damage in the past six months.

O'Neill ... a Vietnam veteran for a close-to-home war.

Herald Sun News article written by Michael Wilkinson 1974.

$2mil. DAMAGE
SCHOOL CRIME SQUAD TREBLED

By PETER FITZGERALD

The State Government plans to treble the Education Department's securities staff in a bid to combat arson and vandalism in schools.

The Education Minister, Mr Thompson, told me the present staff of two will be increased to seven.

Mr Thompson and the department's assistant director-general (building), Mr Neville Barwick, said there were about 35 problem schools out of 2240 Victorian State schools.

When I discussed arson and vandalism figures with Mr Thompson, Mr Barwick and the director-general, Dr L. W. Shears, for 2½ hours, they stressed that most schools were well looked after by children.

Herald Sun News article written by Peter Fitzgerald.

School crime squad trebled

Continued from P. 1

While Mr O'Neill's security department only deals with offences against school property, he says "the rest of the school crime picture is a pretty heavy scene."

"We hear from teachers about boys as young as nine running protection rackets from six-year-olds and extorting their tuckshop money on the threat of physical violence.

"This is a common occurrence.

"Also that even teachers are not safe from assault by bigger students.

"While this is not common yet, it is happening.

"To stand outside some schools at lunchtime and see the girls drive off with men is an eye-opener.

"From what we hear there is every reason to suppose that some Melbourne schoolgirls are operating prostitution rings in their schools.

"Our security patrols helped by private watching organisations and police are finding about 150 children every weekend illegally loitering on school property.

"And often they are sitting up against a wall drinking alcohol or having sex.

"The extent of drugs in schools is worrying," he says.

Mr O'Neill's statement confirms disturbing reports I have been hearing for some time from teachers about violence in Melbourne State schools including standover rackets, bashings, prostitution and promiscuity.

One standover racket involved a 16-year-old boy using a home-made knife with a seven-inch blade to extort the tuck-shop money of 12-year-old boys.

An example of school vice was a lunch-hour prostitution ring using homes where both parents were away at work.

From inquiries I have made, many teachers believe the number of emotionally disturbed and aggressive children is increasing and they want the expansion of the school medical service before school violence reaches unmanageable proportions.

This list shows figures for arson and attempted arson from January 1 to November 21 this year.

Date	School	Damage $
3. 1.1975	T.S. Shepparton	3000
5. 1.1975	P.S. Fawkner	250,000
19. 1.1975	H.S. Wodonga	71,000
23. 1.1975	P.S. Bundig	15,000
4. 2.1975	P.S. Gowerville	1500
12. 2.1975	P.S. Fitzroy North	2000
1. 4.1975	H.S. Glenroy	85,000
1. 4.1975	H.S. Newlands	100
23. 4.1975	H.S. Footscray	1,000,000
26. 4.1975	T.S. Preston	3000
28. 4.1975	GHS Malvern	200
7. 5.1975	P.S. Portland	100,000
24. 5.1975	P.S. Syndal South	6000
29. 5.1975	P.S. Syndal South	100
15. 6.1975	P.S. Malvern	30,000
25. 6.1975	P.S. Templestowe Valley	200
30. 6.1975	H.S. Oak Park	2500
2. 7.1975	H.S. Highett	60
6. 7.1975	P.S. Box Hill South	800
12. 7.1975	P.S. Gladstone Views	385
17. 7.1975	H.S. Frankston	50
19. 7.1975	P.S. Echuca	10
19. 7.1975	P.S. Maralinga	50
20. 7.1975	H.S. Richmond	100,000
22. 7.1975	P.S. Mentone	50
26. 7.1975	T.S. Preston East	—
27. 7.1975	P.S. Burwood Heights	60
28. 7.1975	P.S. Oberon South	1450
3. 8.1975	T.S. Templestowe	5
7. 8.1975	P.S. Kilsyth	40
10. 8.1975	T.S. Templestowe	5
11. 8.1975	P.S. Flora Hill	20
12. 8.1975	P.S. Kilsyth	5
14. 8.1975	T.S. Tottenham	—
15. 8.1975-18.8.1975	H.S. Ararat	—
16. 8.1975	P.S. Monterey	5
17. 8.1975	P.S. Essex Heights	5
17. 8.1975	P.S. Heidelberg West	50
24. 8.1975	P.S. Box Hill South	20
24. 8.1975-6.9.1975	P.S. Belvedere Park	40
26. 8.1975	H.S. Ringwood	5
27. 8.1975	P.S. Auburn South	20
30. 8.1975	P.S. Preston North-East	5
30. 8.1975	P.S. Wattle Glen	10
31. 8.1975	T.S. Mitcham	20
1. 9.1975	P.S. Parktone	25
6. 9.1975	P.S. Heidelberg West	1000
6. 9.1975	P.S. Cheltenham Heights	20
9. 9.1975	H.S. Heidelberg	200
11. 9.1975	H.S. Eltham	207,000
13. 9.1975	H.S. Heidelberg	20
17. 9.1975	T.S. Jordanville	250
17. 9.1975	P.S. Ballarat Special	5
18. 9.1975	P.S. Noojee	30,000
19. 9.1975	P.S. Healesville	60
20. 9.1975	P.S. Kilsyth	10
15.10.1975	P.S. St. Albans Heights	—
19.10.1975	P.S. Norlane	100
25.10.1975	H.S. Lalor	—
3.11.1975	T.C. Swinburne	—
7.11.1975	P.S. Watsonia Special	20
9.11.1975	H.S. Moe	200
10.11.1975	H.S. Oakleigh	135,000
16.11.1975	P.S. Ringwood North	30
Total: 64 — 16 offenders charged		**$2,048,360.**

Page 2 of Herald Sun News article.

FORM No. 73

VICTORIA POLICE

Bureau of Criminal Intelligence,
P.O. Box 2763,
MELBOURNE, VIC. 3001,
AUSTRALIA.

14th April, 1980.

TO WHOM IT MAY CONCERN

This letter is to introduce Mr. Colin O'NEIL, Senior Security Officer for the Education Department for the whole of the State of Victoria, Australia.

Mr. O'NEIL is to undertake a world study tour specifically orientated towards Law Enforcement, Security and Modern Technology related to Law Enforcement.

Mr. O'NEIL has strong, professional and social ties with Law Enforcement groups throughout the whole of Australia.

My object in providing this introduction for Investigator O'NEIL, is to seek the co-operation of fellow Law Enforcement officers coming into contact with Investigator O'NEIL and ask all to offer him all possible assistance.

Phillip C. Walliss
Phillip C. WALLISS
Detective Inspector,
Bureau of Criminal Intelligence,
MELBOURNE, AUSTRALIA.

Letter written by Detective Inspector Phillip Walliss, Vic Police Bureau of Criminal Intelligence. 14th April, 1980.

SECURITY AND COMMUNICATIONS – A NEW LOOK

Following a spate of major fires in the early 1970s, the Department established a Security Section and appointed Mr Colin O'Neill as Senior Security Officer.

Colin's broad charter was that he be responsible for the overall prevention and detection of crime against school buildings and property.

Prior to his appointment, Colin undertook various administrative duties in a number of branches within the Office of the Chief Commissioner of Police, and also served two years with the Australian Army, which included twelve months' active service in Vietnam.

With an initial staff of three officers and a limited funding source to engage contract security firms, Colin initiated programs involving patrols and surveillance of school property, provision of security rooms and engraving school equipment.

Field operations and experimentation with numerous types of alarm systems became an every day (and night) occurrence for Colin O'Neill. Following an extensive overseas study tour, this finally lead to the introduction for the first time in any Australian school system, of a silent alarm intruder detection system.

This system, devised and implemented by Colin has grown to a total of 900 schools connected to the Security and Communications Central Control room, which is manned 24 hours a day, 365 days a year.

The success of the system has been acknowledged by Departments of Education in NSW, South Australia, Queensland and Western Australia. The latter State introduced the system for its schools with Colin's aid in 1984.

Since the inception of the silent alarm intruder detection system, a total of 3200 offenders have been apprehended on school property, and charged with offences including arson, burglary, and wilful damage.

The integrity of the system can be further proven by the excellent support given by the Victoria Police Force through direct access to D24, Helicopter and Dog Squad services.

Up to June 1984, the system, in terms of personnel to man the control room and conduct field operations, was undertaken by contract security companies under the direction of Colin O'Neill.

Security and Communications for Victorian State Schools took a new direction as from 1 July 1984 by directly employing its own staff to man the Central Control Room, attend alarm activations and conduct field operations. The new team will be fully operational by the end of March 1985.

Headquarters for Security and Communications is currently located in leased premises in Collingwood and by June of this year will be relocated to permanent quarters within the State Schools Nursery Site of Glen Waverley.

In concluding this article it would be remiss of me not to acknowledge the support given to Colin O'Neill by his administrative staff Ms Lyn Hutchins and Mr Mark Swift and also the protective support given directly to him by "EDO" (Education Department Officer), Colin's trained German Shepherd dog.

Finally, I extend my compliments and thanks to Colin O'Neill for his remarkable foresight, complete dedication to school security and wish him well in his new position as Manager, Security and Communications Group.

Neville Rohan

Education Security Newsletter.

SCHOOL 'SLEEP' PATROL NABS 7

By ALAN ROWE,
Herald Education Reporter

Education Department security men are sleeping on the job in western suburbs schools — and catching school-breakers in the act.

Last weekend and on a weekend in April they made "on-the-spot" arrests of school-breakers leading to 12 charges of burglary and theft being made against six boys and a youth.

The officer in charge of the Education Department's security section, Mr Colin O'Neill, said today: "Our tactics are to catch them in the act. Then there is no way they can escape prosecution."

His officers staked out schools in the northern and western suburbs and the Geelong area and made arrests.

Mr O'Neill said: "These are schools where there have been repeated break-ings.

"We are sleeping in the schools and catching offenders we believe could be responsible for other community crimes as well as school breaking."

On Friday, an officer slept overnight in a western suburbs primary school and stayed till Saturday afternoon when he surprised a youth, 19, and a boy, 14, who broke in a window.

As a result of these arrests, two other boys, aged 14 and 15, were also charged.

The charges included five counts of burglary involving a calculator, stationery and office equipment worth about $200, and one count of theft of a bicycle from a school.

The youth would appear in a magistrate's court and the boys in the Children's Court, Mr O'Neill said.

In mid-April, a security officer staying the weekend in a western suburbs primary school caught two 13-year-old boys breaking in on a Saturday night.

Another boy, 14, was also charged with the 13-year-olds with six counts of burglary from canteen supplies, audio-visual equipment and stationery and stores items worth $400.

The offences dated back to last October.

The three boys would appear before the Children's Court, Mr O'Neill said.

Herald Sun News article by Alan Rowe.

1986 visit to Los Angeles Police Airwing.

Entry to Lebanon, 1986.

Israel army on the Lebanese border.

Lebanon in background with Israel's security fence to the left.

Nigel at Israel Lebanon border.

With my beautiful wife Michelle, her brother Tony, best friend Miranda, her sister Bernadine, and my mate, Nigel. 12th March 1988.

School fires lit to get days off – judge

By CHRISTINE GILES

TWO youths caused more than $500,000 damage to their high school so they could get days off, the County Court heard yesterday.

The court was told the youths, now 17 and 19, lit four fires at Frankston High over eight months.

The fires were lit during commando-style operations, avoiding guards who had been called in to patrol the area.

They had used a Molotov cocktail, a home-made bomb and an army bag containing fire accelerants and a variety of tools.

Judge Nixon yesterday sentenced the 17-year-old and Evan Rees Williams, 19, formerly of Cecil St, Frankston, to detention in a youth training centre.

He said Williams had a grudge against teachers at and wanted to "get back at those who had crossed his path".

Judge Nixon sentenced Williams to 2½ years' detention and the 17-year-old to 18 months.

He also ordered Williams to pay $527,427 and the 17-year-old $156,736 in compensation to the Education Ministry.

Williams had pleaded guilty to two counts of burglary, four counts of arson and one count of attempted arson.

The 17-year-old pleaded guilty to one count of arson and one count of attempted arson.

Judge Nixon said both had told police they had assignments and tests due and they were trying to delay them.

The court heard more than 700 senior students were given days off and teachers had to be relocated because of the fires, lit between January 9 and August 4 last year.

Judge Nixon said when the youths were caught by police trying to light a fifth fire on August 12 last year, they had a home-made bomb consisting of 30 .22-calibre bullets wrapped in a sock.

"The conduct in which the two of you engaged was abhorrent," Judge Nixon said.

Herald Sun News article by Christine Giles. 26th June, 1993.

Sky police tackle young vandals

By GREG THOM

POLICE have launched an airborne attack on arson and vandalism at schools and railway stations.

The number of flying hours for the police helicopter has been doubled in an effort to arrive more quickly at school break-ins.

The campaign has been immediately effective, with 10 youths caught illegally on school grounds over the weekend.

At one school, seven youths were arrested after a police helicopter landed and caught them before they could flee.

Police are co-operating with the Education Department to fight vandalism by working in areas that are particularly troublesome.

The airwing operations room at Essendon airport has been fitted with a radio tuned to transmissions by Education Department security staff so trouble-spots can be quickly identified and the helicopter sent in.

The blitz comes as figures released by the Education Department show a rise in school property damage.

Fire, theft, burglary and vandalism have cost the department more than $32 million since 1985.

In the past two years, property crimes have cost the department $10 million. Half the damage bill was caused by fires, despite arson accounting for only one in 50 offences.

In the year to June 1992 there were 3680 incidents in which schools were damaged, including 136 fires.

The police helicopter now has an extra one hour of flying time per shift available, taking to three the number of hours the helicopter can patrol.

With 10 shifts a week, the increase means the helicopter can be airborne for an extra 10 hours, most of which will be spent patrolling the streets.

"The police helicopter is basically a flying divvy van," Sen-Sgt Gary Lindsey of the police airwing said.

"We can land at a troublespot within minutes, where it would take ground units longer to get there."

Sen-Sgt Lindsey said the extra hour of flying time was a huge boost to "astro patrolling" which usually suffered at the hands of other demands on the helicopter.

"We normally use up our flying time pretty quickly for things like rescues, searches, surveillance and drug crops," he said.

"There are always great demands on our resources from other police. This will allow us to do a bit of pro-active policing."

Sen-Sgt Lindsey said the helicopters are costly to operate, with the expense of aviation fuel and the need for maintenance after 30 hours of flying.

"Vandalism at schools and railway stations has always been a problem. We are going to spend a lot of time on them and hopefully reduce some of the damage."

Assistant Commissioner (Traffic and Operations Support) Frank Green said the extra flying time had been allocated by juggling his department's budget.

"We are manipulating the dollars to suit demand," he said.

"Last weekend showed the effectiveness of astro-patrolling. When a security alarm goes off, we are able to be above the school very quickly."

Herald Sun News article by Greg Thom 26th February 1993.

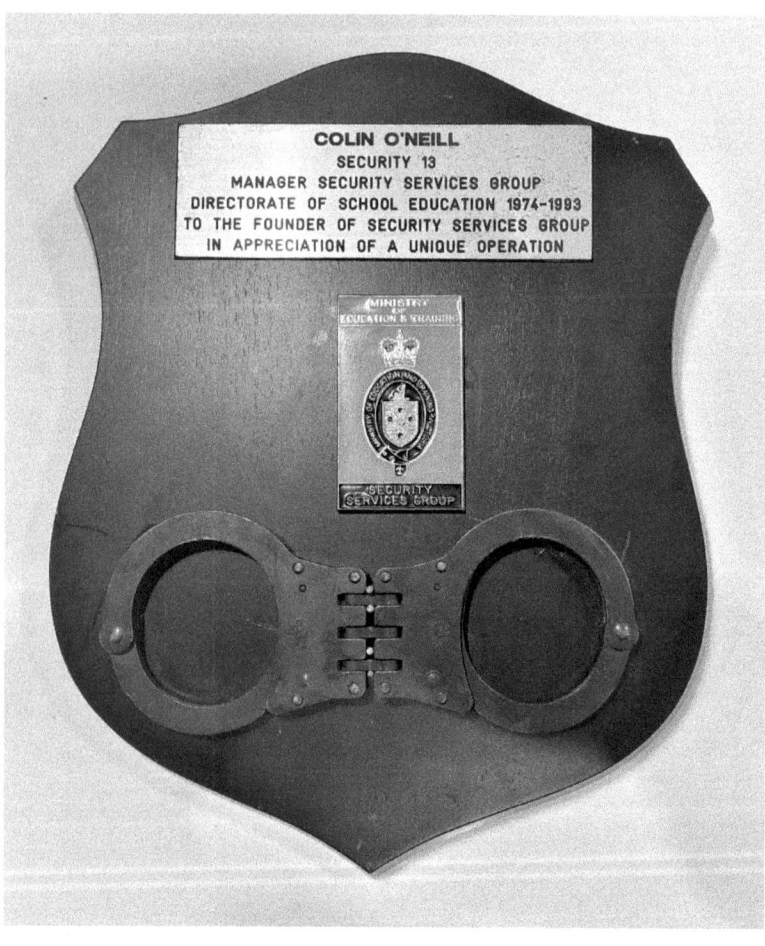

In Appreciation shield presented to me from the Directorate of School Education upon my resignation, 16th September, 1993.

34

The Final Chapter

On 10 August, 1990, following her promotion to the position of Deputy Premier and, after serving in the education portfolio, Joan Kirner was appointed as Victoria's first female state premier. During her term as Minister of Education, Mrs Kirner introduced the Victorian Certificate of Education, which I was now studying to obtain at night school.

This journey of seeking a higher education for myself largely stemmed from following my 1986 study tour to Israel. On my return, I determined that my education qualifications or lack thereof, needed to be improved so I studied part time, achieving fair results with mostly passes.

However, one subject in which I excelled with a high distinction, was legal studies. Following my exposure to our legal system, in particular the two defining arrests, I decided to apply for entry to the Monash University Law Faculty and sat an entrance exam, hoping to be selected to commence the first year of a law degree. To say my application and entrance exam was not successful is an understatement, as I think I finished in the last 50 following the assessment.

My interest in studying, perhaps as an alternative to detecting school crime 24 hours a day, seven days a week, prompted me to commence a Bachelor of Criminal Justice Administration at Phillip Institute of Technology (PIT) in Coburg in 1990. I successfully completed the first two years of this degree, achieving eight high distinctions, much to my amazement. As La Trobe University was seeking candidates to undertake a law degree, applications were invited to become a law student under their newly created Faculty of Law, commencing in 1992.

One of the criteria was, not only education qualifications, but they were looking for students with a background in law enforcement. Of the 900 or so who applied, only 30 were successful and once again, to my amazement, I was one of the chosen 30. With two years of credits towards an arts degree following my time at PIT, I transferred over to La Trobe. Providing I put my head down and bum up, so to speak, I would qualify at the end of 1994 with a Bachelor of Arts and a Bachelor of Laws after three more years of study.

Not forgetting I was a father to a young son turning one in March, 1992, I now had to balance my duties as Manager of the Security Services Group with studying, effectively full-time. Luckily, they supported me with one day a week's study leave to attend La Trobe.

By the end of 1991, we had relocated our control room from Mt Waverley to larger premises in Beaumaris. I was now responsible for our school security operations and a total staff number of 29 employees, which included 24 officers for control room, patrol and under-cover surveillance duties.

I was still the project coordinator for the design and supervision of all silent intruder detection systems installed in our schools, monitored by our control room seven days a week, 24 hours per day. Our arrest rate was averaging at least

120 offenders per month but, of course, school fires were still a problem and despite our best efforts, there seemed to be no solution on how to bring them under control.

I had to justify my ADM 6 public service classification and in March, 1992, I was required to collate and submit a 19-page job description questionnaire to the Public Service Board of Victoria. This included providing details of the objectives and functions of my role, the type of equipment I was required to have knowledge of, skill requirements, the role of my subordinates and even position dimensions, including our security budget, which was now around the $1.5 million mark.

During her term as premier, Mrs Kirner was unable to improve her government's popularity with the Victorian electorate and the state's financial insolvency was around $3.5 billion per year. This was despite the government of the day selling off trains and trams to then lease them back, followed by the sale of the State Bank of Victoria to the Commonwealth Bank of Australia and three years of reducing schoolteacher numbers and the public school system overall. Mrs Kirner was effectively a "premier-in-waiting" and on 6 October, 1992, her Labor Government was soundly defeated with the Jeff Kennett-led Liberals winning a 16-seat majority in the lower house.

Unfortunately, her lasting legacy was the introduction of 50,000 poker machines into Victoria, following the passing of legislation in 1991. The thinking behind this so-called initiative was to provide access to such facilities in Victoria, rather than having our adults spend their hard-earned money over the border in New South Wales.

Kennett didn't muck around and passed in excess of 30 pieces of legislation, which saw a much-welcomed overhaul of workers compensation with the introduction of a Workcover Bill, significant reform of the industrial relations system, including the establishment of an Employee Relations Commission, even the abolition of the 17.5% employee leave loading, the abolition of unsworn statements by defendants, and new standards for public sector employees with Public Sector Management legislation. His government also reduced the number of gaming machines in Victoria to 30,000 with rules providing for adults-only access and no public promotion, including a ban on advertising.

In addition, on 20 November, 1992, Kennett announced the Liberal Government would close or merge a total of 56 schools, abolish around 4,000 teaching positions and terminate nearly 4,000 school cleaners, together with 830 administrative staff. While our charter was the prevention and detection of school crime, somehow, our group became involved in patrolling schools that were selected for closure.

This included the Ardoch-Windsor Secondary College, which managed a large program for homeless students, and the Northland Secondary College, formerly Preston East Technical school, which had a highly credentialed record in Aboriginal education and was used as an example in submissions to the Royal Commission into Black Deaths in Custody.

As parents, teachers and students were not impressed, our charter was to ensure everyone remained calm during this period of upheaval. The Victorian Secondary Teachers and the Federated Teachers Union of Victoria were very unhappy and organised a number of teachers' strikes, all to no avail. The public, especially the many workers being made redundant, were also unimpressed with Kennett's massive state funding cuts and over 100,000 marched on state parliament to voice their opposition. Despite this protest being the largest since the Vietnam War Moratorium, Kennett remained unmoved.

In early 1993, I introduced a program titled School Watch into a number of selected schools and it was loosely based on the very successful Neighbourhood Watch initiative. My parents were members of their local community program and, on one occasion, I had attended their monthly meeting and presented the functions of the school security group.

Neighbourhood Watch in Victoria was introduced as a result of a pilot program which commenced in Frankston in June, 1983. Its main objective was seeking assistance from local residents in an attempt to reduce crime, in particular burglary and theft. The idea of School Watch was to stimulate local interest, particularly from residents living in proximity to schools to keep a watchful eye out. Although this borrowed idea had some merit, it was really another attempt, albeit unsuccessful, in thinking outside the square trying to reduce school crime. In particular, arson.

In January, 1993, my family relocated from East Hawthorn to Mt Martha on the Mornington Peninsula, partly due to my intention to limit the number of hours I was working, particularly responding to silent alarm call outs at all times of the day and night. I was still actively involved though and would often work varying shifts, including night shifts. I would like to say this was solely due to my dedication but it was also about finding a work and study balance, so either an afternoon or night shift that would work in with my study regime, in particular when attending day and afternoon lectures and tutorials at La Trobe.

Victoria Police members were also once again placed in difficult situations with Peter Gibb's escape from the

Melbourne Remand Centre in March 1993. Gibb was a well-known crook, having previously escaped from Pentridge Prison in 1981, where he was on remand for murder and armed robbery. His latest escape with another crook, Archie Butterley, was ably assisted by prison officer Heather Parker. It didn't end well for them with Butterley shot dead in circumstances never determined by the coroner and the arrests of Gibb and Parker after a shootout with police.

Five police officers, including Sergeant Trevor Berryman and his police dog Shamus, were ultimately recognised for their bravery, whilst Gibb and Parker would serve lengthy terms of imprisonment. Gibb didn't last long after being released as he died from an assault in 2011.

Frankston was unfortunately placed in the public spotlight on many occasions due to a number of murders. There were two, still unsolved, murders in the early 1980s; the first being Allison Rooke when her naked body was found in scrubland on 5 July, 1980. Fifteen months later in October, 1981, Frankston North resident, Joy Summers, disappeared and her remains were found on 22 November, 1981. Similar to the three unsolved Tynong North murders, $3 million still remains as a reward leading to the conviction of the person(s) responsible for these unsolved murders. A number of suspects fell under the police radar for these killings, one being a person by the name of Harold Janman. He denied any involvement and there was certainly no credible evidence to connect him, despite failing two police lie detector tests.

It should be noted that years later, Bandali Debs was also considered by police to be a suspect regarding the Tynong North and Frankston murders. He was convicted of the 1998 murders of police officers, Sergeant Gary Silk and Senior

Constable Rod Miller, who were part of Operation Hamada at the time. When initially bugged by police as part of the murder investigation, Debs was heard bragging about how to kill a woman, saying, 'Put the rod in the mouth ... blew her brains away ... close the mouth there's no noise ... I've done it.'

Two of his other murder victims were both female and their bodies were dumped off main roads, similar to the six unsolved murders.

Debs was also questioned by police for the murder of Sarah MacDiarmid as was triple murderer, Ashley Coulston, but no evidence could connect either of them to any of these despicable crimes. Coulston, who brutally murdered three young people in Burwood, was sentenced to three consecutive life sentences and will never be released.

Unfortunately, another murderous rampage was to take place on 31 July, 1993 when I was working night shift and we were patrolling schools in the Frankston area. Apart from a vast number of police units also in the same location, the streets of Frankston and surrounding areas were very quiet due to a five-month period of attacks on females, including another spate of murders.

The first murder had occurred in June, 1993 when the body of Elizabeth Stevens was found with her throat slashed and a criss-cross pattern carved into her chest. What followed next was equally as horrific when Deborah Fream was abducted on Thursday 8 July, 1993 and her body found four days later, once again with similar injuries.

The final and third victim was 17-year-old schoolgirl, Natalie Russell, who was abducted on her way home from attending John Paul College on Friday, 30 July, 1993. Tragically she was later found with her throat slashed after being strangled. Luckily, the low life murderer, Paul Denyer), left behind incriminating evidence as he lay in wait for his victim, notably his empty car which was observed and recorded by patrolling police. Denyer was subsequently sentenced on these three counts of murder and on appeal to a non- parole period of 30 years.

Denyer was also considered a suspect in the disappearance of Sarah MacDiarmid but he denied any involvement. It would appear Denyer was eliminated as a suspect in the murder of Michele Brown, who disappeared from around the Frankston Railway station on her 25th birthday on 1 March, 1992. Her body was found two weeks later in a shed at the back of a gun shop in Playne street, Frankston. Denyer, who now dresses in prison as a woman with long hair and wanting to be known as "Paula", was also accused of four rapes in April 2012 involving inmates believed to have intellectual disabilities. Hopefully, this low life will never be released.

I was now blessed with two young sons, two-year-old Hayden and newborn, Patrick. Rajah had not changed his aggressive canine habits and our concern was whether he could be trusted around our two young children. The decision was made to rehouse him to a Police Dog Squad member, who would use him for breeding purposes.

Although this left me without four-legged protection when responding to silent school alarms, Michelle and I really had no choice but to part company with Rajah. At least he was going to a good home. In addition, as I was effectively studying for a law degree full time, I had already decided my days as Manager of the Security Services Group were coming to an end.

My final arrest was to take place in the early hours of the morning at Mount Martha Primary School when the portable buildings were entered, activating a two section multi break alarm. I was only living a few minutes away and, on arrival at the school, I observed a rather large Māori male in the corridor between the two connected portables. Aware that police back up was only a few minutes away, I decided to keep him under observation.

The offender quickly changed my decision when he gathered his ill-gotten goodies and began to leave the portables. Leaving me with no choice, I had to introduce myself but he took off down the road adjoining the school with me giving chase. Unfortunately for him, he only made it to a roundabout near the school when he saw a police divvy van approaching so, realising the game was up, he lay down on the road.

Although he was my last arrest, after 19 years of working in security, I had no doubt there would be many more who would suffer the same fate, as our total school silent alarm arrests were now in the order of almost 10,000 since their inception.

The game was also up for me on Thursday, 16 September, 1993 when I accepted a redundancy package, one of many available in the Kennett Government's attempt to reduce the number of public sector personnel. My final chapter as Manager, Security Services Group for the Directorate of School Education Victoria, was over when I left the Victorian Public Service to complete my final year of a law degree and start another interesting chapter in my life.

Acknowledgements

In writing this book, reference to my army service in Vietnam certainly brought back a lot of memories, some good and some not so pleasant. When recently visiting Cerberus Naval Base for a football match, I had an uneasy feeling, as it was not unlike a typical army base and brought back the reality and memories of my national service.

My heartfelt thanks must go to Alan "AB" Pearce for his perusal of my recollection of our time served in Vietnam, in particular with 1 Australian Field Hospital, Vung Tau. Little did we know at the time that we would remain great mates into our old age and hopefully, for many more years to come. I make special mention of the assistance afforded to me by Denise Bell and Paul Danaher, two of the authors of the much-credentialed book titled *Call Sign Vampire*, which tells the largely unknown service of those attached to the Australian Field Hospital during the Vietnam War. It certainly brought back a lot of memories, not only for me, but also other returned Vietnam veterans. My book contains a number of amazing photographs and thank you to each of the veterans who provided them for publication from the various pages of *Call Sign Vampire*, namely Ian Dann (pg. 27), Alan Dodds (pg. 33), Murray Lovett (pg. 51), Rob Watson (pg. 133-134), Roger Nation (pg.135), Margaret Young (pg. 191), Alan "AB" Pearce (pg. 224) and Dave Wittner (pg. 40).

The contribution from my good friend, Jack Higgins, clearly

demonstrated what he and other veterans were confronted with, not only on contact with the VC, but on returning home. Thank you, Jack for your service and valued friendship.

Unfortunately, my mate, Ross Clark, did not survive Vietnam and I trust his family will get some comfort from my recollection of our time together, especially the street and backyard cricket we enjoyed so much. Rob Watson, sadly has also passed away and my reference to Rob in this book is also my thanks to him for his mateship. Vale also to Murray Lovett - Rest in peace - Lest we forget.

I recall Neville Barwick when he was Assistant Director General for the Ministry of Education, saying to me during my time as Head of School Security that I should write a book. At the time, we were experiencing a number of arson incidents and, of course, responding to silent school alarms and placing offenders under arrest.

Thank you, Neville. I do regret not writing this book earlier and also not keeping an extensive diary as the detail and story line set out is, in many ways, based on my own personal recollection but supported by a number of press cuttings and corroborating contributions.

My 19 years with the Ministry of Education was time well spent with now lifetime friends, Graeme White and Nigel Buckley. They both were valuable sources of assistance and learned counsel, not only during our time involved with school security, but on checking the factual content and based on their experiences in arresting school crooks. My heartfelt thanks and gratitude go to them and here's to many more years of valued friendships.

I must also thank Age journalist, John "Sly of the Underworld" Silvester, for his many informative articles on crime and its infamous identities and also his "Naked City" podcast and articles. Anthony Dowsley and Andrew Bolt of the Herald Sun also need to be acknowledged for their enlightening articles and podcasts on criminals, long forgotten and those of today.

A huge thank you to an amazing young woman who was the final key to the puzzle of publishing. Alana Lambert of Book Burrow - you have been my saviour in this unknown world. Also to Samantha Elley, I owe you my thanks for your professional editing skills.

My family, who I dearly love, have always been a source of support and inspiration. My amazing sister, Susan, for her input in respect of our early days and to my two beautiful daughters, Karen and Alison, who have given me five wonderful grandchildren to love. My two sons, Hayden and Patrick, have grown into fine young men who have always given me their never-ending love, encouragement and loyalty.

Kudos to our much-loved dogs. Firstly Edo, who certainly saved me from several dangerous situations when chasing and arresting school crooks, our beautiful Golden Retriever Tully, our first family dog who showed us so much love and loyalty and helped heal our hearts during many difficult and sad times with the loss of friends and family members and, finally, our amazing rescue Doberman, Pickle, who taught us all about resilience and never ending love over the four years she was in our lives. They have all now crossed the rainbow bridge and no doubt are eating schmackos, doing zoomies and telling tales of how much we loved them and they loved us in return.

To my loving and supportive wife, Michelle, I owe her so much, especially for her steadfast belief in me. She not only experienced the ongoing stressful drama of me being called out in the middle of the night to confront and catch school crooks, but her contribution as an editor and her input into this book, deserves a big thank you. This book would not have been possible without her guidance, with a number of suggested amendments, of course, so thank you and love you to the moon and back.

Mind you, she had a bit of a chuckle when I was admitted to practice law on April Fool's Day but that is another story for another day.

Bibliography

- Banks, Keith (with Ben Smith), *Drugs Guns & Lies*, Allen & Unwin 2020.
- Bezzina, Charlie, *The Job Fighting Crime from the Front Line*, The Slattery Media Group 2010.
- Bowman, John S(Ed), *The Vietnam War – Day by Day*, Bison Books Ltd. 1989.
- Brown, M. Macgladre, S. & Sutton C, *You're Leaving Tomorrow*, Random House Australia Pty Ltd 2007.
- Cameron, M. *A Look at The Bright Side*, Detail Printing 1988.
- Caulfield, Michael (Ed. *Voices of War*, Hodder Australia, 2006.
- Dapin, Mark, *The Nasho's War*, Penguin Books, 2014.
- Davis, T. & Kennedy, A. & Kennedy, E, *The Holden Heritage*, Edition February 2007.
- Dennis, P & Gray, J (Eds), *The Australian Army and the Vietnam War 1962-1972*, Army History Unit.
- Doyle, J & Grey, J. & Pierco, P, *Australia's Vietnam War*, Texas A & M University Press 2002.
- Faulkner, A, *Stone Cold*, Allen & Unwin 2016.
- Fitzroy Legal Service, *The Law Handbooks*, FLS 2017-2022.
- Ford, Justine, *The Good Cop*, Pan Macmillan 2016.
- Hardy, J, *The History of Family Law in Australia*, Society, 2016.

- Haran, P & Kearney, R, *Crossfire An Australian Reconnaissance Unit in Vietnam*, New Holland Publishing (Australia) Pty Ltd 2001.
- *Flashback Echoes from a Hard War*, New Holland Publishing (Australia) Pty Ltd 2003.
- Haran, P, *Trackers*, New Holland Publishers (Australia) Pty Ltd 2009.
- Hoser, Raymond, *Victoria Police Corruption*, Kotabi Australia 1999.
- Hosking, M, *Rescued from Vietnam. A Veteran's Recovery from PTSD*, Xiibris 2016.
- Laffin, J, *The Australian Army at War 1899-1975*, Osprey Publishing London 1982.
- Leonard, B. (Ed), *Their Service Our Heritage The Story of the Medicos*, Westpac Subbranch of the RSL 1998.
- Mallett, Ashley, *The Diggers' Doctor; The fortunate life of Col. Donald Beard AM, RFD, ED (Retd)*, Booktopia 2014.
- Mason, Robert, *Chickenhawk*, Viking Press 1983.
- Mollison, C.S, *Long Tan and Beyond*, Cobb's Crossing Publications 2004.
- O'Brien, Kerry, *Kerry O'Brien A Memoir*, Allen & Unwin 2018.
- Pederson, Peter, *The Anzac Spirit From Gallipoli to the Present Day*, Carlton Books Ltd 2010.
- Pemberton, G(Ed), *Vietnam Remembered*, Lansdowne 1990.
- Petraitis, Vikki, *Inside the Law 25 years of true crime writing*, Clan Destine Press 2019.
- Quaedvlieg, Roman, *'Tour de Force'*, Penguin Random House Australia 2020.
- Rintoul, Stuart, *Ashes of Vietnam*, William Heinemann Australia, 1987.

- Rowe, John, *Vietnam The Australian Experience*, Time Life Books, 1987.
- Searle, Rod & Bell, Denise & Danaher, Paul, & Anderson Greg, *Call Sign Vampire: The Inside Story of an Australian Field Hospital During The Vietnam War*, (1 Aust) Field Hospital Incorporated 2021.
- Sharpe, Alan & Encel, Vivienne, *Murder: 25 True Australian Crime Stories*, Kingsclear Books Pty Ltd 1997.
- Simpson, J, *We Chose to Speak of War and Strife*, Bloomsbury Publishing 2016.
- Souter, J. Giangreco, D.M & MacDougall, A.K.(Eds), *The Vietnam War Experience*, The Five Mile Press Pty Ltd 2007.
- Tate, D, *The War Within*, Murdoch Books Pty Ltd 2008.
- Thurgar, J & Wright, C(Ed), *Welcome Home*, Austwire Communications Pty Ltd 1988.
- Webb, Emily, *Suburban True Crime - Australian cases you'll never forget and some you've never heard of*, Big Sky Publishing Ltd 2022.
- Williams, Dr Brian, *Somebody Knows Something: On the Trail of the Tynong North and Frankston Serial Killer*, New Holland 2020.

Magazines, Journals, Reports & Articles

- Alcohol and Drug Foundation, *The Role of Drug Education In Schools* (10 March 2020).
- Amphora, Reservoir High School Magazine (1964).
- Architects Conversation Consultants, *Conserving Eltham Courthouse*, (20 March 2020).
- Atlus Obschura, How Bamboo Sticks Help Vietnamese Shoulder Mighty Loads (January 2020).
- Australian Food Timeline, *1968 Courage Beer Launched*.
- Australian Government Department of Foreign Affairs and Trade, *Developmental Assistance in Vietnam*.
- Australian Government Department of Veterans Affairs, Vietnam Veterans Family Study – Spouse and partners of Vietnam Veterans – Summary of findings from the Vietnam Veterans Family Study (2014) (Australian Institute of Family Studies 2021).
- Australian Institute of Criminology, *Crime At Schools Proceedings of a Seminar In Canberra* (2-4 June 1987).
- Australian Pesticides Map (undated).
- Australian Veterans' Children Assistance Trust, *Our Story* (2022).
- Australian Women's Weekly 'Vandalism in Schools' (6 October 1982).

- AVURG, Colin Twelftree Hands Over after 24 Years of Service in AVVRG.
- BITE Magazine, *Bashing the Nash*.
- Blumberg, Arnold, Sapper Attack – The Elite North Vietnamese Unit (2 January 2017)
- Bray, Rosie, The Man's a Legend – A Special Fanfare for Howard John Cornish OAM 2017.
- Burgess, Carolyn, Luscombe Bowl – The Concert Stage.
- Community Veteran Justice Project, *B52 Rained Fire In Vietnam*.
- Consulting Specifying Engineers, *Fire Protection In Schools* (21 October 2015).
- Contact Magazine, Chapter 36.
- Digger History, Air Support/ Vietnam.
- Dung, T. *Cu Chi Tunnels* (2002).
- Education Department, *Framework (Vic)* No 3 (April 1985).
- Factory Direct Models, Army's Floating Helicopter Repair Workshop.
- Facts and Details, American Soldiers in the Vietnam War: Daily Life, Special Forces, Sex and Drugs.
- Foreign Affairs and Security, Bad Moon Rising – How Australians Avoided a Massacre at Nui Le.
- Hartley J & Neesham, H, *Vietnam Vanguard* (Australian National University).
- Henderson, K, The Base Operations Building at the US Army Airfield at Vung Tau (1964).
- History Net, Vung Tau-Vietnam's Hottest R & R Destination. (undated).
- HQ 1ATF: *Punch A Postie* (undated).
- Hughes, John, Vandalism and Arson – Is There and Answer, (26 October 1982).

- Issue No 11, Two Hundred Years (Vietnam The Unwinnable War (Bay Books Pty Ltd)
- Justice Quarterly, Police Officers in Schools; Effects on School Crime and the Processing of Offending Behaviours (3 October 2011).
- Learning from the Past, *Ardoch High School* (St Kilda East) (2021).
- Library of Congress, Long Binh Post and the Vietnam War.
- Los Angeles Police Department, – Protecting the Children – Our Future.
- Mc Culloch, *Behind the Headlines* (3 June 1987).
- McNab, Duncan, Digging up the past: The gruesome bid to cover up the murder of Melbourne solicitor Roger Wilson (15 December 2019)
- Medical Association For Prevention of War, *Australian Veterans Health: Vietnam* (August 2012)
- Military History, *Battle of Binh Ba*.
- Monument Australia, Royal Australian Army Medical Corps.
- MRFA, US Naval Support Activity Attachment 1965-1971.
- Murderpedia, Christopher Dale Flannery
- News and Resources, *Drug Driving- The Lick Test* (10 March 2010).
- O'Donnell, J, AP Suoi Nghe, Phuoc Tuy Province Vietnam 1967-09 Houses in Various Stages of Completion.
- Old Parade, Just Doing My Job – Michael Pratt Tells (5 July 2017).
- OTU Association, The Officer Training Unit- A Short History.

- Phivolcs, 1968 August 02 MS 7.3 Casiguran Earthquake.
- Police Integrity, Past Patterns- Future Directions -Victoria Police and the Problem of Corruption and Serious Misconduct, Victorian Government Printer 2007.
- PSY Warrior SGM H. Friedman (Ret), *The 'White Mice' of Vietnam*.
- Pubmed (MD Stanton), Drugs, Vietnam and The Vietnam Veteran: An Overview.
- Quora, How was Singapore Effected by the Vietnam War?
- RAAMC History, School of Army Health.
- Royal Commission Into the Failure of West Gate Bridge (August 1971).
- Ryan, R, You're Messing Up My Mind. Why Judy Jacques Avoided the Path of Pop Diva (1964).
- Sixties Project, Glossary of Military Terms from the Vietnam War (Generation Inc 1996).
- Stewart, A. War Time Magazine, Tragedy at An Nhut (July 2004).
- Tate, Donald, The Minefield: Australia's Greatest Military Blunder of the Vietnam War.
- U.S. Department of Justice, Drugs- The Role of the Australian Bureau of Criminal Intelligence (1993).
- U.S. Office of The Historian, Ending the Vietnam War 1969-1973.
- Victims of Crime Commissioner, *Annual Report 2018-2019*
- Victims of Crime Commissioner, *Annual Report 2020-2021*.
- Victoria Police Department, *Annual Report 1976*.
- Victoria Police Management Services Bureau, *Police in Victoria 1936-1980*, National Library of Australia.

- Vietnam WBB, Napalm and Agent Orange.
- Villard, Dr E, Were Viet Cong Prisoners Tossed From Helicopters (16 February 2022).
- War History Online, Liquid Fire – How Napalm was Used in the Vietnam War.
- -The Bell UH-1 Huey Gunship.
- Way, Nicholas, What Happened to Kennett's IR Reforms (5 December 1994).
- Wings Autumn 2012, *Caribous in Vietnam*.

Australian War Memorial Website Publications

- www.awm.gov.au
- Army Nurses in Vietnam DPR 206 1971
- Australian Army Training Team Vietnam.
- Australian Casualties in the Vietnam War, 1962-72.
- 1st Australian Civil Affairs Unit- Dedication.
- Australian Medical Aid to Villagers After Viet Cong Attack- (Corporal Colin O'Neill), DPR/TV/1042 (18 March 1969).
- *AP Suoi Nghe Medcap*, DPR/TV/824 (April 1968)
- *Baria Begins to Recover* DPR/TV/774 (February 1968).
- *Cordon and Search of Binh Gia*, DPR/TV/762 (December 1967).
- *It Looks Ridiculous But Isn't (Hats in Vietnam)*, DPR/TV/1249 (September 1969- February 1970).
- Langford, S, Appendix: The National Service Scheme, 1964-1972 (25 February 2021).
- Last Post Ceremony Commemorating The Service of Private Wayne Edward Telling 2790880(6 June 2019)
- *Medcap in Ngai Giao*, DPR/TV/1133 (1 July 1969).
- Medcap at Refugee Village, DPR/TV/852 (1968).
- Operation Ainslie DPR/TV/692.
- Phouc Tuy Province Saigon River- Baria.

- TET Turning Point.
- Vietnam Orphans Sing (December 1969).
- Vietnam War 1962-1975.
- Wilcox, DC, Life at the Dat.

Other Principal Reference Websites

- Anzac Web Portal anzacportal.dva.gov
- Australian Veteran Matters www.austvetmatters.net
- Battle of Long Tan.com
- callsignvampire.co.au
- Department of Veterans' Affairs (DVA) www.dva.gov.au
- Digger History Website: Unofficial History of the Australian and New Zealand Armed Services.
- NAA.Gov.Au.
- Trove.
- Vietnam War.Govt.NZ.
- Vietnam Veterans Association of Australia www.vvaa.org.au
- Wikipedia www.wikipedia.org

Transcript of Interviews

- Australians At War Film Archive, *Transcript of Interview LTCOL Brian Leslie Cornish* (DOI 18 November 2003).
- Australians At War Film Archive, *Transcript of Interview Colin O'Neill* (DOI 26 March 2004).
- Australians At War Film Archive, *Transcript of Interview Colin Twelftree* (DOI 6 May 2004).
- State Library South Australia, *Transcript of Interview Marie Boyle* (DOI 26 September 2007).

Newspaper References

The Age

- The West Gate Bridge collapses (16 October 1970).
- 50 Police to face charges: Beach Inquiry (13 October 1976).
- The After Dark Bandit Strikes Again in Victoria (28 April 1979).
- Pentridge Prisoners Escape and Hold Family Hostage (18 April 1983).
- Cain Declares State of Emergency to Break Strike (6 August 1983).
- Fugitive Mad Max Dies in Shootout (26 February 1986).
- Five Die in Jika Jika Fire (31 October 1987).
- The Riddle of A Top Bloke Turned Killer (10 December 1987).
- Sentence for School Burners (Frankston High School) (26 June 1992).
- Hundreds of School Closures in Victoria (5 December 1992).
- Fearless law enforcer loses battle with illness (21 October 2002).
- Date Aside Tigers Get Jack's Number (13 November 2003).
- Around the World in 54 Years (1 April 2004).
- The Myth of a Clean Police Force (12 June 2004).
- One dead, gunman at large after city shooting (19 June 2007).
- Party girls' world collided with violence (20 June 2007).

- Sarah's Flame Still Burns Strong on the Eve of the Heat Breaking 20 Year Anniversary (10 July 2010).
- Criminal Peter Gibb 'bashed over practical joke' (24 January 2011).
- The Real Animal Kingdom (12 February 2011).
- It is never too late for justice (3 June 2011).
- Top Honour for officer shot twice by escaping prisoners (13 September 2011).
- Kieran Walshe to Quit Police Force (14 February 2012).
- Top Traffic Cop to Leave Force After 44 Years (15 February 2012).
- Serial Killers Parole Bid Refused (13 December 2012).
- Serafettin Huseyin Found Guilty of Ferocious Hatchet Attack on Wife (8 March 2014).
- Principal of Key Banker School Tells IBAC He's Done No Wrong (5 May 2015).
- New evidence could spark fresh probe into notorious police slaying of Graeme Jensen (17 December 2015).
- Veterans Affairs: Promised changes are too little too late (26 October 2017).
- 35 Years on From Ash Wednesday (15 February 2018).
- Bernie the Attorney Came from the School of Hard Knocks (8 March 2018).
- Where the bodies are buried (18 October 2018).
- You're Nicked: Victoria's First Undercover Cop (3 November 2018).
- Australia's Last Bushrangers Were Twins (27 April 2019).
- Serving Detective Accuses Police Command of Intentionally Derailing Murder Inquiry (8 July 2020).
- The 40-year murder mystery (8 August 2020).

- Phil Cleary Giving Men a Sporting Chance to End Violence Against Women (16 June 2021).
- Her shoelaces were still on fire: Incredible act of courage and compassion (11 March 2022).
- The conflicting accounts Roberts, Debs and prosecutors gave of Silk- Miller shootings (11 July 2022).
- Cold case reward up to $1 million: Answers sought on 1992 Frankston Murder (25 August 2022).
- Someone knows: How detectives and a change of conscience can crack a cold case (9 September 2022).
- 'Ragtag team's courage under fire' (5 November 2022).

The Argus Melbourne
- *Cherry Bobs Game* (3 January 1938).

AP News
- Gunman Storms Kindergarten, Takes Children Hostage (10 May 1989).

The Australian
- Entire School Kidnapped (6 October 2002).

Blue Mountain Gazette
- James Bazley Prime Suspect in Donald Mackay Murder Dies (2 November 2018).

Brisbane Times
- Tell Him He's Dreaming-Lawyer Loses $250k Dennis Denuto Defamation Case (21 November 2015).

The Canberra Times
- Leading Citizen to Make Draw (4 March 1965)
- Boy Charged Over School Fire- Melbourne (24 April 1975).
- Victoria Cuts Planned School – Building Program (25 September 1975).
- *Vandals No Class* (9 December 1975).
- School Fire Melbourne (Maidstone State School) 13 January 1976).
- Compensation to Church Ordered (15 September 1976).
- School Fire (Tottenham Technical School) (10 June 1978).
- *School Security* (16 November 1979).
- Fire Information School Doveton Fires (15 September 1980).
- Spate of Arson in Melbourne (30 October 1981).
- Arson Costs $130 million a Year (31 December 1981).
- Arson Suspected in $1million School Fire (Glenroy High School) (26 April 1983).
- Arson Conference – A $700 Million Problem (28 April 1983).
- Lionel Rose Fined (19 June 1983).
- School Fire 2 Charged (Swan Hill High) (24 November 1987).
- School Fire Damage Bill to Top $3m (20 November 1989).
- *Fire Deliberately Lit* (Frankston High School) (4 July 1990).
- Arsonist Gets 10 Years (R. Saville) (28 August 1990).

The Courier
- The Story of a Prisoner, Police Officer and a Four-Legged Mate (26 May 2018).

Courier Mail
- Meet Bernie 'the Attorney' Balmer and his mate Mick Gatto (31 May 2013).

Daily Mail Australia
- Evil Paedophile who Kidnapped, Abused and Murdered six-year-old Girl Sheree Beasley Dies in Prison (9 November 2021).

Daily Telegraph
- Police probe death of notorious criminal Peter Gibb (24 January 2011).

The Exchange Post
- Flashback Friday: The Exchange in Vietnam (25 March 2022).

The Herald Sun
- School Fires Lit to Get Days off – Judge (Frankston High School) (26 June 1992).
- Sky Police Tackle Young Vandals (26 February 1993).
- David Robin's Widow Welcomes Verdict on Murder (30 May 2008).
- Serial Killer Paul Denyer accused of jail rape (8 May 2012)
- Peter Robert Gibb ran with Trevor John Smith, suspected killer of Fr George Scerri (1 June 2012)
- Man Who Took Kindergarten Kids Hostage in 1988 is back in Jail after Hatchet attack on Wife (13 June 2012).
- The List of Hoddle Street Victims Shot Dead by Julian Knight in 1987 (8 March 2013).

- Killers Bandali Debs and Ashley Mervyn Coulston linked to unsolved murders (10 March 2015).
- Queen's Birthday Honours: Greensborough's Howard Cornish (17 June 2017).
- What happened in missing years of a monster? (31 July 2021).
- Jim Bazley Grim Secrets of the Dead (6 February 2022).
- *Playing it Cruel* (17 April 2022).
- Facts to disturb every decent- minded person (29 October 2022).
- The Massacre and Miracle of Queen Street (11 December 2022).

The New Daily
- Easey Street Murder House Sells (30 June 2017).

The News Bayside
- *Cold case murder* (19 October 2021).

New York Times
- Saigon's Gold Mine PX is Going out of Business (27 April 1975).

Nunawading Gazette
- Arson Ruled Out in School Fire (Mitcham Primary School (15 December 1992).

The Observer
- Children At Risk at Most New Schools Built without Sprinklers (14 April 2019).

The Standard
- Naringal's Ray Smith tells of his Ash Wednesday Triumph (9 January 2020).

The Sydney Morning Herald
- Seven draft resisters released from jail- quick action by Govt (7 December 1972).
- Home again – to end an era (21 December 1972).
- Truth Still a Casualty of a Just War (30 June 2003).
- Worship No More, Your Honour Will Suffice (3 May 2004).
- Sex and the City; Take A Walk on Sydney's Steamy Side (17 December 2007).
- Worst Peril Since Ash Wednesday (6 February 2009).
- Six women murdered but still no conviction (17 August 2013).
- The PM, The Cop, The Punch and the 5- Year- Cover- Up (26 May 2019).
- *Evil Unmasked* (27 November 2020).
- Barrister with a Heart of Gold (11 February 2021).

The West Australian
- Serial Killer Paul Denyer quizzed on four jail rapes in just six weeks (26 July 2012).

Young Arcade
- Students Lit Fires (Frankston High School) (16 June 1992).
- Miscellaneous Press cuttings (School Security - Undated 1974- 1993)
- Bittlemam, Jackie, School Fire: Arson Theory.

- Cogdon, K. & Newsome, B, School in New Arson Probe (Mitcham Primary School).
- Deighton, Matt, A Bloke Who Did His Best (Laurie Ratz).
- Fitzgerald, Peter, $2Mil Damage – School Crime Squad- The School Destroyers.
- Harris, Steve, Education Reporter, Electronics May Help School Kidnappers.
- International Express, Bid To Sue The Parents of School Fire Thugs.
- Joachim, Kenneth, The Protectors Silent Sentinels Keep the Firebugs from Your School.
- Pankhurst, Tim, School Guards Go On Unpaid.
- Rowe, Alan Herald Education Writer, Six Boys Faces Charges Crackdown on Vandals.
- School Sleep Patrol Nabs 7.
- Traps… Parents Work in Ruins.
- Skeggs, Phil, Anger Over Compo for Law Breaker (John Didik).
- Trengrove, Kim, Its Quiet for Kiddy Crime.
- Walker, Graeme, $1/2m. Fire Razes School.
- Wilkinson, M, It's war to Stop Damage to Our Schools.
- Wilson, Tony, A Hotline on School Firebugs.
- School Blaze Damage $70,000; Classroom Fire Bill is $3mill'What's the Damage?

About the Author

Colin served in Vietnam as a National conscript during 1968-69. On his discharge from the Army, he resumed working for the Victoria Police Department as an unsworn member. In 1974, Colin was appointed Head of School Security for the Victorian Education Department in the prevention and detection of school crime.

He then entered the legal profession, being admitted to practice in 1996 as a Barrister and Solicitor mainly practicing in the areas of crime, family violence and industrial relations. He retired in 2022 and lives on the Mornington Peninsula in Victoria with his wife, Michelle.

www.ingramcontent.com/pod-product-compliance
Lightning Source LLC
Chambersburg PA
CBHW042321090526
44585CB00025BA/2787